BARRON'S

HOW TO PREPARE FOR THE

EMT

BASIC EXAM

Chief Will Chapleau, EMT-P RN, TNS
Chief, Chicago Heights, Illinois Fire Department

BARRON'S

All inquiries should be addressed to:
Barron's Educational Series, Inc.
250 Wireless Boulevard
Hauppauge, NY 11788
http://www.barronseduc.com

International Standard Book Number 0-7641-2261-4

Library of Congress Catalog Card Number 2002038592

Library of Congress Cataloging-in-Publication Data
Chapleau, Will.
How to prepare for the EMT basic exam / by Will Chapleau.
p. cm.
Includes index.
ISBN 0-7641-2261-4
1. Emergency medicine—Examinations, questions, etc. 2. Emergency medical
technicians—Licenses—United States—Study guides. I. Title.

RC86.9 .C426 2003
616.02'5'076—dc21

2002038592

PRINTED IN THE UNITED STATES OF AMERICA
9 8 7 6 5 4 3 2 1

Dedication

This book is dedicated to every new First Responder. In an uncertain world, one certainty is that we will respond to protect and save the lives of those in need everywhere. I wish you good fortune and safety as you begin your journey.

Special thanks goes to my wife, Kathy, who has patiently supported my career path, one that certainly makes her life more complex than she expected. Her review of these pages was most helpful in finding errors I missed after repeated readings. To my children Abby, Paul, and Alex, thank you for your patience and encouragement as my work on this book meant so much time away from you.

To every First Responder, EMT, Paramedic, Firefighter, Police Officer, Nurse, and Doctor I have had the pleasure to work with during the past 30 years, thank you. You have enhanced my professional life, and are key factors in what I do.

Contents

Preface

Prehospital care is a relatively young profession. Over the last 30 years, the profession has evolved from what was a transportation service provided by responders with limited training or none at all, to specially trained professionals ranging from First Responders to Advanced Life Support.

Emergency Medical Technicians, or EMT-Bs, form the backbone of the U.S. Emergency Medical System and comprise the largest number (more than 500,000) of EMS Responders. EMT-B is a prerequisite for employment with ambulance services all over the United States and many police and fire departments. Most job surveys show the EMT-B as a growing profession with job opportunities all over the country.

This book is intended to help the EMT-B candidate prepare for the licensure or certification examination. Each chapter begins with a listing of the U.S. Department of Transportation Curriculum Objectives and a review of covered materials. The multiple-choice questions are drawn from the Objectives and are intended to give you an opportunity to practice the type of questions you are likely to face in the exam. Throughout the book there will also be scenario questions to give you a chance to apply what you have learned to real-life situations. It is our hope that this book will assist you in your preparation to become an EMT-B.

About the Author

Will Chapleau is the chief of the Chicago Heights Fire Department in Chicago Heights, Illinois. He has been involved in emergency services for over 30 years as a firefighter, paramedic, educator, and administrator. He has authored numerous texts and journal articles on fire and EMS topics, lecturing in these areas all over the Americas, Europe, and Asia. He is on the Board of Directors of the National Association of EMTs and the National Association of EMS Educators and is the chairman of the Prehospital Trauma Life Support Program which provides prehospital trauma training in over 30 countries.

CHAPTER 1

Introduction to Emergency Care

Objectives

This chapter and the sample/practice questions will help readers determine if they are able to

1. define Emergency Medical Services (EMS).

2. differentiate the roles and responsibilities of EMT-Bs from other prehospital care providers.

3. describe the roles and responsibilities related to personal safety.

4. discuss the roles and responsibilities of the EMT-B toward the safety of the crew, patient, and bystanders.

5. define quality improvement and the EMT-B's role in this process.

6. define medical direction and the EMT-B's role in the process.

7. state the specific statutes and regulations in their state regarding the EMS system.

Emergency Medical Services Systems

Prehospital care providers work within emergency medical service systems to provide emergency care to people all over the world who suddenly become sick or injured. This system is built on the training of the Emergency Medical Technician. Emergency Medical Technicians are trained to assess, stabilize, and transport patients to appropriate medical facilities to receive definitive care. They interact with other health care professionals such as doctors, nurses, and so on.

Health Care System

An EMT-B is a part of the health care system that includes trauma centers, burn centers, pediatric centers, poison centers, and other specialty centers. It is important that you, as an EMT-B, understand your local protocols in determining which facility to transport your patient to in an emergency. You also may be involved in nonemergency transport or transfers of patients between these facilities and/or patients' homes.

Public Safety Personnel

You will also work closely with other public safety personnel such as police and fire personnel. Close communication and cooperation with these agencies will be imperative to ensure the safety of EMT-Bs, their teammates, and their patients.

The U.S. Department of Transportation (DOT) standardized and contracted for the national curriculum that all EMT-B courses follow. The National Highway Traffic Safety Administration (NHTSA) technical assistance standards are the components essential to any EMS System. These include

- ✔ regulation and policy.
- ✔ resource management.
- ✔ human resources and training.
- ✔ transportation.
- ✔ facilities.
- ✔ communications.
- ✔ public information and education.
- ✔ medical direction.
- ✔ trauma systems.
- ✔ evaluation.

911 Systems

All of the above-listed components are essential, but of greatest importance is public information and education. The community served by EMS must understand what the system is designed to do, how it is used appropriately, and how it best serves the community.

Access to EMS across much of the United States is through 911 systems. Callers into 911 systems have the potential for important information stored within the system to be available to responders dispatched to care for them. There are areas of the country, however, that do not have coverage by 911 dispatch centers, and they may still use conventional phone numbers to access EMT-Bs for response. An important part of educating your community will be orienting them to the communication and dispatch system that covers them.

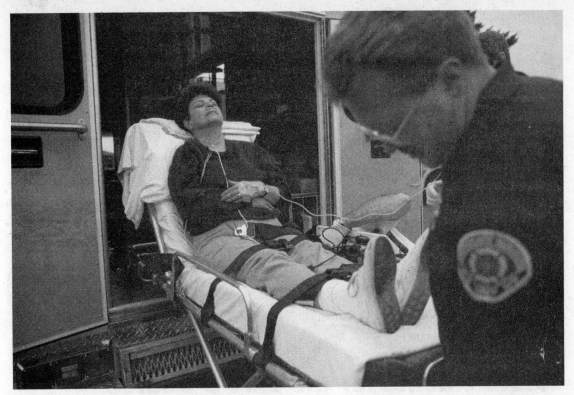

An important part of an EMT-B's duties is the safe transport of patients to a variety of care facilities.

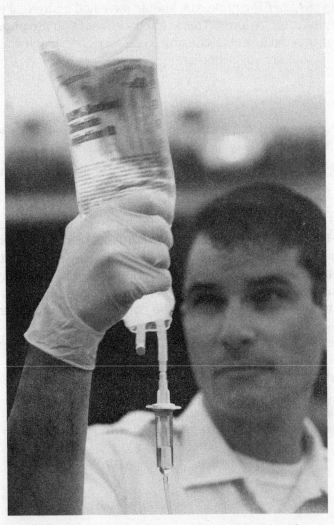

The EMT-B must be able to make critical decisions based on accurate assessment.

Levels of Care

The care given by prehospital care providers has four levels:

1. First Responders give initial care, which might include bleeding control or CPR, and typically do not transport patients.

2. EMT-Basics (EMT-Bs) provide basic life support at the scene and during transport to the hospital.

3. EMT-Intermediates (EMT-Is) provide some advanced life support care such as intravenous fluid administration, limited medications, and in some cases, defibrillation.

4. EMT-Paramedics (EMT-Ps) provide advanced life support (ALS), which includes advanced airway control such as intubation, defibrillation, cardioversion and pacing capabilities, intravenous fluids, medications, and invasive techniques for airway support and control.

Requirements for the EMT-B Course

As you enter(ed) your EMT-B course, you should have had a physical examination and review of your immunization records. This is to ensure that you are physically up to the job and that you are protected against exposure to diseases for which vaccines are available. The immunizations that are suggested are

✔ tetanus,
✔ hepatitis B,
✔ common diseases such as measles, chicken pox, and mumps,
✔ any other vaccines that may be available to you, plus
✔ TB testing.

Roles and Responsibilities of the EMT-B

The roles and responsibilities of the EMT-B include

✔ personal safety.
✔ safety of your crew.
✔ patient assessment.
✔ patient care based on assessment findings.
✔ lifting and moving patients safely.
✔ transport/transfer of care.
✔ record keeping and data collecting.
✔ patient advocacy (patient rights), patient as a whole.

The EMT-B's first responsibility is personal safety. The EMT-B will first have to determine the safety of a scene and take proper precautions to protect against exposure to any patient body fluids. Proper training in lifting and moving patients safely will enable you to move patients while minimizing the risk of injury to yourself. This is a very important part of your job as back injuries are the most common career-ending injury. Determining whether or not the scene is safe includes making sure that other responders (such as police or fire personnel) have done their job to make the scene safe and secure before the EMT-B arrives. This also includes protection from blood-borne pathogens. The EMT-B's safety is the priority. You can be of no help to the sick and injured if you become a patient yourself.

You will be called on to make assessments of the sick and injured and your treatments will be based on the needs of your patient determined through this assessment.

Personal Attributes

To ensure confidence and convey an image of well-trained professionals, EMT-Bs should work to maintain a neat, clean, and positive image. It is the responsibility of the EMT-B to attend continuing education and refresher courses as required to maintain licensure and keep skills and knowledge base up to the highest possible levels. It is also important to remember that in caring for patients, their needs must always be the priority. This priority is met only if it can be done without placing the EMT-B's safety in jeopardy. The EMT-B also needs to keep up to date with local, state, and national issues that affect EMS. EMS is affected by the activities of a variety of legislative and commercial entities and it is important to know what will affect the EMT-B's ability to care for patients.

Quality Improvement

The DOT curriculum defines Quality Improvement as "a system of internal/external reviews and audits of all aspects of an EMS system so as to identify those aspects needing improvement to assure that the public receives the highest quality of prehospital care."

The roles of the EMT-B in quality improvement include

✔ documentation.
✔ running reviews and audits.
✔ gathering feedback from patients and hospital staff.
✔ conducting preventative maintenance.
✔ continuing education.
✔ skill maintenance.

Medical Direction

A physician is responsible for the clinical and patient care aspects of an EMS system and every ambulance service must have physician medical direction. This medical direction is provided in two ways.

1. **Online medical direction.** This is direct medical direction over patient care during an EMS run via phone or radio communication.

2. **Offline medical direction.** Medical direction is also provided through establishing protocols and standard operation guidelines/orders.

The medical director is also responsible for reviewing quality improvement. The EMT-B's relationship with the medical director is important, as the EMT-B is the agent of the medical director. As an extension of the medical director, the EMT-B carries out the medical director's orders through following protocols, standard guidelines, or direct orders.

State and Local Legal Issues

Each state has a law in place that establishes the practice of prehospital care. Associated with that law are rules and regulations that dictate how EMT-Bs are to be trained and licensed. The regulations also describe the authority of the medical director and what the minimum practice levels are for EMT-Bs throughout the state.

Scenario

You are called to a scene of an industrial accident to treat a man who has severed a large blood vessel in his right forearm. As an EMT-B, what should you be doing as you approach this scene?

Solution

Scene safety is first. The EMT-B should first make sure that the hazard that created the injury, or any other hazard, has been secured. The EMT-B should also be wearing any special equipment (such as helmet, goggles, etc.) that this industrial situation requires. Scene safety also includes body substance isolation (BSI) and, at the very least, the EMT-B should be wearing gloves and protective eye covering. Masks or gowns may be necessary in particularly messy situations.

Review Questions

1. Emergency medical services is

    (A) emergency medical care provided in prehospital settings.
    (B) emergency medical care provided in emergency departments.
    (C) emergency medical care provided by specially trained prehospital care providers.
    (D) A & B.

2. Emergency Medical Technicians-Basics (EMT-Bs)

(A) are trained to provide Basic Life Support (BLS) to the sick and injured and transportation to the appropriate medical facility.

(B) provide a limited amount of Advanced Life Support (ALS) to the sick and injured and transportation to the appropriate medical facility.

(C) provide Advanced Life Support (ALS) to the sick and injured and transportation to the appropriate medical facility.

(D) are first on the scene to provide emergency care to the sick and injured prior to the arrival of transporting agencies.

3. Emergency Medical Technicians-Paramedics (EMT-Ps)

(A) provide BLS to the sick and injured and transportation to appropriate medical facilities.

(B) provide a limited amount of ALS to the sick and injured and transportation to appropriate medical facilities.

(C) provide ALS to the sick and injured and transportation to appropriate medical facilities.

(D) are first on the scene to provide emergency care to the sick and injured prior to the arrival of transporting agencies.

4. First Responders

(A) provide BLS to the sick and injured and transportation to appropriate medical facilities.

(B) provide a limited amount of ALS to the sick and injured and transportation to appropriate medical facilities.

(C) provide ALS to the sick and injured and transportation to appropriate medical facilities.

(D) are first on the scene to provide emergency care to the sick and injured prior to the arrival of transporting agencies.

5. EMS and the EMT-B are a part of the health care system that includes

(A) doctors.
(B) nurses.
(C) hospitals and special-care facilities.
(D) All of the above.

6. The NHTSA technical assistance standards list the necessary components of an EMS system, the most important of which is

(A) regulation and policy.
(B) facilities.
(C) communication.
(D) public information and education.

7. The EMT-B's first responsibility is to

(A) the EMS system medical director.
(B) the patient.
(C) personal safety.
(D) the employer.

8. Medical direction is provided

(A) online via phone or radio communications.
(B) offline via protocols and standing orders or guidelines.
(C) by physician medical directors.
(D) All of the above.

9. Prior to entering an EMT-B program, the EMT-B should

(A) have a physical exam performed by a physician to determine overall fitness for the job.
(B) obtain a complete immunization record.
(C) receive immunizations recommended by the EMT-B program.
(D) All of the above.

10. Body substance isolation (BSI), or universal precautions, refer to

(A) precautions to prevent your exposure to blood-borne pathogens.
(B) precautions to prevent your exposure to all body substances and anything the patient may have been exposed to.
(C) precautions to prevent exposure to airborne pathogens.
(D) precautions to prevent exposure to anything the patient may have been exposed to.

Answers to Review Questions

1. **D** Objective 1
While EMT-Bs are trained specifically to work in the prehospital setting, many are employed in emergency departments as aides or technicians assisting physicians and other allied health care personnel.

2. **A** Objective 2
EMT-Bs are trained to provide Basic Life Support, which includes CPR and AED; patient-assisted medications; the use of oxygen, activated charcoal, and glucose; control of bleeding; and fracture management, but does not include the use of manually operated defibrillators, advanced airway adjuncts, or intravenous drug administration.

3. **C** Objective 3
EMT-Ps, or Paramedics, are trained to provide ALS or Advanced Life Support. ALS includes administration of intravenous fluids, advanced airway management, manually operated defibrillators and cardioverters, and possibly the use of external pacemakers. They are trained to monitor EKG rhythms and to recognize and treat life-threatening rhythms.

4. **D** Objective 2
First Responders are individuals trained because they are likely to be at the scene of an emergency when it occurs. Their training is meant to be a bridge covering the minutes spent waiting for trained transporting prehospital care providers to arrive.

5. **D** Objective 2

EMT-Bs and other prehospital care providers are a part of the health care provider team that includes physicians, nurses, and other allied health care providers who care for the sick and injured. It is important for EMT-Bs to conduct themselves as professional members of this team realizing that how they perform and how they document their performance is a part of a team effort.

6. **D** Objective 1

Of all of the things essential to a functioning EMS system, public information and education is the most important as it educates people about how to access the system, what is the appropriate use of the system, and how they can contribute to positive outcomes. Public information and education also plays a role in prevention, educating people about how to take better care of themselves and prevent injuries.

7. **C** Objective 3

Above all else, the EMT-B must be concerned with safety. This is first for himself or herself, then for other team members, and then for the patient. Emergency work is a dangerous business; many First Responders lose their lives every year. We cannot complete our mission of caring for others if we become patients ourselves.

8. **D** Objective 1

Medical direction is a number of things. First, the physicians providing direction for EMS systems must develop plans and protocols for the treatment of patients using prehospital care in the regions they are responsible for. These protocols are offline medical control, or what all the providers in the system understand as standard treatments with no need to call in for orders. Second, they have to oversee the education of the prehospital care providers within those regions. Third, they must organize online medical control to follow the protocols they have approved.

9. **D** Objective 3

Before making first patient contact, all health care workers should make sure they are physically capable of doing the job and that they have protected themselves as much as possible from diseases to which they might be exposed.

10. **B** Objective 3

BSI includes whatever precautions are appropriate to the risk of exposure to harmful body substances. This can be as simple as gloves, but may also include eye protection, masks, or gowns.

CHAPTER 2

Well-being of the EMT-B

▌ Objectives

This chapter and the sample/practice questions will help readers determine if they are able to

1. list possible emotional reactions that the EMT-B may experience when faced with trauma, illness, death, and dying.

2. discuss the possible reactions that a family member may exhibit when confronted with death and dying.

3. state the steps in the EMT-B's approach to the family confronted with death and dying.

4. state the possible reactions that the family of the EMT-B may exhibit due to the outside involvement in EMS.

5. recognize the signs and symptoms of critical incident stress.

6. state the possible steps that the EMT-B should take for protection from blood-borne pathogens.

7. explain the need to determine scene safety.

8. discuss the importance of body substance isolation (BSI).

9. describe the steps the EMT-B should take for personal protection from airborne and blood-borne pathogens.

10. list the personal protective equipment necessary for each of the following situations:

    ✔ hazardous materials,
    ✔ rescue operations,
    ✔ violent scenes,
    ✔ crime scenes,
    ✔ exposure to blood-borne pathogens,
    ✔ exposure to airborne pathogens.

■ Emotional Aspects of Emergency Care

Death and Dying

The EMT-B must be prepared for the emotional aspects of the work. This includes dealing with death and dying. People faced with death, either their own or that of someone close to them, go through stages toward acceptance. These stages are

- ✔ Denial—"No, not me."
- ✔ Anger—The EMT-B may be the target of this anger. It is important to be tolerant and not become defensive. Good listening skills and empathy will be key to helping them though this.
- ✔ Bargaining—An attempt to postpone the death for a time, to make a deal: "I'll be a better person if you just bring him back."
- ✔ Depression—Characterized by sadness and/or despair, with the patient becoming quiet and withdrawn.
- ✔ Acceptance.

While the patient may have accepted death at this time, he or she may still be very sad or unhappy. The family will require a great deal of support at this point. In dealing with dying patients and their families, the EMT-B needs to address the patients' needs by treating them with dignity and respect. They will want to share in decisions about their care, so communication is key. Patients also have a need and a right to privacy, which should be given as much as possible.

The family of the dying patient may express rage, anger, and/or despair. The EMT-B should listen empathetically and speak using a gentle tone of voice while being careful not to falsely reassure. Holding the patient's hand or a gentle touch on the arm may also serve to show genuine concern and attention to his or her needs. Let the patient and the family know that everything that can be done will be done, and give as much comfort as possible.

■ Stressful Situations

Examples of situations that may cause stress to the EMT-B may include

- ✔ mass casualty situations.
- ✔ infant and child trauma.
- ✔ amputations.
- ✔ infant, child, elder, or spousal abuse.
- ✔ death or injury of a coworker or other public safety personnel.

The EMT-B will experience personal stress as well as having to deal with patients, bystanders, and family members who are experiencing stress.

■ Stress Management

EMT-Bs must be able to recognize the warning signs of stress in themselves and their coworkers, such as:

✔ irritability toward coworkers, family, and friends.
✔ inability to concentrate.
✔ difficulty sleeping and/or nightmares.
✔ anxiety.
✔ indecisiveness.
✔ guilt.
✔ loss of appetite.
✔ loss of interest in sex.
✔ isolation.
✔ loss of interest in work.

Lifestyle changes can be helpful in dealing with job stress and "burnout." Changing your diet by reducing sugar, caffeine, and alcohol intake, avoiding fatty foods, and increasing carbohydrates will help. Exercising and practicing relaxation techniques, meditation, or visual imagery can also help reduce or regulate stress. In any case, balancing work, recreation, family, and health promote personal and career longevity.

Friends and Family

Friends and family of the EMT-B can either help him or her to deal with stress or they can contribute to the stress. They may have a lack of understanding of the EMT-B's work, which can contribute to a fear of separation and being ignored. Irregular work schedules and the complications to family life of being on call make it difficult to plan activities and may cause those close to the EMT-B to feel they can't count on him or her. Wanting to share and not feeling that you'll be understood can be frustrating and hurtful.

You can address this by requesting shifts that allow more time with friends and family and making an effort to express the things you need to share with your family, while making sure to hear them and their concerns as well. If you can't seem to get a handle on this, seek professional help before things get too far out of hand.

Critical Incident Stress Debriefing (CISD)

Critical incident stress debriefing teams are teams of peer counselors and mental health professionals who can be called together to help emergency care workers deal with critical incident stress. The meeting must be held within 24 to 72 hours to be effective and will consist of open discussions of feelings, fears, and reactions. This is not a critique or an investigation and all of the information and discussions are confidential. The team will make recommendations or suggestions to help the care workers overcome the stress of the incident. These sessions are designed to accelerate the normal recovery process after a critical incident and succeed through venting feelings in a nonthreatening environment.

Comprehensive critical incident stress management includes

✔ preincident stress education.
✔ on-scene peer support.
✔ one-on-one support.
✔ disaster support services.

✔ defusing.
✔ CISD.
✔ follow-up services.
✔ spouse/family support.
✔ community outreach programs.
✔ other health and welfare programs such as wellness programs.

Check with your EMS system on how to access CISDs in your area.

Scene Safety

The first part of scene safety is BSI, or body substance isolation. For the protection of yourself and your patients you should

✔ wash hands before and after patient contact.
✔ use eye protection (glasses or goggles).
✔ wear vinyl or latex gloves.
✔ use heavier gloves for cleaning the vehicle and equipment.
✔ wear gowns when there is a body fluid splash potential, and change uniforms when exposed.
✔ wear masks to protect against inhaled hazards.
✔ wear a special HEPA mask which filters out very fine particulate matter when treating patients with tuberculosis.
✔ have patients with a respiratory disease wear surgical masks if they don't interfere with breathing or oxygen delivery.

You should also familiarize yourself with OSHA (Occupational Safety and Health Administration) and state regulations regarding BSI and rules on notification of exposure.

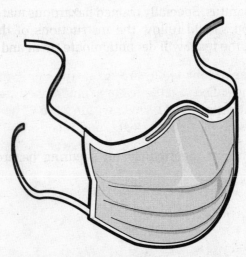

A variety of masks is indicated in handling sick and injured patients. A special HEPA mask is worn when handling confirmed or suspected cases of tuberculosis.

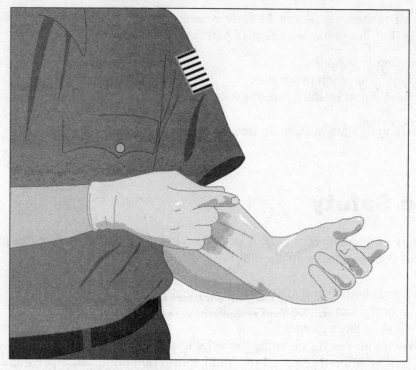

Gloves are like an EMT's second skin and should be worn with every patient contact.

Personal Protection

In dealing with hazardous materials, your most important equipment will be binoculars and the "Hazardous Materials, the Emergency Response Handbook," published by the U.S. Department of Transportation. Use the binoculars to find the placard on container(s) and use the guidebook to determine the hazards. Unless you are specially trained to deal with hazardous environments, don't enter a hazardous scene. Even if you are trained, you cannot approach the hazards without HAZMAT (hazardous material) suits and self-contained breathing apparatus. Specially trained hazardous materials teams are in control of these scenes, and you should follow the instructions of the team. Should there be patients for you to treat, the team will decontaminate them and deliver them to you.

Rescue

Safe rescue depends on first identifying and securing hazards. These hazards might include

- ✔ electricity.
- ✔ fire.
- ✔ explosions.
- ✔ hazardous materials.

These hazards must be secured before rescue can be accomplished. To effect rescue safely, the EMT-B should be wearing full protective clothing including

✔ turnout gear.
✔ puncture-proof gloves.
✔ a helmet.
✔ eye protection.

There are many circumstances in which the
EMT-B must wear eye protection.

In confined space or entrapment situations, special rescue teams must be used. In the case of violence at the scene, police should secure the scene before the EMT-B enters. If you know that the scene is a violent one, ask Dispatch if police are on the scene before you get there. If not, inform them that you will be "staging" or waiting a safe distance away until police secure the scene. Violent scenes can present hazards from the perpetrator of a crime, family, or bystanders. If you find yourself at a crime scene, do not disturb the scene any more than necessary for patient care.

▉ Scenarios

1. You are called to the scene of a motor vehicle collision; the victim is trapped in the car. The extrication team has gained access but you are being called on to remove the victim from the vehicle. What do you as an EMT-B have to do in order to work on this scene?

Solution

The EMT-B needs to take personal protection precautions that are appropriate to the scene. In this case, besides BSI precautions, turnout gear including helmet, gloves, coat, boots, and eye protection must be worn when removing the victim from the car.

2. You've arrived on the scene where a child has died. The mother is sitting quietly in the corner by herself and the father is shouting that the rescuers are all idiots and don't know what they're doing. What do you think is happening here and what should you do?

Solution

The mother appears to be in the depression stage of acceptance, while the father is in the anger phase. You should have the child quickly prepared for transport and try to make time or have someone else make time to listen to and be empathetic toward the family.

3. You have arrived at the scene of a hazardous materials incident. Should you go to the patients?

Solution

In hazardous materials incidents special training and equipment are needed. The patients will be decontaminated and brought to you.

▬ Review Questions

1. The wife of a man who was found dead at the scene is repeating the phrase, "No, he's not dead. He can't be," over and over again. Which stage of acceptance of death and dying would you say she is in?

    (A) Denial
    (B) Anger
    (C) Bargaining
    (D) Depression
    (E) Acceptance

2. While at the hospital with the family of a patient who has just died after a long fight with cancer, you hear the son say, "She had a good life, and she's not in pain anymore." This sounds as though he's reached the stage of

    (A) denial.
    (B) anger.
    (C) bargaining.
    (D) depression.
    (E) acceptance.

3. You are preparing to transport a patient in full cardiac arrest and continuing CPR. The family asks you, "Will he be all right?" An appropriate response from you would be

    (A) "I'm sure he'll be fine."
    (B) "Everything's going to be OK."
    (C) "We'll do everything we can."
    (D) "The hospital might be able to bring him back."

4. Patients suffering from extended terminal illness

    (A) should not be involved in decisions about their care.
    (B) need to be involved in decisions about their care.
    (C) are often enraged about loss of control over their life.
    (D) Both B & C.

5. Rage, anger, and despair are

    (A) common responses to death.
    (B) uncommon responses to death.
    (C) inappropriate responses to death.
    (D) None of the above.

6. Your partner has been unable to sleep, has been having trouble making decisions, and seems to have lost interest in work. You should consider this:

   (A) none of your concern.
   (B) a normal response to work.
   (C) signs of stress and possible burnout.
   (D) a signal that you need a new partner.

7. Diet can be a factor in your ability to deal with stresses of your work. Your diet should

   (A) be high in caffeine and sugar to increase energy.
   (B) be high in fat for muscle strength.
   (C) include alcohol to help you relax.
   (D) have increased carbohydrates.

8. You and your partner are having trouble dealing with a call you had last shift. You should

   (A) request a leave of absence.
   (B) call in sick.
   (C) seek alternative employment.
   (D) seek access to a critical incident stress debriefing team.

9. In order for it to be effective, critical incident stress debriefing should take place within

   (A) 1 week of the event.
   (B) 1 month of the event.
   (C) 24–72 hours of the event.
   (D) 72–96 hours of the event.

10. Body substance isolation should include

    (A) gloves.
    (B) eye protection.
    (C) masks if needed.
    (D) All of the above.

■ Answers to Review Questions

1. **A** Objective 2

The first stage of dealing with death and dying is denial. People faced with their own death or the death of someone close to them may express a variety of denials. This may be evident in the EMT faced with the death of a patient as well.

2. **E** Objective 2

When a person is able to verbalize both a recognition of death or imminent death and to relate feelings about it, it becomes clear that he or she is beginning to accept the possibility of death.

3. **C** Objective 3

Honest straightforward responses that are not unnecessarily blunt or cruel are the best. Do not lie to the family or make promises you can't keep, but do not blurt out unfeeling statements either.

4. **D** Objective 3

An aspect of illness that brings on anxiety and depression in terminally ill patients is the sense of loss of control. Doctors, nurses, and technicians are constantly telling them what they must and must not do. We should take every opportunity to give these patients information to help them to make decisions about their own care and give them back some control over their life.

5. **A** Objective 2

Rage, anger, and despair are all common responses to death and can be exhibited throughout the stages of reaching acceptance.

6. **C** Objective 5

Stress related to our work and the possibility of job burnout are occupational hazards. Changes in our behavior can be clues that we, or the people we are working with, are in trouble.

7. **D** Objective 5

Emergency medical care is extremely stressful and physical. In order for you to be at your best and to work safely, health and nutrition are important. While many of your coworkers may rely on sugar and caffeine, carbohydrates are the real source of stamina and energy.

8. **D** Objective 5

EMT-Bs may face society at its worst on a daily basis. They also witness society at its best in the people who respond to these emergencies. When faced with horrific situations, such as the death of a child or coworker, critical incident stress debriefing sessions should be a matter of policy and convened whenever situations fitting these criteria occur.

9. **C** Objective 5

Time is critical. The debriefing must be done while the events are fresh in everyone's mind, before they are buried deep or there is serious psychological damage.

10. **D** Objective 8

In order to protect yourself from spattering blood, coughing, and sneezing patients, or even to keep patients from getting your cold, eye protection, gloves, and masks should be used.

CHAPTER 3

Medical, Legal, and Ethical Issues

▨ Objectives

1. Define the EMT-Basic scope of practice.

2. Discuss the importance of Do Not Resuscitate (DNR), Advance Directives, and local or state provisions regarding EMS application.

3. Define consent and discuss the methods of obtaining consent.

4. Differentiate between expressed and implied consent.

5. Explain the role of consent of minors in providing care.

6. Discuss the implications for the EMT-B in patient refusal of transport.

7. Discuss the issues of abandonment, negligence, and battery, and their implications to the EMT-B.

8. State the conditions necessary for the EMT-B to have a duty to act.

9. Explain the importance, necessity, and legality of patient confidentiality.

10. Discuss the considerations of the EMT-B in issues of organ retrieval.

11. Differentiate the actions that an EMT-B should take to assist in the preservation of a crime scene.

12. State the conditions that require an EMT-B to notify local law enforcement officials.

▨ Scope of Practice

The EMT-B's scope of practice is to render basic life support (BLS) to the sick and injured. The EMT-B's scope of practice also includes legal duties to the patient, the medical director, and the public. The EMT-B must provide for the well-being of the patient by rendering necessary interventions outlined in the scope of practice dictated by the laws in your state and your medical director and referenced to the national standard curricula. The EMT-B's legal right to function may also be contingent on medical direction by radio or phone communications or protocols.

The EMT-B's ethical responsibilities are

✔ to meet the physical and emotional needs of the patient and maintain skills to the point of mastery.
✔ to attend continuing education and refresher programs.
✔ to critically review performances, seeking ways to improve response time, patient outcome, and communication.
✔ honesty in reporting.

Advanced Directives

DNRs, or do not resuscitate orders, are documents expressing patients' wishes to not be resuscitated if found pulseless and nonbreathing. Patients have a right to refuse resuscitation and you should know your state, local, and EMS system rules on what constitutes a legal "Do Not Resuscitate" order. In general, a written order from a physician is the model used. If there is any doubt, the EMT-B should begin resuscitation efforts.

Consent

The EMT-B must have consent to treat; there are three different types of consent to be familiar with:

1. **Expressed consent** is verbal consent given by a patient of legal age. The patient must be informed of the steps of the procedure and the risks of treating or not treating. All conscious mentally competent adults must give this type of consent.

2. **Implied consent** is assumed in unconscious patients requiring emergency care. It is based on the assumption that the patient would give consent to life-saving care if he or she were able to do so.

3. **Children and mentally incompetent adults** must have consent given by a parent or legal guardian. You should also review your state laws regarding emancipation and the age of minors in your state. In life-threatening situations where there is no guardian present, treat the patient using the rule of implied consent.

Assault and Battery

Specifically regarding medicine, assault is the threat of touching or treating another without consent. Battery is actually touching or treating another without consent.

Refusals

Patients have a right to refuse care. They may withdraw from care at any time, even if they regain consciousness and want you to discontinue care. Refusals may be given by mentally competent adults following the rules of expressed consent. This means you must explain the possible complications should they refuse or discontinue care. Again, when in doubt, treat. Documentation is important in protecting the EMT-B in refusals. Before leaving the scene, try again to persuade the patient and make sure the patient is able to make a rational, informed decision. This means that the patient must not be under the influence of drugs, alcohol, illness, or injury. Consult medical direction as your protocols dictate and consider assistance from the police, if needed. Document any findings and care given and have the patient sign a refusal of care form.

Abandonment

Abandonment is terminating care without assuring the continuation of care at the same level or higher.

Negligence

Negligence is deviation from the accepted standard of care resulting in further injury to the patient. In order for negligence to be found, all of these components must be present:

- ✔ duty to act.
- ✔ breach of duty.
- ✔ injury or damages inflicted.
  - • physical
  - • psychological
- ✔ the actions of the EMT-B caused the injury or damage.

Duty to Act

For duty to act to be present, a contractual or legal obligation must exist. It is implied if a patient calls for an ambulance and it is confirmed that the ambulance will be sent. It is also implied once treatment on the patient begins.

Formal obligation occurs when an ambulance service has a written contract with a municipality or an individual.

Legal duty to act may not apply but there still may be moral or ethical considerations. In some states, duty to act is established when an EMT sees that someone is in need of care. Documentation again is important in determining when duty to act is established. Know the rules regarding this in your state.

Confidentiality

Your patient's history, your assessment, and treatments provided are confidential information and cannot be shared with anyone not involved in the patient's care unless released in writing by the patient. Release is not required if state law requires reporting as in criminal assaults (rapes or gunshots) or if a legal subpoena is produced.

Special Situations

Organ Donors

One example of a special situation the EMT-B will face is the organ donor. Organ donors may have a card expressing their wishes or they will have signed a space on their driver's license. First and foremost, you should not treat the organ donor any differently than you would any other patient. Your role in these situations is to identify the patient as a potential donor in your communication with the hospital and then to the team that receives your patient. You can also reassure the family that you will do your best to honor their wishes.

Medical Identification Insignia

EMT-Bs should also be on the lookout for medical identification insignia. Bracelets, necklaces, or cards can identify the patient as a diabetic, heart patient, or having any significant medical condition. They may also list medications the patient may be taking or allergies.

Crime Scene Evidence

At a crime scene the patient's needs are the EMT-B's first priority. Dispatch should be notified that you have happened upon the scene of a crime if they are not aware of that fact. Do not disturb anything at the scene unless patient care makes it necessary. Document any observations you may have about the scene. Your patient care may involve removing the patient's clothing; if so, avoid cutting through, rips, tears, or bullet or knife holes that may have been made in commission of the crime.

Complying with the Law

While it differs by state, each state will have situations or events that must be reported. Infant, child, elder, and/or spousal abuse, wounds resulting from a crime, and sexual assault are examples of required reporting situations. You will need to familiarize yourself with the laws in your state.

Scenarios

1. You're treating an unconscious male patient on the street. You've determined that the man is in critical condition and should be transported immediately. The police have been unable to locate family to give consent for treatment and transport. What should the EMT-B do in this case?

Solution

The EMT-B should treat and transport this critical patient. As an EMT-B, you can treat an unconscious patient under implied consent.

2. An off-duty EMT-B drives by the scene of a motor vehicle collision with injuries. Has this EMT-B violated any law by not stopping to help?

Solution

In most states, "duty to act" must be established in order for the EMT-B to be required to render aid; so in most states this EMT-B would not be in violation. It is important that all EMT-Bs examine their own state laws, as there are laws in some states that require medically trained individuals to stop and render aid.

3. An alert adult male who was struck in the head with a rock allowed you to bandage his head but he is refusing transport. What should you do in this situation?

Solution

Alert adult patients have the right to refuse treatment and/or transport at any time during their care, so even though you have begun treatment, he has the right to tell you that's all he wants. You should encourage him to go to the hospital and advise him of the possible complications that could result from not going to the hospital. Once you've informed him of the dangers of not going to the hospital, have him sign a release and have family and/or police officers sign as witnesses.

Review Questions

1. The EMT-B's scope of practice is ultimately determined by

(A) the state the EMT-B practices in.
(B) the National Department of Transportation.
(C) the U.S. Department of Health, Education, and Welfare.
(D) the EMT-B's employer.

2. You come upon a patient without pulses or respirations. The family presents you with a DNR. You should

(A) begin resuscitation.
(B) honor the patient's wishes and withhold resuscitation.
(C) contact medical control to verify the DNR.
(D) Both B & C.

3. When patients verbally consent to treatment, what type of consent are they giving?

(A) Implied
(B) Expressed
(C) Informed
(D) Mutual

4. The rules of expressed consent and refusals are that the consent or refusal of care

(A) need only be verbalized.
(B) must be an informed consent or refusal.
(C) may be expressed by someone other than the patient.

5. If you walk away from a patient who is in obvious need of care, you may be guilty of

(A) assault.
(B) battery.
(C) abandonment.
(D) larceny.

6. Which of the following establish duty to act?

(A) While on duty you are dispatched to a call.
(B) You stop to render care for someone in distress.
(C) You accept your EMT-B license or certificate.
(D) A & B.

7. While at breakfast at the end of a shift, you and your coworkers discuss the call you made on a prominent local citizen and the restaurant staff overhears you relate the story of the call as well. This is a violation of

(A) patient confidentiality.
(B) laws of consent.
(C) rules of licensure.
(D) duty to act.

8. You are called to the scene of a crime. In regard to evidence, you should

(A) alter your care of the patient to preserve evidence.
(B) care for your patient while avoiding unnecessary corruption of evidence.
(C) collect evidence and then care for the patient.
(D) wait for the police to collect evidence and then care for the patient.

9. Medical identification insignia:

(A) are used to pick up prescriptions.
(B) are used to convey insurance information.
(C) give medical caregivers vital patient history information.
(D) administer medication.

10. While patients have the right to refuse care, in order to do so

(A) the patient must be informed of risks.
(B) the patient must be mentally competent.
(C) the patient must be of the age of consent.
(D) All of the above.

▩ Answers to Review Questions

1. **A** Objective 1
While there is a national curriculum for the EMT-B, laws or statutes in each state ultimately determine how EMT-Bs are trained, what they are allowed to do, and how they maintain licensure or certification.

2. **D** Objective 2

The laws on what constitutes a valid DNR vary from state to state, and the medical director for each EMS system has policies and procedures regarding DNRs. The overall objective is, whenever possible, to honor the wishes of patients and their families. The final word on that will come from medical direction.

3. **B** Objective 3

Consent given verbally by the patient is expressed consent.

4. **B** Objective 6

In order for expressed consent to be ethical and legally valid, it must be informed consent. Informed consent means that the pros and cons or benefits of treatment and possible negative effects of not receiving treatment have been presented to the patient and that the patient is able to understand them as presented.

5. **C** Objective 7

Once you receive a request for aid, you are obligated to see that call through to the end. That means that you must be with the patient until you turn care over to someone at an equal or higher level. Failing to do that constitutes abandonment.

6. **D** Objective 8

Depending on the situation, several things establish duty to act. First, if you are on duty and being paid to respond to care for patients, the moment you receive the call, the duty to act is established. If you are off duty, duty to act is established once you make patient contact. You are not obligated (in most states) to stop and care for injured when off duty. Once you make patient contact, however, the patient has a right to expect that you will usher him or her into the system for further care. Note: Some states may have a law in place requiring health care providers to render aid to citizens in distress. You must be familiar with the laws in your state.

7. **A** Objective 9

You are bound ethically and legally to protect patient confidentiality. You cannot discuss the misfortune of your patients with friends or family outside of professional exchanges as a part of their care.

8. **B** Objective 11

Crime scenes are complex situations. The EMT-B has the dual duty to care for the patient and not unnecessarily disrupt the crime scene. The priority is patient care. No care essential to the patient should be withheld or impaired by the need to protect evidence. However, the integrity of the scene should be kept in mind as the EMT-B moves about the scene so as not to disrupt the scene any more than absolutely necessary.

9. **C** Objective 10

Medical identification can be a bracelet, necklace, or card that carries important information about the patient's medical history. Histories of diabetes, heart disease, or seizure disorders, along with allergies or medications the patient may be taking, are among the things that may be listed.

10. **D** Objective 6

The right of patients to refuse care is being stressed increasingly in healthcare situations. In order for patients to refuse care, however, it is important that they are informed of the risks of refusing care, and the patient must be competent and of legal age of consent.

CHAPTER 4

The Human Body

Objectives

1. Identify the following topographic terms:

   - Medial
   - Lateral
   - Proximal
   - Distal
   - Superior
   - Inferior
   - Anterior
   - Posterior
   - Midline
   - Right and left
   - Mid-clavicular
   - Bilateral
   - Midaxillary.

2. Describe the anatomy and function of the following major body systems:

   - Respiratory
   - Circulatory
   - Musculoskeletal
   - Nervous
   - Endocrine

Anatomical Terms

In order to review the anatomical terms you need to know, we should start with normal anatomical position, or the position the body is in when these terms and landmarks are identified.

Correct anatomical position is a person standing facing forward with palms facing forward.

Midline is an imaginary line drawn down the center of the body, through the nose and umbilicus (belly button), dividing the body into right and left halves.

Midaxillary lines are imaginary lines on both sides of the body, drawn from the armpit to the ankle, dividing the body into anterior (front) and posterior (back).

The word **torso** refers to the chest and abdomen.

Medial means toward midline, and **lateral** means away from midline. A cut on the inside of the thigh is medial, while one on the outside of the thigh would be lateral.

Proximal and **distal** are used to describe where something lies on an extremity. Toward the fingers or toes would be distal, while something near where the extremity attaches to the body would be proximal.

Superior and **inferior** refer to where something is in relation to the whole body. Superior is toward the head; inferior is toward the feet.

Note: When using the words right and left, remember that this means the patient's right and left. So in order to grab the patient's right and left hands with your right and left hands with the patient facing you, you'll have to cross your hands.

Unilateral refers to one-sided; **bilateral** refers to both sides.

Dorsal is another term for the back of something such as your hand, while **ventral** would mean the front side (your palm).

Plantar is another term that refers to the feet, while palmar refers to the hand.

If you are lying on your stomach you are in a **prone** position; while on your back you are **supine**.

Fowler's position is a sitting position; **Trendelenburg** is sitting with your knees elevated.

The **shock position** is supine with the legs higher than the heart (elevating the legs or tilting the bed).

The Skeletal System

The skeletal system gives the body shape, protects vital organs, and provides the support needed for us to be able to move. The skeletal system is made up of seven sections.

✔ The skull houses and protects the brain.
✔ The face is made up of the orbits (around the eyes), nasal bone, maxilla (upper jaw), mandible (jawbone), and zygoma (cheekbones).
✔ The spinal column is made up of 5 sections containing 33 vertebrae in all. The division is as follows:

Cervical   7

Thoracic   12 (one for each rib)

Lumbar   5

Sacral   5

Coccyx   4

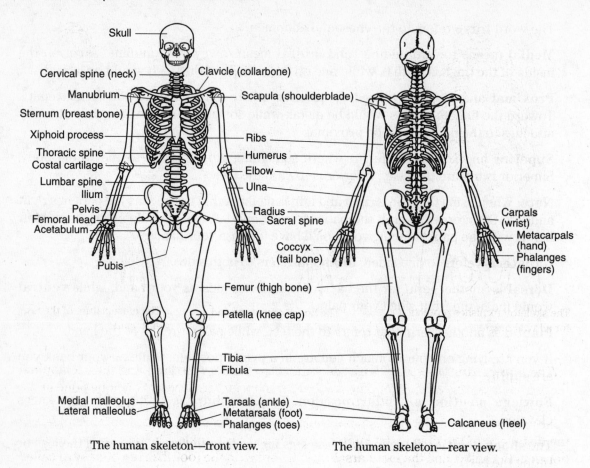

The human skeleton—front view.   The human skeleton—rear view.

All of these vertebrae are separated by flexible disks with the exception of the sacrum and coccyx (sometimes called the sacrococcygeal spine), which is a single fused bony mass.

The thorax or chest is made up of the 12 ribs, which come out of each side of the 12 thoracic vertebrae. Ten of these come together at the sternum in the center of the anterior chest. The last two float freely. The sternum is divided into three parts: the manubrium (top), body (middle), and zyphoid (inferior portion).

The pelvis consists of the iliac crests (pelvic wings), pubis (which is the anterior portion you can palpate), and the ichium, which is inferior and posterior. This is the bone you hurt when you fall on your buttocks.

The upper extremities consist of the clavicles or collarbones, the scapula (shoulderblade), and the acromion process or the tip of your shoulder. Your upper arm is the humerus, the olecrenon is the bone at your elbow (the proximal end of the ulna), and the radius and ulna are in your forearm. The distal end of the radius is at your thumb side, and the ulna is on the other side of your forearm. The small bones in your wrist are the carpals, the bones in your hand are the metacarpals, and your finger bones are the phalanges.

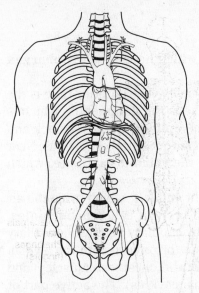

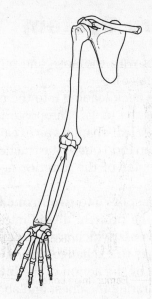

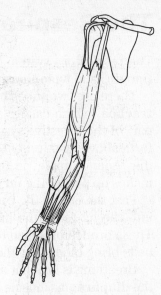

The skeleton furnishes protection for all vital organs.

The bones of the arm and hand.

The musculature of the arm and hand.

The lower extremities start with the greater trochanter (the ball) and the acetabulum (socket) that form the hip joint. The trochanter is the proximal end of the long bone in the thigh, the femur. The kneecap is the patella and the lower leg is made up of the tibia (shinbone) and the fibula. The distal end of the fibula is a knob on the outside of the ankle and the distal end of the tibia is the knob on the inside of the ankle. The tarsals are the small bones in the ankle, and the metatarsals are the bones in the foot. The toe bones are called phalanges, like the fingers.

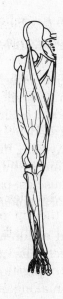

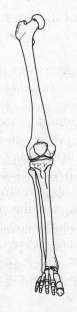

The musculature of the body.

The musculature of the leg and foot.

The bones of the leg and foot.

Two bones come together in a **joint**. The two types that we are concerned with are the ball-and-socket and hinge type. The hip and shoulder joints are ball-and-socket; the knee is a hinge joint.

■ The Respiratory System

The respiratory system starts with the nose and mouth, which house the **oropharynx** (mouth) and **nasopharynx** (nose).

There are two tubes in the neck leading into the chest cavity. The anterior tube is the **trachea**, which carries air to the lungs. The posterior tube is the **esophagus**, which is part of the digestive system. A leaf-shaped valve, called the **epiglottis**, moves back and forth above these tubes to keep food out of the trachea and air out of the esophagus. Near the "Adam's apple" in the center of the anterior neck is the **cricoid cartilage**, which makes up part of the **larynx**.

Past the larynx the trachea splits into two **bronchi**, right and left, which bring the air into the lungs. In the lungs the bronchi divide into small bronchi called **bronchioles**. These bronchioles lead to **alveoli**, which are surrounded by capillary beds. The capillary beds bring blood into the lungs to exchange carbon dioxide for oxygen with the alveoli.

Breathing is brought about by the action of the **intercostals** (chest wall muscles) and the **diaphragm** (muscle separating the chest and abdominal cavities). The active part of breathing is inspiration; it is brought about by the contraction of these respiratory muscles, which increase the size of the chest cavity bringing air into the lungs. The passive part of breathing is brought about by the relaxation of these muscles decreasing the size of the chest cavity, forcing the air out of the lungs.

During each breath, oxygen-rich air enters the alveoli, while oxygen-poor blood arrives in the lungs at the **capillaries** surrounding the alveoli. The oxygen in the alveoli is then exchanged with the carbon dioxide in the capillaries and the oxygen is carried by the blood out to the body, where the opposite exchange takes place in the capillaries in all of the body's tissues.

Normal breathing rates are: Adult 12–20 breaths per minute

Children 15–30 breaths per minute

Infants 25–50 breaths per minute

Breathing should be effortless; any sign of effort is an indication of respiratory distress. Breathing should have a regular rhythm with adequate and equal chest wall expansion. Breath sounds can confirm the presence and quality of respirations.

Inadequate respirations can be indicated by irregular rhythm or rates outside the normal range. Cyanosis, cold and clammy skin, diminished or absent breath sounds, unequal or inadequate chest wall expansion, or increased effort to breathe also indicate respiratory distress. Use of accessory muscles, particularly in children, is also a sign of respiratory distress. Agonal, or occasional gasping breaths, are usually the type of breathing seen just before a patient dies.

Special considerations for infants and children include smaller airways in which the tongue takes up proportionally more space. The trachea is narrower and softer, making it more easily obstructed by foreign bodies or positioning. The criocoid cartilage is less rigid in infants. The chest wall is also softer, making infants rely more on their diaphragm to breathe.

The Circulatory System

The circulatory system is made up of the heart (the pump), the blood vessels that carry the blood, and the blood itself.

The Heart

The heart is a four-chambered muscle. The top two chambers are called the **atria**. The bottom two are called the **ventricles**. The right atrium receives oxygen-poor blood from the veins and the left atrium receives oxygen-poor blood from the lungs. The atria contract, forcing the blood into the ventricles, then the ventricles contract. The right ventricle pumps blood to the lungs to exchange carbon dioxide for oxygen; the left ventricle sends the blood into the arteries to carry the blood out to the body where oxygen will be exchanged for carbon dioxide in the capillaries in the body's tissues.

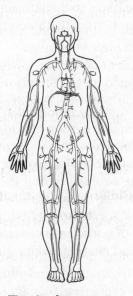

The circulatory system.

Blood Vessels

Arteries are double-walled tubular muscles that carry blood from the heart to the body's tissues. The largest artery is the **aorta**, which comes from the left ventricle and is comprised of ascending and descending portions in the chest. The **coronary arteries** run from the aorta to the heart muscle supplying the heart with blood. The **pulmonary arteries** are the only arteries that carry oxygen-poor blood, carrying blood from the right ventricle to the lungs. The **carotid arteries** branch off from the ascending aorta and carry blood to the brain. The **femoral arteries** branch off from the abdominal aorta and carry blood into the lower extremities. The **brachial arteries** run from the ascending aorta into the upper extremities. The **radial arteries** run from the brachial arteries along the radial bones toward the hands. Wherever an artery runs over a bone or muscle and comes close to the surface of the skin, a pulse can be palpated. Smaller extensions of arteries are called **arterioles**. Examples of arteries are

Carotid = either side of the neck

Brachial = inside the elbows

Radial = anterior, thumb side of wrist

Posterior tibial = medial aspect of ankle, posterior to distal tibia

Dorsalis pedis = top of the foot

Veins are single-walled tubular muscles that carry oxygen-poor blood back to the heart. Smaller veins are called **venules**. Between the venules and the arterioles are the **capillaries**, where the exchange of oxygen and carbon dioxide take place. At the tissue levels, nutrients and waste are also exchanged. The **pulmonary vein** is the only vein that carries oxygen-rich blood from the lungs to the left atrium. The largest veins are the **inferior** and **superior vena cava**, which bring the blood back to the heart from the body.

Blood

Blood is made up of red blood cells, white blood cells, and platelets. Red blood cells give blood its color and carry oxygen and/or carbon dioxide. White blood cells are part of the body's defense against infection. The platelets are part of the body's clot-forming capability.

Blood pressure consists of **systolic** and **diastolic** pressures. The systolic pressure represents the pressure within the arteries during the contraction of the heart and the arteries. The diastolic is the pressure in the arteries between the contractions.

Inadequate circulation is shock, or **hypoperfusion**. This lack of perfusion can be recognized by changes in the level of consciousness (restlessness, nervousness, agitation, and mental dullness), pale, cool, and clammy skin, rapid weak pulses, nausea and vomiting, and rapid, shallow breathing.

The Musculoskeletal System

Like the skeletal system, the muscular system gives the body shape, protects internal organs, and provides for movement. There are three types of muscle:

✔ **Voluntary** or skeletal muscle is attached to bones, forms the major muscle mass of the body and can be instructed by the nervous system and the brain to be contracted or relaxed at command of the individual.

✔ **Involuntary** or smooth muscle can be found in the walls of tubular structures such as the gastrointestinal tract, urinary system, and blood vessels. The individual has no control over these muscles, but the nervous system instructs them to function to move food, blood, or waste material through them.

✔ **Cardiac** muscle is a highly specialized muscle. It is found only in the heart and can tolerate only brief interruptions of blood flow. Most important, cardiac muscle can function independent of control from the brain or nervous system.

The Nervous System

The nervous system includes the brain and the nerves that connect the brain to every other part of the body. The components are the **brain**, the **spinal cord**, and the **peripheral nervous system** that includes sensory nerves that bring information back to the brain and motor nerves that carry the brain's instructions to the body.

The Skin

The skin protects the body from the environment, bacteria, and other organisms. It plays a role in temperature regulation and is a huge sensory organ, collecting information about heat, cold, pressure, and pain, and sending it back to the spinal cord and the brain. The skin is made up of three layers: the **epidermis** is the outermost and thinnest layer that is made up of cells that die, flake off, and replace themselves; the **dermis** is the next layer and contains sweat and sebaceous glands, hair follicles, and nerve endings; the deepest layer is the **subcutaneous layer**, which is made up of fat cells that store nutrients and water and is responsible for the contours of the exterior of our bodies.

The Endocrine System

The endocrine system secretes chemicals such as insulin, adrenalin, and other hormones that regulate various body functions.

Scenarios

1. You are giving aid to a male patient who was struck by a car. During your exam you notice swelling and deformity to his right thigh. This injury most likely has involved what structure?

Solution

You would suspect that this patient has broken the largest long bone in his body, the femur. You should also check for pulses and sensation below the injury (ankle) to make sure nerves and blood vessels have not been disrupted.

2. Your patient is complaining of tenderness in the right upper quadrant of his abdomen after being involved in a fistfight. What injuries do you suspect?

Solution

The liver is the largest solid organ and takes up most of the right upper quadrant and part of the left upper quadrant. You might also suspect injury to the ribs, gallbladder, kidneys, and colon.

▪ Review Questions

1. Correct anatomical position is

  (A) the back of the body facing you, palms toward you.
  (B) the front of the body facing you, palms forward.
  (C) the back of the body facing you, palms facing away from you.
  (D) the front of the body facing you, palms away from you.

2. The imaginary line drawn from the top of the head down the middle of the body through the nose and belly button is the

  (A) midline.
  (B) axillary line.
  (C) inline.
  (D) waistline.

3. If something is unilateral, it is

  (A) on one side only.
  (B) above the waist.
  (C) on both sides.
  (D) below the waist.

4. If you were trying to describe something as toward the head, you would say:

  (A) inferior.
  (B) proximal.
  (C) superior.
  (D) distal.

5. A patient lying on his or her back is in what position?

  (A) Supine
  (B) Prone
  (C) Recumbent
  (D) Lateral

6. The spine is made up of _____ vertebrae?

  (A) 25
  (B) 30
  (C) 33
  (D) 40

7. There are _____ cervical vertebrae?

  (A) 4
  (B) 5
  (C) 7
  (D) 12

8. The _____ vertebrae are fused together into a bony mass.

   (A) cervical
   (B) sacral
   (C) coccyx
   (D) Both B & C

9. The forearm bone that ends at the thumb side of the wrist is the

   (A) metacarpal.
   (B) carpal.
   (C) radius.
   (D) ulna.

10. Finger and toe bones are all called

   (A) metacarpals.
   (B) carpals.
   (C) tarsals.
   (D) phalanges.

Answers to Review Questions

1. **B** Objective 1
The correct anatomical position is palms turned forward, making the palms the anterior and the backs of the hands the posterior surface of the hands.

2. **A** Objective 1
The imaginary line drawn down the middle of the body dividing the left from the right is the midline.

3. **A** Objective 1
Unilateral means one-sided; bilateral means two-sided.

4. **C** Objective 1
The superior of the body is toward the head; the inferior is toward the feet.

5. **A** Objective 1
A patient lying on his or her back is said to be supine; a patient on his or her stomach is prone.

6. **C** Objective 2
There are 7 cervical, 12 thoracic, 5 lumbar, 5 sacral, and 4 coccyx vertebrae for a total of 33 vertebrae. The sacrum and coccyx are fused into one bony mass.

7. **C** Objective 2
There are 7 cervical vertebrae.

8. **D** Objective 2
The sacrum and coccyx are fused into one bony mass.

9. **C** Objective 2
There are two bones in the forearm: the radius and the ulna. At the distal ends of the bones, the radius is on the thumb side of the wrist and the ulna is on the fifth finger side of the wrist.

10. **D** Objective 2
The bones that make up the fingers and toes are called phalanges.

CHAPTER 5

Baseline Vital Signs and SAMPLE History

Objectives

1. Identify the components of vital signs.
2. Describe the methods to obtain a breathing rate.
3. Identify the attributes that should be obtained when assessing breathing.
4. Differentiate between shallow, labored, and noisy breathing.
5. Describe the methods to obtain a pulse rate.
6. Identify the information obtained when assessing a patient's pulse.
7. Differentiate between a strong, weak, regular, and irregular pulse.
8. Describe the methods to assess the skin color, temperature, condition (capillary refill in infants and children).
9. Identify the normal and abnormal skin colors.
10. Differentiate between pale, blue, red, and yellow skin color.
11. Identify normal and abnormal skin temperature.
12. Differentiate between hot, cool, and cold skin temperature.
13. Identify normal and abnormal skin conditions.
14. Identify normal and abnormal capillary refill in infants and children.
15. Describe the methods to assess the pupils.
16. Identify normal and abnormal pupil size.
17. Differentiate between dilated (big) and constricted (small) pupil size.
18. Differentiate between reactive and nonreactive pupils and equal and unequal pupils.
19. Describe the methods to assess blood pressure.
20. Define systolic pressure.
21. Define diastolic pressure.
22. Explain the difference between auscultation and palpation for obtaining a blood pressure.

23. Identify the components of the SAMPLE history.

24. Differentiate between a sign and a symptom.

25. State the importance of accurately reporting and recording the baseline vital signs.

26. Discuss the need to search for additional medical identification.

General Information

You will need to collect general information on your patient. This information will include the chief complaint, or why EMS was called. This information also includes age, sex, and race.

Vital Signs

Baseline vital signs include assessing breathing, pulse, skin, pupils, and blood pressure and a reassessment of these vital signs.

Breathing

In obtaining a breathing rate, it is important that the patient not know you are counting his breaths or it may influence the rate of breathing. Count the breaths over 30 seconds and double that to obtain the rate of breaths per minute. You should also note the quality of breathing.

- **Normal breathing** would be average chest wall movement without use of accessory muscles.
- **Shallow breathing** would have slight movement of the chest wall.
- **Labored breathing** would be evidenced by obvious increased effort to breathe. Sounds such as grunting or stridor (a harsh sound) may be heard and the use of accessory muscles can be seen. In infants and children nasal flaring and supraclavicular and intercostal retractions are common. Patients may also gasp for breath. Noisy respirations can include snoring, wheezing, gurgling, and crowing sounds.

Pulse

In all patients over one year old, the pulse you obtain initially would be the **radial pulse**. Once you obtain the radial pulse, assess its rate and quality. As with breathing, count the pulse for 30 seconds and double it to get the rate per minute. The quality of the pulse should be described as weak or strong. You should also determine whether the rhythm is regular or irregular. If you are unable to get the radial pulse, check for a **carotid pulse**. When assessing the carotid it is important to check only one at a time and not to use excessive pressure, particularly in geriatric patients.

Skin

Assess skin color to determine tissue perfusion. You can examine nail beds, oral mucosa, and/or conjunctiva. In infants and children, you can check the palms and soles. Normally, skin color should be pink. Pale skin indicates poor perfusion. Bluish, or cyanotic, skin indicates poor tissue perfusion and/or inadequate oxygenation. Red or flushed skin can occur because of exposure to heat or carbon monoxide poisoning. Yellow, or jaundiced, skin indicates illness involving the liver.

Skin temperature should be assessed by placing the back of your hand on the patient's skin. Normal skin should feel warm. Abnormal skin temperatures would include: Hot, which would indicate fever or exposure to heat; cool, which would indicate poor perfusion or cold exposure; and cold, which would indicate exposure to extreme cold. Normal skin condition would be dry. Wet, moist, or extremely dry skin would be abnormal.

In infants and children less than six years old, you should assess **capillary refill** to evaluate tissue perfusion. This is done by pressing on the skin or nail beds and counting the seconds it takes for the initial color to return. In infants, this should take two seconds or less. More than that would be abnormal.

Pupils

Briefly shine a light into your patient's eyes and evaluate the size and reactivity of the pupils. A large pupil would be described as dilated, while small would be constricted. The pupils should be described as equal or unequal and reactive or nonreactive to light.

Blood Pressure

The blood pressure reading includes the **systolic** and **diastolic** values. When **auscultating** the blood pressure, the first sound heard is the systolic pressure, which represents the pressure in the arteries during contraction of the heart. The disappearance of sounds is the diastolic pressure, which represents the pressure in the arteries between the contractions of the heart. When using palpation, only the systolic pressure is obtained. Blood pressures should be obtained in all patients over the age of three.

It is important to remember that general physical condition may be more important than the vital signs, particularly in children. Noting that the patient is unresponsive or in respiratory distress is more descriptive of the patient's condition than the numbers.

Also of importance is reassessing the patient's vital signs. This should be done at least every 15 minutes and every 5 minutes if the patient is unstable. You should also recheck vitals after every treatment or intervention. This will enable you to determine whether the patient's condition is worsening or improving and measure the effectiveness of your treatments.

■ SAMPLE

SAMPLE is an acronym that will help you remember the parts of the patient history you need to obtain.

S = Signs and symptoms

A = Allergies

M = Medications

P = Pertinent past history

L = Last oral intake

E = Events leading to the injury or illness

NOTE: A sign is measurable, such as a pulse or the color of the skin. Symptoms are descriptions by the patient of how he or she feels, any discomfort or disability. Examples of symptoms would be nausea, chest pain, or light-headedness.

Medical Identification

As mentioned earlier, many patients who want others to be aware of their medical history will wear or carry medical identification. These bracelets, necklaces, cards, or other forms of identification alert EMTs to conditions such as diabetes, heart disease, or allergies, as well as letting you know that patients may have other special needs or disabilities. EMTs should be on the lookout for medical IDs, particularly if the patient is unconscious and/or unable to give a history.

Scenarios

1. Your partner has asked you to obtain a blood pressure on your patient. How do you go about that?

Solution

After confirming the location of the brachial pulse in the arm you have selected, place the cuff around the arm so the bladder is centered over the anterior surface of the forearm. (Many cuffs have arrows showing how to line it up.) Once done, put the bell of your stethoscope over the place on which you felt the pulse and pump the cuff up to about 150 mm hg. Place the earpieces of the stethoscope in your ears and listen as you slowly let the air out of the cuff. The first sound you hear is the systolic pressure and the last you hear is the diastolic pressure.

2. Your partner asks you to check the pupils on your patient. How would you go about doing that and what are you looking for?

Solution

You are looking to determine PERL—Pupils Equal and Reactive to Light. In order to do this, hold one of the patient's eyes open at a time and move the light across the eye from the outside (lateral) to the inside (medial). Check to see the size of the pupil before the light is shone into it and how it responds, then compare the eyes.

3. It appears that your patient has an injury to his knee. You've been asked to check the circulation and sensation below the injury. How would you do that?

Solution

You need to check for pulses distal or below the injury to check for the posterior tibial or dorsalis pedis. Also check to see if the nerves are intact by asking the patient to wiggle his toes and see if he can feel you touching the inside and outside of his toes.

▬ Review Questions

1. In assessing the patient's respiratory rate, the EMT-B should observe the rise and fall of the chest, counting the number of breaths for

   (A) 10 seconds and multiply by 6.
   (B) 15 seconds and multiply by 4.
   (C) 30 seconds and multiply by 2.
   (D) 60 seconds and multiply by 2.

2. Normal respirations can be characterized by

   (A) average chest wall motion, not using accessory muscles.
   (B) slight chest or abdominal wall motion.
   (C) an increase in effort of breathing.
   (D) the use of accessory muscles.

3. To obtain a pulse in a conscious patient, the EMT-B should assess the

   (A) carotid pulse.
   (B) brachial pulse.
   (C) radial pulse.
   (D) femoral pulse.

4. In all patients less than one year old, the _____ pulse should be assessed.

   (A) carotid
   (B) brachial
   (C) radial
   (D) femoral

5. To determine perfusion, the patient's skin should be assessed. If normally perfusing, the skin should be

   (A) pink, warm, and dry.
   (B) pale, cool, and moist.
   (C) pink, cool, and moist.
   (D) pale, warm, and dry.

6. Capillary refill should be assessed in patients less than six years old. Normal capillary refill time is

   (A) < than 10 seconds.
   (B) < than 6 seconds.
   (C) < than 4 seconds.
   (D) < than 2 seconds.

7. When checking the patient's pupils, big pupils are considered

  (A) dilated.
  (B) constricted.
  (C) midrange.
  (D) reactive.

8. If you are auscultating, you are

  (A) feeling for tenderness or distension.
  (B) listening with a stethoscope.
  (C) feeling for a pulse.
  (D) shining a light into the patient's eyes.

9. Blood pressure should be obtained in

  (A) all patients.
  (B) all patients over the age of 18.
  (C) all patients over the age of 10.
  (D) all patients over the age of 3.

10. In critical patients, vital signs should be reassessed

  (A) every 5 minutes.
  (B) every 10 minutes.
  (C) every 15 minutes.
  (D) only when requested by medical control.

Answers to Review Questions

1. **C** Objective 2
Irregularities in rhythm will cause inaccuracies in the count that increase with the shortness of the time measured. Counting the breaths or heartbeats felt over 30 seconds gives a fair chance of reasonable accuracy.

2. **A** Objective 3
Respirations should be effortless. Any time a patient's breathing draws attention to itself with signs of obvious effort, that is a sign of distress.

3. **C** Objective 5
The easiest pulse to gain quick access to in a conscious patient is the radial pulse. If the patient is unresponsive, the carotid pulse is larger, stronger, and more easily obtained.

4. **B** Objective 5
It is difficult to feel a carotid pulse in an infant because of the shortness of the neck and the rolls of baby fat. The radial pulse may also be obscured by the baby fat at the wrist. The most reliably obtained pulse in infants is the brachial. On the infant it is found superior and medial to the anterior antecubital fossa or inside of the elbow.

5. **A** Objective 8
Normally, skin is pink, warm, and dry. Hypoxia can cause the skin to be pale, cool, and moist. Environmental conditions can also change the skin, as in flushed and warm when exposed to heat and pale and cool when exposed to cold. Allergic reactions may also cause the skin to be flushed or reddened.

6. **D** Objective 8
When compressed, the blood is squeezed from the capillary beds, causing the skin to blanch or become pale. The time it takes for the color to return to the compressed area is the capillary refill time, which should be less than two seconds. Longer than that implies poor perfusion or possibly shock.

7. **A** Objective 16
The size of the pupil changes when exposed to light. In normal room light they should be mid-sized; when exposed to brighter light they constrict, and with minimal light they dilate.

8. **B** Objective 19
Auscultation means listening. The EMT-B will use a stethoscope to listen to the lungs when evaluating a patient's breathing and to hear the pulse over the brachial artery while obtaining a patient's blood pressure.

9. **D** Objective 19
Obtaining blood pressures are less accurate assessments in patients under the age of three; closer attention will be paid to their heart and breathing rates.

10. **A** Objective 25
Since the condition of critical or serious patients can change rapidly, it is important to monitor them closely for signs of change. In order to do that it is necessary to repeat vital signs every 5 minutes. In noncritical patients, vital signs should be checked every 15 minutes (**C**).

CHAPTER 6

Lifting and Moving Patients

Objectives

1. Define body mechanics.

2. Discuss the guidelines and safety precautions that need to be followed when lifting a patient.

3. Describe the safe lifting of cots and stretchers.

4. Describe the guidelines and safety precautions for carrying patients and/or equipment.

5. Discuss one-handed carrying techniques.

6. Describe correct and safe carrying procedures on stairs.

7. State the guidelines for reaching and their application.

8. Describe the correct reaching technique for logrolling patients.

9. State the guidelines for pushing and pulling.

10. Discuss the general considerations of moving patients.

11. State situations that may require the use of an emergency move.

12. Identify the following patient carrying devices:

    ✔ Wheeled ambulance stretcher
    ✔ Portable ambulance stretcher
    ✔ Long spine board
    ✔ Basket stretcher
    ✔ Flexible stretcher

Body Mechanics

Proper lifting techniques include the basic safety precautions of using your legs and not your back to lift, and keeping the weight as close to your body as possible. The guidelines for lifting include taking the patients' weight into consideration and whether or not you need additional help. You should always lift without twisting, with your feet properly positioned, while communicating clearly and frequently with your team members.

Lifting cots and stretchers calls for using the proper amount of people to help. When possible, consider a stair chair when traversing stairs for safety and patient comfort. Before placing the patient on the device, try to determine the patient's weight. The team should consist of an even number of people to provide balance when lifting. You should also make sure you know the weight limitations of your equipment and what to do when patient weight exceeds the limits of your gear. When lifting, use the power-lift or squat-lift position, maintaining your back locked in normal curvature and position. Even with weak knees or thighs, the power lift can be helpful. Feet should be flat and evenly spaced to distribute the weight. When you lift, it is important that the upper body come up before the hips.

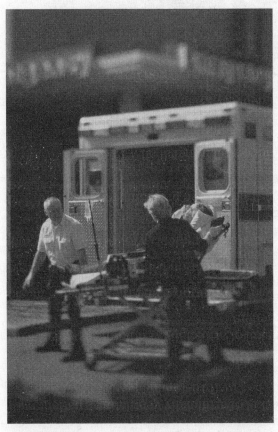

The selection of the proper stretcher facilitates the safe transport of patients.

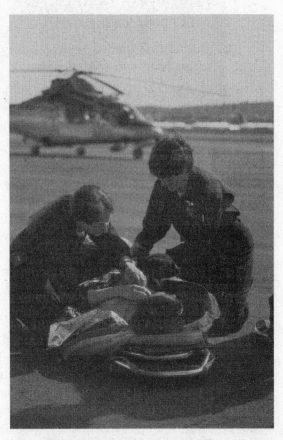

In any emergency situation, there must be sufficient personnel present to achieve the required objectives.

The power grip maintains the maximum surface of your hands in contact with what you are lifting. Always avoid bending at the waist.

When carrying, it is important to use devices that can be rolled whenever possible. Know the weight that your device and your team are capable of lifting. Weight close to your body, good communication with your team members, back in proper position, refraining from twisting when lifting, and bending at the knees and not the back while avoiding hyperextension of the back are all essential.

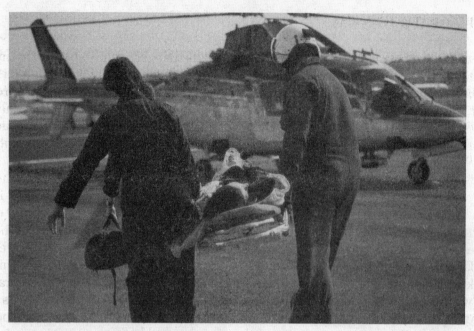

The EMT-B should always be fit and practiced enough to handle a stretcher properly.

Use correct lifting techniques and choose teammates of similar strength and height for best results.

The one-handed technique calls for picking up and carrying the patient with the back in the locked-in position while avoiding leaning to either side to compensate for the imbalance.

As mentioned, correct procedure on stairs should include the use of a stair chair when possible with the back in locked-in position, flexing at the hips, not the waist, while bending at the knees. As with all lifts and carries, keep weight and arms as close to the body as possible.

When reaching, avoid reaching overhead and a hyperextended position. Do not twist while reaching and keep the back in a locked-in position. You should avoid reaching more than 15 to 20 inches in front of the body. Situations where strenuous effort is required to be maintained for longer than a minute should be avoided.

When reaching to perform a logroll maneuver, lean from the hips with your back straight, using your shoulder muscles to help with the roll.

You should push whenever possible rather than pulling with your back in locked-in position, keeping the line of pull through the center of the body by bending your knees. Keep the weight close to your body while pushing from the area between the waist and shoulder. If the weight is lower, use the kneeling position. Avoid pushing or pulling if the weight is in an overhead position. Keep your elbows bent and close to the sides.

Types of Moves

The EMT must be able to determine the kinds of moves to be undertaken when handling various categories of patients.

Emergency Moves

Emergency moves are used when there is an imminent danger to the patient if not moved immediately. Fire or danger of fire or explosion, an inability to protect the patient from hazards, or the need to gain access to another patient in need of lifesaving care are reasons for using emergency moves. Emergency moves are used when there is an immediate threat to life. They should be used when the patient has an altered mental status, inadequate breathing, or shock. If there is no threat to life, nonurgent moves using normal precautions should be used.

Using emergency moves may aggravate spine injuries, so moving the patient by pulling him or her in the direction of the long axis of the spine can limit the hazard. It is not possible to completely protect the spine without immobilization devices; therefore emergency moves should be used only when there is imminent danger to the patient or the rescuers, or there is another patient in more imminent need who necessitates the movement of the patient. If the patient is on the ground (or floor), pull on the patient's clothing in the neck and shoulder area, put the patient in a blanket, and drag the blanket, or drag the patient with your hands under the patient's armpits, grasping the patient's forearms.

Urgent moves include using rapid extrication from a vehicle. This entails getting behind the patient, providing in-line immobilization, while a second EMT applies a cervical collar (c-collar) and a third places a long board under the patient and then moves into the passenger seat. The second EMT supports the thorax as the third frees the patient's legs from the gas and brake pedals. As the EMT at the head and neck directs, the patient is rotated in several short coordinated moves to bring his or her back square to the doorframe. At this point, another EMT must take the head and neck from the EMT in the backseat, as he or she can no longer maintain cervical immobilization while the patient is being moved to the board. While the end of the board is supported, the team lowers the patient from a sitting position down to supine. The patient is then moved onto the board in short movements that allow the team to maintain in-line immobilization.

Nonurgent Moves

Nonurgent moves are used when there is no suspicion of spinal injury. These moves include the direct ground lift, in which the rescuers, side by side, slide their arms under the patient at the neck, lower back, just above the buttocks and the knees, and lift the patient to their chests. Another nonurgent move is the extremity lift in which a rescuer at the patient's head comes from behind and places his or her hands under the patient's arms and grabs the patient's wrists. The second rescuer grabs the patient under the knees and the two rescuers lift the patient together.

Transferring a Supine Patient

Transferring a supine patient from a bed to your stretcher is a variation of the direct ground lift. The stretcher is placed perpendicular to the bed with the head of the stretcher at the foot of the bed. After sliding the patient to the edge of the bed, the two rescuers lift the patient in the same manner as the direct ground lift and rotate toward the stretcher. The draw sheet method depends on the strength of the draw sheet and the weight of your patient. It is widely used to transfer patients from a stretcher to a bed or vice versa. In this method, the top sheet is loosened from the bed, then the cot is pushed up to the bed as the rescuers reach across the stretcher, grasping the sheet firmly at the head, chest, hips, and knees. The patient is then gently slid onto the bed.

Equipment Used in Lifting and Moving

The equipment used in lifting and moving patients includes stretchers or cots, which are commonly used for transport as well as movement to and from the ambulance. The stretchers have collapsible wheel assemblies and are stable only on even terrain. Once collapsed, these stretchers can be carried up and down stairs by two or four rescuers. Two rescuers would lift from the feet and the head, while each of four rescuers would lift at each corner of the stretcher. When loading stretchers into an ambulance, always ensure that there is sufficient lifting power available. It is also important to lift with your legs, maintaining your back in a straight, upright position. Avoid twisting and lifting at the same time. If you are loading an ambulance that includes multiple stretchers, hanging stretchers should be loaded first. All patients and cots should be secured before the ambulance moves.

Other devices for lifting and carrying include portable or collapsible stretchers and stair chairs for bringing patients out of buildings in a sitting position. Long backboards are used to immobilize spine-injured patients and short boards are used for patients who must be extricated from a vehicle or other compartment and brought out onto a long board. Scoop stretchers split at the center and scoop the patient up. Flexible stretchers are just that—flexible enough to assist in moving patients in awkward situations. As with any piece of equipment, all of these should be tested according to manufacturer's recommendations.

Patient Positioning

Unresponsive patients without a spine injury should be placed in the recovery position. This has the patient on his or her side to help keep the airway open. Patients with chest pain or respiratory distress should be placed in a sitting position. Spine-injured patients should be immobilized on a long board in a supine position. Patients in shock may benefit from elevating the foot end of their stretcher. Pregnant patients may suffer from postural hypotension. Placing a pregnant patient on her left side in the left, lateral recumbent position should relieve this. Uncomfortable, nauseated, or vomiting patients should be placed in a position of comfort or the position they best tolerate with an EMT in position to monitor the airway.

Scenarios

1. You are called to assist lifting a patient on a cot. Is it acceptable to bend at the waist as you lift the cot?

Solution

Proper body mechanics require that you bend at the knees and lift with your back straight. Bending at the waist puts you at risk for serious back injuries.

2. You and your partner are confronted with moving a patient in respiratory distress down several flights of stairs. What is the best way to do this?

Solution

When taking patients down stairs, whenever possible, it is best to use a stair chair device or, at the least, a chair. The patient can be transferred to a sitting position on your cot when you reach the street level.

3. You have arrived at the scene of a burning vehicle with the victim still inside the vehicle. After donning proper clothing and being given the signal to proceed by the fire department, how would you remove the victim from the car?

Solution

Whenever there is an immediate danger to the patient if not moved, emergency moves are to be used. These are manual moves using minimal equipment to move the patient without delay.

▉ Review Questions

1. Proper lifting includes

(A) bending at the waist and lifting with your back.
(B) bending at the knees and lifting with your back.
(C) bending at the waist and lifting with your legs.
(D) bending at the knees and lifting with your legs.

2. When lifting, your feet should be

(A) turned inward and widely spaced.
(B) flat and evenly spaced.
(C) turned inward and evenly spaced.
(D) flat and widely spaced.

3. In order to accomplish a power lift, you must

(A) wear special armbands.
(B) grip with your hands in opposite directions.
(C) keep as much of the surface of your hands in contact with the stretcher.
(D) keep your arms as far from your body as you can.

4. When moving patients, you should not work with the patient farther than

(A) 5–10 inches from your body.
(B) 10–15 inches from your body.
(C) 15–20 inches from your body.
(D) 20–25 inches from your body.

5. Whenever possible, it is best to

(A) push your patients.
(B) pull your patients.
(C) push or pull your patients.
(D) not push or pull your patients.

6. The type of move to be used if your patient is in imminent danger is

(A) an urgent move
(B) a nonurgent move.
(C) an emergency move.
(D) a standard move.

7. An unresponsive patient in a car, following a motor vehicle collision, with a rapid weak pulse and ineffective respirations, should be removed from the vehicle using

(A) an urgent move.
(B) a nonurgent move.
(C) an emergency move.
(D) a standard move.

8. A patient with normal vital signs and complaints of back pain when moving should be moved using

(A) an urgent move.
(B) a nonurgent move.
(C) an emergency move.
(D) a standard move.

9. Unconscious patients without spine injury potential should be placed

(A) on their back.
(B) on their stomach.
(C) on their side.
(D) sitting up.

10. Patients with difficulty breathing, without spine injuries, should be placed

(A) supine.
(B) prone.
(C) in a recovery position.
(D) in a sitting position.

Answers to Review Questions

1. **D** Objective 2
Proper lifting techniques call for keeping the back straight and bending at the knees to protect your back. Lifting with your legs is safer than bending your back and lifting with your arms and back.

2. **B** Objective 2

Keeping your feet flat and evenly spaced ensures that your legs are in proper lifting position, preventing unnecessary strain to the leg muscles and a solid platform to distribute the weight you are lifting.

3. **C** Objective 2

The intention of the power lift is to position your hands in a way that keeps as much of the anterior surfaces of your palm and fingers on the handle or bar you are lifting.

4. **C** Objective 7

Working further than 15–20 inches away from your body does not allow you to use your body to distribute the weight you are lifting. The weight will be creating excessive strain on your arms and back.

5. **A** Objective 9

Pushing patients allows you to use the weight of your body to move the patient. Pulling depends too much on your arms and back.

6. **C** Objective 11

Generally you should take your time moving patients in order to protect their injuries and prevent further harm. When there is immediate danger to the patient, emergency moves allow for rapid movement with caution reasonable to the circumstances.

7. **A** Objective 11

Patients in critical condition may require rapid movement to get them to definitive care. The moves used in these patients are called urgent moves and the patient needs care urgently.

8. **B** Objective 11

The types of moves appropriate for most patients, taking full precautions to ensure no further harm, are called nonurgent moves. These moves are not time-critical, while urgent and emergency moves are.

9. **C** Objective 10

One of the most common complications in unconscious patients is airway obstruction due to vomiting. Placing unconscious patients on their side, or even turning the backboard to the side, allows gravity to assist in keeping the airway clear.

10. **D** Objective 10

Breathing is facilitated by the lungs being pulled open. Standing or sitting allows gravity to assist in pulling the lungs into open position and making breathing easier. Conversely, lying on one's back creates pressure against the chest cavity, making breathing more difficult.

CHAPTER 7

Airway

■ Objectives

1. Name and label the major structures of the respiratory system on a diagram.

2. List the signs of adequate breathing.

3. List the signs of inadequate breathing.

4. Describe the steps in performing the head-tilt chin-lift maneuver.

5. Relate the mechanism of injury to the opening of the airway.

6. Describe the steps in performing the jaw thrust maneuver.

7. State the importance of having a suction unit ready for immediate use when providing emergency care.

8. Describe the techniques of suctioning.

9. Describe how to artificially ventilate a patient with a pocket mask.

10. Describe the steps in performing the skill of artificially ventilating a patient with a bag-valve mask system while using the jaw thrust maneuver.

11. List the parts of the bag-valve mask system.

12. Describe the steps in performing the skill of artificially ventilating a patient with a bag-valve mask for one and two rescuers.

13. Describe the signs of adequate artificial ventilation using the bag-valve mask.

14. Describe the signs of inadequate artificial ventilation using the bag-valve mask.

15. Describe the steps in artificially ventilating a patient with a flow-restricted, oxygen-powered ventilation device.

16. List the steps in performing the actions taken when providing mouth-mouth and mouth to stoma ventilations.

17. Describe how to measure and insert an oropharyngeal airway.

18. Describe how to measure and insert a nasopharyngeal airway.

19. Define the components of an oxygen delivery system.

20. Identify a nonrebreather face mask and state the oxygen flow requirements for its use.

21. Describe the indications for using a nasal cannula vs. a nonrebreather face mask.

22. Identify a nasal cannula and state the flow requirements needed for its use.

Anatomy Review

The respiratory system begins at the mouth and nose and ends with the capillary beds surrounding the alveoli in the lungs. To review: The mouth and nose open into the oropharynx and nasopharynx, joining to form the retropharynx or the back of the throat. The epiglottis covers the esophagus when we breathe to allow the air to enter the trachea and keep it out of the digestive tract. While swallowing, it covers the trachea to keep solids and fluids out of the respiratory tract. Further down, the trachea is the larynx and cricoid cartilage. Beyond that the trachea divides into the right and left bronchi, one leading into each lung. The bronchi divide into bronchioles, which lead to groups of alveoli, each of which is surrounded by a capillary bed.

Breathing is facilitated by the contraction of the intercostals and diaphragm muscles. As the muscles contract, the lungs expand and air is drawn into the lungs. As the muscles relax, the chest shrinks and the air is forced out.

The cells in every body tissue require oxygen and need to off-load carbon dioxide to function. Blood is circulated to the lungs where the capillaries off-load the carbon dioxide to the alveoli and take oxygen from the alveoli. The carbon dioxide is exhaled and replaced with oxygen with inhalation.

In order for adequate oxygen to reach our body's cells, we need to maintain adequate breathing. Normal rates for adults range from 12 to 20 breaths per minute, while for children it is 15 to 30, and 25 to 50 for infants. Breathing also needs to have a regular rhythm, with clear breath sounds and equal and adequate expansion of both lungs. Breathing should be effortless.

Breathing is inadequate if there is an increased effort to breathe, the rate is outside normal parameters, the rhythm is irregular, or the lungs inflate inadequately or unequally. The patient's skin may become pale, blue, cool and/or clammy if breathing is inadequate.

Infants and children have some significant differences affecting their airways. First, all of the structures are smaller and more easily obstructed. Infants' and children's tongues are larger and take up more of the pharynx. Their trachea are narrower and softer, making obstruction more likely. Cartilage and muscles are also less developed and infants and some children may depend more on the diaphragm to breathe.

Opening the Airway

When there is no suspicion of spinal injury, the head-tilt chin-lift method of opening the airway should be used. If there is a possibility of injury to the spine, the jaw thrust should be used.

To perform the head-tilt chin-lift maneuver, place your hand on the patient's forehead and tilt the head back. Place your other hand under the bony part of the patient's jaw and lift the jaw up.

To perform the jaw thrust maneuver, kneel above the supine patient's head, placing your elbows on the surface on which the patient is lying, with one hand on each side of the patient's head. Grasping the angles of the patient's lower jaw on both sides, move the jaw upward and forward.

Suctioning

Gloves and eye protection are a must when providing suction. Suction is performed to remove blood, fluids, or other materials from the airway. It is important that you know the operation capabilities and limitations of your equipment, which can be as simple as a turkey baster or as complex as a multiple pressure-setting, battery-powered unit. When using commercial battery-powered or mounted suction units, the preferred suction tip or catheter is the hard or rigid "tonsil tip" suction catheter. This has a large orifice that will allow removal of debris from the airway. The soft "French" catheters have a stopcock to apply or release suction, but have a narrow internal diameter and are useful only for light secretions.

Whatever the device, you should premeasure from the corner of the mouth to the earlobe to determine how much of the catheter should be inserted into the airway. Once done, turn on the suction unit and insert the suction catheter. Once fully inserted to the depth premeasured, apply suction and keep the catheter moving around the airway, gradually withdrawing from the airway. Suction should not be applied for more than 15 seconds at a time to allow for adequate ventilations. If suction is needed continuously, suction for 15 seconds alternating between 2 minutes of uninterrupted ventilations. It is a good idea to rinse the catheter with saline between suctioning to clear the tube.

Artificial Ventilation

When providing artificial ventilation for a patient, there should be equal rise and fall of both sides of the chest, the rate of ventilation should fall within the normal rate range for your patient, and you should see the patient's color and heart rate return to normal. Inadequate ventilations won't produce adequate rise and fall of the chest and the patient's color and heart rate will continue to be abnormal.

Studies have shown that the most effective means of providing ventilations of adequate volume are, in order of effectiveness, mouth-to-mask devices; two-person bag-valve masks; flow-restricted, oxygen-powered ventilation devices; and one-person bag-valve masks, in that order. After providing for body substance isolation, whatever the device, the most important and first point after opening the airway is to obtain and maintain a seal around the mouth. Using the thumb and forefinger to form a C around the base of the mask, holding it to the face and making a seal is the most effective one-handed method. If there are two EMTs you can use both hands to ensure a seal. Having the device connected to an oxygen source increases the oxygen concentration of each ventilation.

The mouth-to-mask device consists of a mask and a one-way valve that prevents the rescuer from coming in contact with the patient's expired air or airway secretions, and it should also have a nipple to attach oxygen supply.

Bag-valve masks consist of a mask, a one-way valve, a self-inflating bag, and an oxygen reservoir. When attached to an oxygen supply of 15 liters per minute, ventilations of 95%

to 100% oxygen can be obtained. It can be difficult for one EMT to maintain the seal and squeeze the bag, which is why mouth-to-mask and two-person bag-valve masks have better ventilation volumes. Bag-valve masks also come in child and infant sizes to limit the chance of overinflating your patient.

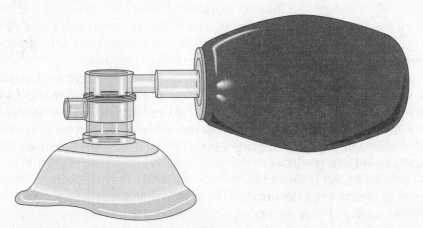

A bag-valve mask is effective for providing breathing assistance to patients requiring artificial ventilation.

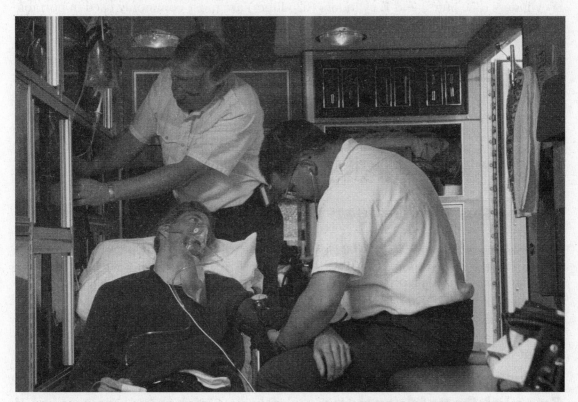

This patient wears an oxygen mask while being prepared for transport to the hospital.

Flow-restricted oxygen-powered ventilators can provide 100% oxygen under pressure to ventilate the patient. The volume delivered will still depend on adequate sealing. The device has a pressure relief valve designed to prevent overinflation.

In patients with stomas as airways you need to either seal around the stoma to ventilate (you will also have to hold the mouth and nose closed) or seal the stoma and have the patient breathe through the mouth and nose.

Airway Adjuncts

You may find it necessary to use an airway adjunct to maintain an open airway. If the patient is unconscious and does not have an active gag reflex, you can use an **oropharyngeal airway**. Select the proper size by measuring from the corner of the mouth to the earlobe. Then insert it into the open mouth with the tip toward the roof of the mouth, rotating it as you insert. You may also insert the airway directly into position without needing to rotate if you hold the tongue down with a tongue blade.

For patients with a gag reflex, you will need to use a **nasopharyngeal airway**. Select a size that is small enough to fit the nostrils and measure the length it should be inserted from the nose to the earlobe. The insertion end is beveled and this bevel should face the center of the nose. Insert the airway allowing the curve of the device to approximate the curve of the airway and stopping at the point determined by your measurement of the distance from the earlobe to the nose.

Oxygen

D cylinders (350 liters) and E cylinders (625 liters) are most commonly used in portable oxygen delivery systems. The inline oxygen in your ambulance is usually attached to an M cylinder (3,000 liters); G cylinders (5,300 liters) and H cylinders (6,900 liters) are also available. Safety includes handling this equipment carefully to avoid damaging the valve assembly and understanding that the contents are under pressure. While oxygen is not flammable, it will increase the intensity of flame if exposed to it.

When changing tanks, remove the assembly from the empty cylinder (2,000 psi is full; anything less than 500 psi is considered empty) and remove the protective seals from the full cylinder. Quickly open and shut the valve at the top of the tank. Attach the regulator to the tank and the oxygen delivery device to the regulator.

Equipment for Oxygen Delivery

Nonrebreathers allow for up to 90% oxygen delivery to the breathing patient. The oxygen flow rate to the device should be adjusted to keep the oxygen reservoir bag filled between breaths. This may require 15 Lpm in the adult patient. This is the preferred device for patients showing signs of hypoxia (lack of oxygen).

Nasal cannulas only can accept 6 lpm of oxygen and will assist only in a slightly better than room air concentration of oxygen delivered. Their use should be limited to the patient who does not tolerate the nonrebreather mask.

Special Considerations

Special considerations are patients with stomas with or without tubes in place. You will need to be prepared to suction, ventilate, and provide oxygen to these patients.

Infants and children may need padding behind their shoulders to keep the airway in line and open because of the size of their head relative to their body. Gastric distension is also more common when ventilating infants and children.

Bleeding can be significant with facial injuries, so keeping the airway clear may be a challenge. Airway obstructions may need to be cleared manually, using abdominal thrusts or back blows as appropriate for the age of the patient and whether they are conscious or unconscious.

Also be aware of dental appliances. Generally, they will need to be left in place in order to get a seal with a mask around the mouth, but watch that they are secure and don't slip into the airway.

Scenarios

1. You are on the scene with a nonbreathing patient. There is no history of injury. How should you proceed to aid this patient?

Solution

As there is no history of head or neck injury, the airway should be opened using the head-tilt chin-left method. Then the EMT-B should "look, listen, and feel" for respirations. If there are none, the EMT-B should clear the airway, using suction if necessary, and provide artificial ventilation.

2. You have opened your patient's airway and are providing ventilations, but the chest doesn't appear to rise and your partner does not hear ventilations when he auscultates the chest. What should you do next?

Solution

Reposition the airway and check the seal around the patient's mouth. An inadequate seal is the most common problem associated with inadequate ventilations.

3. If your patient did have a history of head and/or neck injury, what would you have done differently?

Solution

In patients with possible neck injuries, the head and neck should be immobilized as you open the airway. The technique for opening the airway in a patient with possible head and neck injuries is the jaw thrust method.

Review Questions

1. The leaf-shaped muscle that moves to cover either the trachea or the esophagus is the

(A) alveolus.
(B) epiglottis.
(C) bronchus.
(D) capillary.

2. During inspiration

  (A) the intercostal muscles contract and the diaphragm relaxes.
  (B) the intercostal muscles relax and the diaphragm contracts.
  (C) both the intercostals and diaphragm contract.
  (D) both the intercostals and diaphragm relax.

3. The normal respiratory rate for an adult is

  (A) 12–20 breaths per minute.
  (B) 15–30 breaths per minute.
  (C) 25–30 breaths per minute.
  (D) 25–50 breaths per minute.

4. The normal respiratory rate for a child is

  (A) 12–20 breaths per minute.
  (B) 15–30 breaths per minute.
  (C) 25–30 breaths per minute.
  (D) 25–50 breaths per minute.

5. Signs of increased respiratory effort include

  (A) use of accessory muscles.
  (B) posturing.
  (C) gasping breaths.
  (D) All of the above.

6. Differences in the child and infant airway are

  (A) a larger tongue.
  (B) a smaller tongue.
  (C) narrower airways.
  (D) A & C.

7. In a patient with a potential spine injury, the proper method for opening the airway is

  (A) head-tilt chin-lift.
  (B) jaw thrust.
  (C) A and/or B.
  (D) None of the above.

8. When suctioning a patient, suctioning should be limited to

  (A) a minute.
  (B) 30 seconds.
  (C) 15 seconds.
  (D) There is no limit.

9. The most effective method the EMT-B should use, in terms of volume of air provided for artificial ventilations is

  (A) mouth-to-mask.
  (B) a one-person bag-valve mask.
  (C) a two-person bag-valve mask.
  (D) an oxygen-powered ventilator.

10. The recommended oxygen delivery device for the patient in respiratory distress is

    (A) a nasal cannula.
    (B) a nonrebreather mask.
    (C) a partial rebreather mask.
    (D) a Venturi mask.

▰ Answers to Review Questions

1. B Objective 1
The epiglottis is positioned over the trachea and esophagus. When one swallows, the epiglottis moves to close the trachea, keeping foreign bodies out of the lungs. When one breathes, it moves to cover the esophagus, allowing air to enter the lungs and keeping air from entering the esophagus.

2. C Objective 2
The primary muscles of breathing are the diaphragm and intercostal muscles. As these muscles contract, the lungs are pulled open to allow air to enter the lungs. When these muscles relax, the lungs contract forcing air out of the chest. The sternocleidomastoid muscles are considered accessory muscles to breathing and are often observable in patients with respiratory distress.

3. A Objective 2
Normally, adults breathe 12 to 20 times per minute. More or less than that decreases the overall volume of breathing and the patient will become hypoxic.

4. B Objective 2
Children breathe somewhat faster than adults, ranging from 15–30 times per minute normally.

5. D Objective 3
Patients in respiratory distress will use their accessory muscles and try to position themselves to make breathing easier (posturing). Their difficulty can also be evidenced by gasping breaths.

6. D Objective 4
Infant and child airways are narrower, shorter, and the tongue is proportionately larger.

7. B Objective 4
The jaw thrust is used to open the airway of patients with possible spine injuries. The head-tilt method is inappropriate as it may make neck injuries worse.

8. C Objective 7
Suctioning should be limited to 15 seconds or about as long as you can hold your breath. Your needing a breath is a good indication that the patient needs a breath too.

9. **A** Objective 10

Studies have shown that mouth-to-mouth gives the best volume of breaths but it violates reasonable risk and does not provide BSI. The best method recommended to EMT-Bs is mouth-to-mask, which allows for an easy seal with the mask, good ventilation volume, and the opportunity for supplemental oxygen.

10. **B** Objective 20

Patients in respiratory distress need oxygen and the nonrebreather mask can give concentrations of oxygen of 95% to 100%.

CHAPTER 8

Patient Assessment

SECTION 1—SCENE SIZE-UP/ASSESSMENT

■ Objectives

1. Recognize hazards/potential hazards.

2. Describe common hazards found at the scene of a trauma and to a medical patient.

3. Determine if the scene is safe to enter.

4. Discuss common mechanisms of injury/nature of illness.

5. Discuss the reason for identifying the total number of patients at the scene.

6. Explain the reason for identifying the need for additional help or assistance.

Scene size-up begins with BSI and scene safety. Before you enter the scene it is important to protect yourself from exposure by wearing gloves and eye protection and adding masks and gowns as necessary. Then the scene needs to be evaluated to determine if there are threats to the rescuers or the patient. These threats will have to be stabilized before approaching the patient, which may involve fire or police personnel depending on the nature of the scene. Fire or HAZMAT, unstable surfaces, and other unsafe conditions must be made safe before the EMT-B enters. The EMT-B may also need turnout gear for working in hazardous environments.

As the EMT-B approaches the scene, he or she should be observing for critical information about mechanism of injury or nature of illness. Patients, bystanders, and family can give you an idea about why you were called. You can observe the number of patients before you approach in order to call for additional help. Once you've called for additional resources, you can begin to triage multiple victims. Your observation of the scene and interviews with bystanders and family can help you to determine the mechanism of injury.

SECTION 2—INITIAL ASSESSMENT

■ Objectives

1. Summarize the reasons for forming a general impression of the patient.

2. Discuss methods of assessing altered mental status.

3. Differentiate between assessing the altered mental status in the adult, child, and infant patient.

4. Discuss methods of assessing the airway in the adult, child, and infant patient.

5. State reasons for management of the cervical spine once the patient has been determined to be a trauma patient.

6. Describe methods used for assessing a patient who is breathing.

7. State what care should be provided to the adult, child, and infant with adequate breathing.

8. State what care should be provided to the adult, child, and infant without adequate breathing.

9. Differentiate between a patient with adequate and inadequate breathing.

10. Distinguish between methods of assessing breathing in the adult, child, and infant.

11. Compare the methods of providing airway care to the adult, child, and infant.

12. Describe the methods used to obtain a pulse.

13. Differentiate between obtaining a pulse in an adult, child, and infant.

14. Discuss the need for assessing the patient for external bleeding.

15. Describe normal and abnormal findings when assessing skin color.

16. Describe normal and abnormal findings when assessing skin temperature.

17. Describe normal and abnormal findings when assessing skin condition.

18. Describe normal and abnormal findings when assessing skin capillary refill in the infant and child.

19. Explain the reason for prioritizing patient care and transport.

General Impressions

The initial assessment is made to form a general impression. This is focused on the mechanism of injury or chief complaint. While noting the age, sex, and race of the patient, you determine whether there are any obvious immediate life threats, treating them as you find them. **ABCDE** is used to make sure the patient is evaluated in order of the priorities of Airway, Breathing, Circulation, Disability, and Exposure.

A—Airway

The patient's mental status should be assessed, keeping in mind that if the patient is unresponsive, airway and breathing need to be evaluated immediately. Alert and responsive patients imply open airway and a breathing patient. The acronym **AVPU**, Alert, Verbal, Painful, or Unresponsive, is used to describe the levels of mental status.

In the unresponsive patient, in medical situations, you can examine the airway using the head-tilt chin-lift maneuver and determine if the airway is clear or obstructed. The neck-injured patients should be evaluated using the trauma jaw thrust.

B—Breathing

Breathing is then evaluated. If the patient is breathing, supplemental oxygen may be used and if the patient is not breathing, ventilations should be provided. Breathing patients with ineffective breathing (too many, too few, too weak) should also have ventilations provided. You may need to use airway adjuncts (oro- or nasopharyngeal airways) to maintain an open airway.

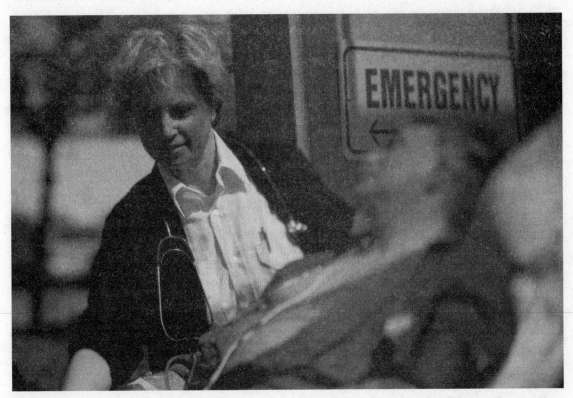

An initial assessment by the EMT at the scene is very important to subsequent approaches to treatment.

C—Circulation

Circulation is checked by finding a pulse and evaluating its quality. In adult conscious patients the radial pulse is checked; in patients less than one year old the brachial pulse is used. If there is no pulse, CPR should begin immediately. If there is a pulse, it should be observed to determine strength, regularity, and general rate (fast or slow).

Next check for bleeding, controlling it as you find the source. The patient's skin condition and color also give information about circulation. Checking the nail beds and around the eyes, if you can, you should normally see pink, dry, and warm skin. Pale or blue skin shows oxygen deficits; a flushed or red appearance can indicate hypertension, fever, or an allergic reaction; yellow skin or jaundice indicates liver problems. Cool or moist skin also hints at inadequate circulation and hot, dry skin may be fever associated with infection.

In infants and children we also check capillary refill, which should be less than two seconds.

D—Disability

In cases of disability, the EMT-B is reminded to assess the patient for any disability such as numbness or inability to move all or part of an extremity during the physical exam. This assessment should also include any other disruption of normal physical activity.

E—Exposure and Environment

The EMT-B must expose the body to conduct an adequate examination and the environment must also be considered. Hot or cold environments present particular hazards both to the patient and the EMT-B when exposing the patient for examination, so this must be considered as well.

The goal here is to determine priority patients. This would include patients with poor general impression, unresponsive patients, patients with inappropriate responses, patients with difficulty breathing or signs of inadequate perfusion (circulation to tissues), complicated childbirth, chest pain, uncontrolled bleeding, or severe pain. Transport should be expedited in priority patients, then focused history and physical exam can be done.

SECTION 3—THE FOCUSED HISTORY AND PHYSICAL EXAM—TRAUMA PATIENTS

Objectives

1. Discuss the reasons for reconsideration concerning the mechanism of injury.
2. State the reasons for performing a rapid trauma assessment.
3. Recite examples and explain why patients should receive a rapid trauma assessment.
4. Describe the areas included in the rapid trauma assessment and discuss what should be evaluated.
5. Discuss when the rapid trauma assessment may be altered in order to provide patient care.
6. Discuss the reason for performing a focused history and physical exam.

The focused history and physical exam focuses on the mechanism of injury you isolated during your initial exam. Significant mechanism such as motor vehicle collision rollovers, high-speed, ejection, pedestrians struck by vehicles, motorcycle crashes, the death of another patient in the same vehicle, falls of more than 20 feet, unresponsive trauma patients, or penetrations to the head or trunk imply life-threatening potentials.

Restraint systems can cause injury that your patient should be evaluated for. Air bags can cause abrasions and other soft tissue injuries in average-size adults and can cause fatal injuries in pediatric patients who should be in car seats in the back of the car. Shoulder harnesses and seat belts can cause abrasions, contusions, and fractures in some situations.

In infants or young children, consider falls of more than 10 feet, bicycle injuries, and vehicle collisions of even moderate energy.

If you've determined that there is a significant mechanism, perform a rapid trauma assessment while continuing support of the c-spine and the airway. If the patient is responsive and in minor to moderate distress, perform a more thorough survey to look for injuries. The acronym **DCAPBTLS** will help you remember what to check for when assessing your patient. Working from the head to the toes, palpate, look, and feel for Deformities, Contusions, Abrasions, Punctures, Burns, Tenderness, Lacerations, or Swelling. The head, neck, and trunk are done first, and then the extremities. As always, life threats should be treated as you find them. Remember to roll the patient to check the back. Once the physical exam is done, vital signs should be obtained along with a SAMPLE history.

SECTION 4—THE FOCUSED HISTORY AND PHYSICAL EXAM—MEDICAL PATIENT

■ Objectives

1. Describe the unique needs for assessing an individual with a specific chief complaint and no prior history.

2. Differentiate between the history and physical exam that are performed for responsive patients with a known prior history.

3. Describe the needs for assessing an individual who is unresponsive.

4. Differentiate between the assessment that is performed for a patient who is unresponsive or has an altered mental status and other medical patients requiring assessment.

In the responsive medical patient, you begin your focused assessment with **OPQRST** or Onset, Provocation, Quality, Radiation, Severity, and Time to describe pain, discomfort, or distress. Next is the SAMPLE history or Signs and Symptoms, Allergies, Medications, Pertinent past medical history, Last intake of food, and Events leading up to calling for help. Vital signs should then be obtained and care should be administered appropriate to your findings under the guidance of medical direction.

In unresponsive patients a rapid assessment is done. The airway should be opened and evaluated and breathing evaluated and/or supplemented as needed. A head to toe assessment is then done by palpating and looking and feeling your way down the anterior and then the posterior of the body. Patient position should be such as to protect the airway as in the recovery position. SAMPLE history should be obtained from family or bystanders.

SECTION 5—DETAILED PHYSICAL EXAM

■ Objectives

1. Discuss the components of the detailed physical exam.

2. State the areas of the body that are evaluated during the detailed physical exam.

3. Explain what additional care should be provided while performing the detailed physical exam.

4. Distinguish between the detailed physical exam that is performed on a trauma patient and the one of the medical patient.

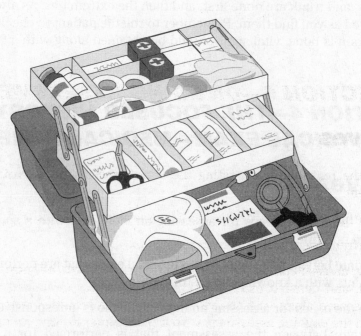

A properly equipped supply kit for any emergency is basic to the
EMT-B's ability to assist patients.

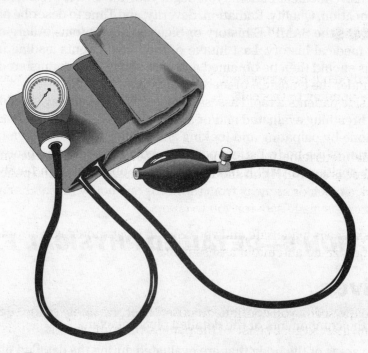

The blood pressure cuff is one of the EMT-B's most important
diagnostic aids.

The detailed physical exam is specific to your patient and his or her illness or injury. You will move from head to toe palpating, looking, and feeling as with the focused exams, but in the focused exams you were looking for life threats particular to the mechanism or complaint; here you will be doing a thorough evaluation in the absence of life threats requiring your attention. At the end of your detailed exam the vital signs should be reevaluated.

SECTION 6—ONGOING ASSESSMENT

Objectives

1. Discuss the reasons for repeating the initial assessment as part of the ongoing assessment.

2. Describe the components of the ongoing assessment.

3. Describe trending of assessment components.

The ongoing assessment is the continuous reassessment of your findings in the initial, focused, and detailed exams. Mental status, airway, breathing, and circulation should be reassessed along with the vital signs. Patient priorities may shift along with your findings in the ongoing assessments. Your treatments, oxygen, airways, and ventilation, for instance, should be reassessed as to their effectiveness in meeting the patient's needs.

Scenarios

1. You are called out for a shooting. The victim is a male. What precautions should you take in responding to this call?

Solution

First, you should determine from Dispatch whether or not police are on the scene and whether the scene is secure. If you should arrive on the scene and the police are not there, you should park a block or so away from the scene and notify Dispatch that you are "staging" until the scene is made safe for you to enter.

2. Once the scene is made safe and you enter it, what should you be doing as you make your scene size-up and initial assessment?

Solution

As you move to the scene you continue to observe for the safety of the scene, for you and your patient, and start to get a sense of the patient's condition by how he is positioned and whether or not he is interacting with people or the environment around him. You are also making sure that there is just one patient. As you approach, you should get from either by-standers or the patient information that describes the mechanism of injury, to enable you to continue your exam. You should quickly determine that the patient is alert and the wound appears to be in and out of the right forearm. The patient is talking and breathing without effort but is understandably agitated.

3. How would you proceed with your assessment of this patient?

Solution

You would first do a rapid trauma assessment to look for immediate life threats.

4. The injury appears to be isolated to the patient's arm and he is not complaining of any other problem, nor are there any other obvious injuries. How would you proceed?

Solution

You would begin your focused trauma assessment. Given the mechanism, the focus is on the area of injury and quickly done.

5. There are indeed entrance and exit wounds in the arm with minimal bleeding but significant pain and swelling. As your partner dresses and splints the injured arm, what should you do next?

Solution

You should get baseline vitals and start the patient on oxygen.

6. The patient's vitals are HR = 96, RR = 20, B/P 120/70. His skin condition is good, pupils are PEARL, and you have him on high-concentration oxygen with 15L to a nonrebreather mask. What is your next job with this patient?

Solution

Next, you would conduct a detailed physical exam, beginning with the patient's head and moving all the way to the feet.

7. What are you checking for as you move through your detailed physical exam?

Solution

DCAPBTLS. As you move from the head to the toes you are checking for Deformities, Contusions, Abrasions, Punctures/Penetrations, Burns, Tenderness, Lacerations, and/or Swelling. You should also reassess the baseline vital signs at the completion of the exam.

8. You are now en route to the hospital. What should you be doing for the patient until you get to the hospital?

Solution

The patient appears to be stable, so vitals should be repeated at least every 15 minutes. Since the mechanism was a gunshot, however, you might want to treat him as a critical patient and repeat the vital signs every 5 minutes.

▬ Review Questions

1. You are dispatched to a scene for a sick person. In regard to BSI, you should

   (A) always wear gloves when approaching any patient.
   (B) get a look at the patient and then determine whether or not gloves are needed.
   (C) not worry about gloves because it's not a trauma run.
   (D) wash hands before and after contact with the patient and gloves will not be necessary.

2. The first step of your scene size-up is to determine if the scene is safe for

   (A) yourself and your crew.
   (B) the patient.
   (C) bystanders.
   (D) other responding agencies.

3. When responding to motor vehicle accidents, the EMT-B should

   (A) wear special turnout gear.
   (B) carefully remove the patient without wearing special clothing.
   (C) have fire or rescue crews wearing protective clothing extricate and deliver the patient to him or her.
   (D) A and/or C.

4. Once you have made certain to protect yourself from the dangers of the scene, the next step is to

   (A) begin your patient assessment.
   (B) protect the patient and bystanders from hazards.
   (C) begin patient treatments.
   (D) begin patient transport.

5. The full definition of scene size-up is an assessment of the scene and surroundings

   (A) as to the nature of the event.
   (B) to determine the number of victims.
   (C) that will provide valuable information to the EMT-B.
   (D) that will determine hazards.

6. Once the scene size-up is completed, if additional help is needed, the call for help is best made

   (A) before entering the scene.
   (B) once all personnel are committed.
   (C) before you leave the scene.
   (D) after you have triaged the scene.

7. Of the following, which are examples of mechanism of injury?

 (A) Motor vehicle accident.
 (B) Chest pain.
 (C) Injury in the head with a baseball bat.
 (D) A & B.
 (E) A & C.

8. Forming a general impression determines priority of care and is based on the EMT-B's immediate assessment of

 (A) the environment.
 (B) the chief complaint.
 (C) the information provided by Dispatch.
 (D) A & B.

9. The next step after forming a general impression is to

 (A) perform a focused assessment.
 (B) perform a detailed assessment.
 (C) determine the presence of life threats.
 (D) transport the patient without delay.

10. If a life threat is determined the EMT-B should

 (A) begin the focused assessment.
 (B) perform the detailed assessment.
 (C) transport without delay.
 (D) treat the life threat.

Answers to Review Questions

1. **A** Section 1, Objective 1
At a minimum, gloves should always be worn when approaching patients. If the amount of body substances one might be exposed to is great, eye protection and maybe even gowns should be worn.

2. **A** Section 1, Objective 3
The first priority for the EMT is always scene safety. The safety of the EMT-B and other crewmembers must be assured before approaching the scene. When the scene is determined to be safe and precautions for continued safety of the team are taken, the scene can be entered and the safety of the patient determined.

3. **D** Section 1, Objective 3
Again safety must be emphasized and vehicle rescue calls for specialized protective clothing. If the EMT-B does not have the appropriate turnout gear (protective clothing), then he or she should wait for fire, police, or rescue personnel to bring the patient to him or her.

4. **B** Section 1, Objective 3
Once the rescuers are made safe, the safety of the patients and bystanders must be assured.

5. **C** Section 1, Objective 4

Scene size-up is an assessment of the scene and surroundings that will provide valuable information to the EMT-B. This size-up includes the environment, the conditions at the scene, hazards, resources, and a first, quick global look at the patient from a distance, if visible.

6. **A** Section 1, Objective 5

The time to make the call for additional help is before you enter the scene. Doing the size-up near the vehicle you arrived in gives you the ability to look over the scene and call for whatever help you need.

7. **E** Section 1, Objective 4

Mechanism of injury is a description of the event that gives the EMT-B the opportunity to examine the energy of the event and the potential for injury.

8. **D** Section 2, Objective 1

Getting a look at the environment you find the patient in and the chief complaint is the basis of forming a rapid, general impression as to the nature and severity of your patient's condition.

9. **C** Section 2, Objective 2

Once the general impression is determined, there should be a rapid assessment for immediate life threats. When life threats are found, they need to be dealt with immediately before continuing with the assessment.

10. **D** Section 2, Objective 1

Life threats need to be treated as they are found. The assessment follows the ABCs. If the airway is not open, open it and check breathing. If the patient is not breathing, breathe for the patient then check for a pulse, and so on.

CHAPTER 9

Communications

▬ Objectives

1. List the proper methods of initiating and terminating a radio call.

2. State the proper sequence for delivery of patient information.

3. Explain the importance of effective communication of patient information in the verbal report.

4. Identify the essential components of the verbal report.

5. Describe the attributes for increasing effectiveness and efficiency of verbal communications.

6. State legal aspects to consider in verbal communication.

7. Discuss the communication skills that should be used to interact with the patient.

8. Discuss the communication skills that should be used to interact with the family, bystanders, and individuals from other agencies, while providing patient care, and the difference between skills used to interact with the patient and those used to interact with others.

9. List the correct radio procedures in the following phases of a typical call:
   - To the scene
   - At the scene
   - To the facility
   - At the facility
   - To the station
   - At the station

The components of a communication system include base stations, mobile radios in vehicles at lower watts (20–50), and portable handheld units that are even lower power (1–5 watts). Repeater stations can boost the signals from mobiles and transmit to base stations. The FCC assigns the frequencies used by emergency personnel. Digital radio equipment is also supplemented with cellular and satellite telephones.

The modern EMT-B has the advantage of a wide range
of sophisticated communication equipment, so is
always in touch with the team or a care facility.

Personal communication between EMTs remains one of the most effective means of
accurate assessment.

The 911 centers or non-911 dispatch centers will receive a call and then dispatch units to respond. Communication from the responding unit should include response, arrival on the scene, transport, and back in service information. Other communications should be directed to other services that are needed, such as the police and/or fire department.

Communication with medical direction may be over the MERCI radio network (a special frequency reserved for communications during transport of basic life support patients) or cell phone. Medical direction is not necessarily at the receiving hospital depending on system design and protocols.

Any communication should be organized, concise, clear, and most important, accurate. Remember to pause for one second before speaking after you press the Push to Talk button, and speak with the microphone two to three inches from your mouth. Any order or transmission that is unclear should be repeated. Good communication assures that adequate resources are at the scene, appropriate orders are given for the patient's needs, and the hospital is prepared to receive the patient.

Identify yourself and whom you are talking to. Speak slowly and in a monotone voice. Use clear, plain English, avoiding repetitive or useless phrases. Keep in mind that radio frequencies are monitored by private citizens, so refrain from using patients' names or any unnecessary descriptions or generalizations. Profanity and slang are inappropriate. Avoid making a diagnosis; rather, describe what you've found and what you've done.

Verbal reports should include the identity of the care provider, time of arrival, patient's age and sex, patient complaint, brief pertinent history of present illness, major past illnesses, mental status, baseline vital signs, pertinent finding of exam, emergency medical care given, and the patient's response to your care.

After the report is given, the EMT-B will continue monitoring the patient and adjusting care as needed based on those assessments. Changes in the patient's condition also must be reported.

The EMT-B must also understand responsibilities involved in the maintenance of communications systems.

In giving the report directly to personnel at the hospital, summarize the chief complaint, history not transmitted previously, and any additional assessments or treatments en route.

In communicating with your patient, make and keep eye contact from a position lower than the patient, if possible. Be aware of your body language while speaking slowly, clearly, and distinctly. Use the patient's proper name and do so from in front of the patient with your lips visible, in case your patient has trouble hearing. Be honest with your patient, move, speak, and act calmly, and give your patient enough time to answer before repeating or moving on.

Special considerations the EMT-B must be prepared to deal with include visual or auditory disturbances and language barriers.

▉ Scenarios

1. Once you have been dispatched, what events should you notify Dispatch of?

Solution

You should notify Dispatch that you are en route, on the scene, leaving the scene for the hospital, arriving at the hospital, and back in service returning to quarters.

2. Once back in quarters, you are informed that it is difficult to understand what you are saying over the radio. What can you do to ensure that you are understood when using a radio?

Solution

Make sure the radio is on and properly adjusted, listen to make sure the frequency is clear before you key the microphone, wait a second before speaking after keying the microphone, and speak with your lips two to three inches from the microphone.

3. You are handing your patient over to the staff of the emergency department. What information should be a part of your verbal report?

Solution

Chief complaint, any history not already given, any treatment provided en route, current vital signs, and any information you may have that was not already given over the radio or cell phone.

▪ **Review Questions**

1. A handheld communication device would be a

(A) base station.
(B) mobile two-way radio.
(C) portable radio.
(D) repeater/base station.

2. A device that receives a signal from a low-power portable or mobile, and transmits it at a higher power on another frequency is a

(A) base station.
(B) mobile two-way radio.
(C) portable radio.
(D) repeater/base station.

3. Which of the following is **false** concerning radio communications?

(A) Speak clearly and slowly in a monotone voice.
(B) Keep transmission brief, less than 30 seconds.
(C) Use plain English.
(D) It is appropriate to use patients' names on the air.

4. Online medical control should be accessed via

(A) radio.
(B) cell phone.
(C) both available radio and cell phones.
(D) landlines only.

5. Giving a report over the radio makes the verbal report on arrival at the hospital unnecessary.

    (A) True.
    (B) False.

6. When communicating with your patient, you should

    (A) make and keep eye contact.
    (B) be honest with your patient.
    (C) tell the patient everything will be O.K. even it's clear everything is *not* O.K.
    (D) Both A & B.

7. In communicating with patients, the EMT-B should avoid

    (A) using the patient's proper name.
    (B) calling the patient "Honey" or "Sweetie."
    (C) speaking too quickly.
    (D) acting nervous or excited around the patient.
    (E) All except A.

8. When with special needs patients, the EMT-B should

    (A) avoid communicating with the patient until a specialist arrives.
    (B) speak slowly and clearly directly in front of the patient.
    (C) just speak more loudly.
    (D) not be concerned with communicating with this patient.

9. In communicating with your dispatcher, you should inform them of

    (A) being en route to and time of arrival at scene.
    (B) being en route to and time of arrival at the hospital.
    (C) leaving the hospital, returning to quarters.
    (D) All of the above.
    (E) None of the above.

10. If you are communicating with a patient, body language can either put your patients at ease or make them uncomfortable or uncooperative.

    (A) True.
    (B) False.

Answers to Review Questions

1. **C** Objective 1
Portable radios include installed vehicle radios, while handheld radios are carried on your person.

2. **D** Objective 1
Handheld and some portable radios transmit with a relatively weak signal. Repeaters pick up the weak signals and amplify them for improved reception within the communication system.

3. **D** Objective 1
Patient confidentialty laws prohibit the use of patients' names over the air.

4. **C** Objective 2
Online medical control involves actually speaking to the medical director or his or her agent via phone or radio.

5. **B** Objective 3
While the radio report prepares the hospital to receive the patient, there should always be a report given during patient exchange. The person who received the radio report may not be the person who takes responsibility for the patient, and the patient's condition may have changed since the radio report.

6. **D** Objective 7
It is important to be honest with your patient while maintaining a calm and cool demeanor. Your patient wants the truth about his or her situation and, if you are calm and professional, the patient may be better able to deal with it. The patient trusting the caregiver has a lot to do with how he or she will improve with care.

7. **E** Objective 7
The EMT-B should make eye contact, speak directly to the patient using the patient's proper name, and introduce himself or herself to the patient. Talking too loud or too quickly, or if the patient senses that the EMT-B is nervous, are not good for patient communication and the patient's confidence in the care provider.

8. **B** Objective 7
Speaking clearly and in clear sight of the patient is always important, but even more so with special needs patients.

9. **D** Objective 8
It is important to communicate with Dispatch throughout your response to a call. This includes informing Dispatch that you are en route to the scene, have arrived on the scene, are en route to the hospital, have arrived at the hospital, are back in service, and are leaving the hospital.

10. **A** Objective 7
Body language communicates to people whether we are passive or aggressive. Clenched fists and pacing communicate anger and agitation, while a relaxed posture and open palms imply relaxed listener.

CHAPTER 10

Documentation

▪ Objectives

1. Explain the components of the written report and list the information that should be included in the written report.

2. Identify the various sections of the written report.

3. Describe what information is required in each section of the prehospital care report and how it should be entered.

4. Define the special considerations concerning patient refusal of care.

5. Describe the legal implications associated with the written report.

6. Discuss all state and/or local record and reporting requirements.

Documentation is important, as it is the permanent record of the history of your patient and your actions with your patient. Continuing medical care and responses to allegations in the future depend on accurate, complete documentation. Also, the minimum data set is a national data set that will allow you to accumulate data for research to determine the future of prehospital care. Minimally, this includes the chief complaint, LOC (level of consciousness), vital signs, including skin color, temperature, and condition, as well as quality of pulses and respiratory effort.

The time the incident is first reported, dispatch time, arrival on scene, time to hospital, and the time care is turned over all have to be documented. Clocks on the units must be synchronized with the Dispatch center. The names of the crew members should also be clearly listed.

All forms should be filled out completely, filling in boxes completely and in narratives, avoiding slang and abbreviations that are not standardized. Remember that these reports represent you and will be read by other health care professionals and possibly legal representatives. Make sure spelling and structure are accurate and professional. Any prehospital report is confidential patient information. Make sure you understand your state laws in regard to patient confidentiality.

If you make a mistake on a report, do not attempt to erase it; draw a line through the error, write the word "error," and initial it. Document any deviation from standard of care and the story behind it.

Never falsify information on a report, as that is a criminal act.

Also document patient refusals of care, including the fact that the patient was informed of possible complications if treatment or transport is withheld. Have the patient and a family member sign the documentation. Patients who have an altered mental state cannot refuse aid. When in doubt about consent or refusal, contact medical control.

Getting all the facts right and recording them accurately is an essential component of teamwork the EMT provides to those who will see a patient later.

At multiple-casualty incidents (MCI) you may not have time to complete the report until after everyone is transported. Your disaster plan should include collecting important information temporarily like triage tags. Your system should also have addendum or special situation forms to document unusual events that call for additional explanation in case there are questions later. Documentation, when reviewed, should be a part of a continuous quality improvement program, which allows us to continually improve our practice by monitoring our performance in the field and the documentation of that performance.

Scenarios

1. At the end of your shift, you are at a local restaurant having breakfast with several coworkers, one of whom is showing the waitress and others at his table a copy of the run report involving an embarrassing situation for the patient. Is this an acceptable activity?

Solution

You should inform your coworker that he is violating patient confidentiality and breaking the law. It is not acceptable legally, morally, or ethically.

2. While finishing your run report at the hospital, you notice that there are no vital signs. Is it acceptable to copy them from the patient's emergency room chart?

Solution

That would be considered falsification of records. If you did not obtain the vital signs, they do not belong in your report.

3. If you suspect abuse of a patient you have transported, what should you do?

Solution

The EMT-Bs are required to report abuse to the facility they transport to. Check your state laws as some states may require that you report the suspected abuse directly to the state agency that investigates the class of abuse you suspect. In any case, you should tell the people that receive your patient and if you are concerned beyond that, you can even report the event directly to the agency independently.

Review Questions

1. The minimum data set is

(A) a national, required minimum data set that must be collected on all EMS forms nationwide.
(B) a locally determined minimum data set.
(C) a minimum set of data determined by each state.
(D) a minimum set of data set by each agency.

2. The EMS report form is

(A) a legal document.
(B) a part of the patient's medical record.
(C) an educational tool.
(D) a source of information for billing.
(E) All of the above.

3. The section of the EMS form that includes date and times is the

(A) run data.
(B) patient data.
(C) narrative.
(D) check boxes.

4. When writing a narrative, it's important that the EMT-B

(A) describe and not conclude.
(B) include pertinent negatives.
(C) include state required reporting elements.
(D) All of the above.
(E) None of the above.

5. When an error is made on the report form, the EMT-B should

(A) carefully erase the mistake and rewrite it.
(B) draw a line through the error, initial it, and write in the correction.
(C) obliterate the error with ink on all copies.
(D) tear up the report form and start over.

6. A competent adult patient wants to refuse your care. Which of the following is true?

(A) Once you are on the scene, no patient can refuse your care.
(B) You should try to persuade the patient to go to a hospital.
(C) You should inform the patient about what might happen if they do not go to the hospital.
(D) All of the above.
(E) B & C.

7. The written report

(A) requires the patient's permission for distribution.
(B) can be turned over to the media when requested.
(C) is subject to release by subpoena.
(D) A & C.

8. While each state has its own requirements, all states will require the reporting of

(A) a communicable disease.
(B) acts of violence or crimes.
(C) abuse.
(D) All of the above.

9. You have decided a patient is competent to refuse care. You should

(A) explain the possible complications of not receiving care.
(B) have the patient sign your report as refusing care.
(C) have someone sign the report as a witness (preferably family).
(D) All of the above.

10. The narrative portion of the report should include

(A) a description of what was found on arrival and assessments made.
(B) treatments given and the results of those treatments.
(C) the patient's name.
(D) the patient's allergies and medications.
(E) A & B.
(F) C & D.

▬ Answers to Review Questions

1. **A** Objective 1
The federal government requires that EMS systems use the minimum data set on their report forms. It is further required that the information be collected by each state and reported to the federal government.

2. **E** Objective 2
The EMS report form is a legal document, a part of the patient's permanent medical record, and a part of internal quality improvement and education for the healthcare providers involved in the patient's care. Care must be taken to protect patient confidentiality throughout.

3. **A** Objective 3
Dates and times are in the section of the report that contains the run data.

4. **D** Objective 3
The EMT-B should be telling a story in a way that provides the information so other health care providers can draw their own conclusions and conduct further assessments or treatments based on their interpretation of the information reported. This requires that the EMT describe rather than conclude, give positive and pertinent negative findings, and report all occurrences or findings required by the state.

5. **B** Objective 3
When an error is made on a written report, a line should be drawn through the mistake with the word "error" written alongside and initialed by the person writing the report. *Never* erase or destroy a written report.

6. **E** Objective 4
While competent adults can refuse care, we should always try to encourage them to be evaluated and treated and, at the very least, inform them of the possible ill effects of not seeking care.

7. **D** Objective 5
The written report is a legal document, part of the patient's medical record, and protected by patient confidentiality rules. Release to anyone other than the patient requires the patient's (or the patient's documented agent) written permission, or a subpoena.

8. **D** Objective 6
Each state does have its own laws dealing with mandatory reporting by public safety and healthcare workers. Communicable disease, rape, and other violent acts or abuse are always required reporting situations.

9. **D** Objective 4
Once you have determined that you will allow a person to refuse care, the patient refusing and a witness should sign your report form in the space provided. Family should be witnesses unless they are not available.

10. **E** Objective 3
The narrative portion of the report should be a brief accounting of the entire call. It should include what was found, assessments and treatments, results of that treatment, and any events that occur up to the time care is turned over to the hospital.

CHAPTER 11

General Pharmacology

Objectives

1. Identify which medications will be carried on the unit.

2. State the medications carried on the unit by the generic name.

3. Identify the medications with which the EMT-B can assist the patient in administering.

4. State the medications the EMT-B can assist the patient with by the generic name.

5. Discuss the forms in which the medications may be found.

The medications that the EMT-B must be familiar with include medications that are carried on the ambulance for the EMT-B to administer and medications prescribed by a physician to the patient that the EMT-B may be called upon to assist with.

The medications that are carried on the ambulance are

✔ **activated charcoal**, which is used in poisonings and overdose,
✔ **oxygen**, which is administered to assist patients with difficulty breathing or patients who may be hypoxic for other reasons, such as trauma,
✔ **oral glucose** for diabetic emergencies.

(Charcoal is covered in the allergies chapter, oxygen delivery is covered in the airway chapter, and glucose is covered in the diabetes chapter.)

The medications prescribed by a physician that the EMT-B may assist with include

✔ inhalers (for COPD—Chronic Obstructive Pulmonary Disease—patients)
✔ nitroglycerin (for chest pain)
✔ epinephrine (for allergic reactions)

(These are covered in depth in the respiratory, cardiac, and allergies chapters.)

In general, medications are known by generic names, which identify all drugs of the same kind, and trade names, which are specific to the manufacturer. An example is ibuprofen, a widely used over-the-counter pain medication that is marketed as Advil by one manufacturer.

The reason that a drug is given is called an "indication." For instance, difficulty breathing is an indication for oxygen. A contraindication for a medication is a reason not to give it. For instance, aspirin is contraindicated for patients with bleeding disorders or stomach problems.

Medications are provided in many forms: nitroglycerin is supplied to us as a compressed powder (a small pill) or a sublingual (under the tongue) spray, epinephrine is a liquid for injection, glucose is carried as a gel, activated charcoal is provided as a suspension, inhalers contain a fine powder, oxygen is a gas, and nebulizers provide a vaporized liquid dose of medication. Each of these drugs is provided in the form that allows it to be absorbed into the system in the best way to address the problem for which the medication is used.

With each medication, the EMT-B should be familiar with the dose (how much to give) and the administration route (how it is given, i.e., oral, injection, sublingual, etc.). The EMT-B should also know the actions of the medication or what the drug should do for the patient. An example would be the action of nitroglycerin for pain relief due to dilation of the coronary vessels. The EMT-B must also know the contraindications of these medications or the reasons not to give them, as in not giving nitroglycerin to a patient with a blood pressure less than 100 systolic.

Before you give any medication you should have done a full set of baseline vital signs, and repeated the set as part of an ongoing assessment. Any changes in the patient's condition after the medications are given must be documented and reported.

Scenarios

1. A patient with chest pain possesses a prescription for nitroglycerin and his wife has handed the pills to you. Are you allowed to give them to him?

Solution

Nitroglycerine is considered a patient assist medication for the EMT-B. If the prescription is written for your patient, and he or she is having chest pain and if the systolic pressure is over 100, the medication can be given to the patient.

2. If your patient's blood pressure was 80/50 but he still had chest pain, could you give the nitroglycerine?

Solution

Blood pressure less than 100 systolic would be considered a "contraindication" or a reason not to give the medication.

Review Questions

1. Activated charcoal, oral glucose, and oxygen are

(A) medications the EMT-B may carry and administer.
(B) medications the patient may possess and the EMT-B may assist with.
(C) common prescription medications.
(D) common "over-the-counter" medications.
(E) Both A & C.

2. Inhalers, nitroglycerin, and epinephrine are

(A) medications the EMT-B may carry and administer.
(B) medications the patient may possess and the EMT-B may assist with.
(C) common prescription medications.
(D) common "over-the-counter" medications.
(E) Both A & C.

3. Which of the following is an example of a generic name of a medication carried on the ambulance?

(A) Glucagel.
(B) Oral glucose.
(C) Nitrostat.
(D) Nitroglycerin.

4. An example of a trade name would be

(A) ibuprofen.
(B) acetaminophen.
(C) aspirin.
(D) Tylenol.

5. A contraindication is

(A) a reason not to give a medication.
(B) a reaction to a medication.
(C) the desired effect of a medication.
(D) an effect other than the desired effect of the medication.

6. Oxygen is carried by the EMT-B as a

(A) solid.
(B) liquid.
(C) gas.
(D) gel.

7. Oral glucose is carried by the EMT-B as a

(A) solid.
(B) liquid.
(C) gas.
(D) gel.

8. Nitroglycerin may be prescribed as

(A) a small pill placed under the tongue.
(B) a spray for use under the tongue.
(C) a liquid to be swallowed.
(D) A & B.
(E) B & C.

9. Which of the following would be a contraindication for assisting the patient in taking nitroglycerin?

(A) Chest pain.
(B) Systolic blood pressure of 90.
(C) The patient has already taken several nitroglycerin tablets.
(D) A & B.
(E) B & C.

10. A young man with difficulty breathing has emptied one of his inhalers and would like you to assist him in using a second. He is shaking so badly he cannot do it himself and you've noticed his pulse is racing. You should

(A) help him use the second inhaler as he is still having distress.
(B) not help him with the second inhaler as the shaking and rapid bounding pulse indicate possible overdose of the medication.
(C) administer oxygen for his respiratory distress.
(D) B & C.

▄▄ Answers to Review Questions

1. A Objective 1
Activated charcoal, glucose, and oxygen are the medications the EMT-B will carry on the ambulance. Activated charcoal is used for poison ingestions, glucose for hypoglycemic patients, and oxygen for medical emergencies including chest pain and difficulty breathing.

2. B Objective 3
Inhalers such as Albuterol prescribed to asthmatic patients, nitroglycerin prescribed to patients with histories of chest pain due to angina, and epinephrine auto-injectors prescribed to patients who are prone to serious allergic reactions are prescribed medications the EMT-B may assist in administering to patients.

3. B Objective 2
Generic names are names common to all brands of the same medication. Oral glucose is the generic name, common to all brands, while Glucagel is a trade name or brand name of one company's version of oral glucose.

4. D Objective 2
Acetaminophen is the generic name of the substance, while Tylenol is the company's name of their acetaminophen product. Another example would be Bayer aspirin.

5. A Objective 1
Contraindications are reasons not to take or give a medication. For example, aspirin is contraindicated in patients with chronic stomach problems or bleeding disorders.

6. C Objective 5
Oxygen is carried as a gas in steel or aluminum cylinders of various sizes.

7. **D** Objective 5
Glucose for use with diabetic patients with altered mental status is supplied as a gel that is easily administered orally.

8. **D** Objective 5
Nitroglycerin is supplied to patients both as a tiny pill to be placed under the tongue and a spray to be applied under the tongue.

9. **E** Objective 3
Nitroglycerin is a powerful medication that causes vasodilation. In patients who already have a blood pressure below 100 systolic it is contraindicated as it may drop the pressure even lower, placing the patient in shock. It is also contraindicated to give a patient nitroglycerin tablets when he or she has already taken several of them. The medications may not have taken effect yet and may cause overmedication.

10. **D** Objective 3
There is a fairly high incidence of patients putting themselves in jeopardy and even dying from overmedication using prescribed inhalers. Signs that the patient may have had enough or too much of the medication are the rapid, bounding pulse and shakiness.

CHAPTER 12

Respiratory Emergencies

Objectives

1. List the structure and function of the respiratory system.

2. State the signs and symptoms of a patient with difficulty breathing.

3. Describe the emergency medical care of the patient with difficulty breathing.

4. Recognize the need for medical direction to assist in the emergency medical care of the patient with difficulty breathing.

5. Describe the emergency medical care of the patient with breathing distress.

6. Establish the relationship between airway management and the patient with difficulty breathing.

7. List signs of adequate air exchange.

8. State the generic name, medication forms, dose, administration, action, indications, and contraindications for the prescribed inhaler.

9. Distinguish between the emergency medical care of the infant, child, and adult patient with difficulty breathing.

10. Differentiate between upper airway obstruction and lower airway disease in the infant and child patient.

By this point, you should already be comfortable with the respiratory system anatomy. A review of anatomy is provided in Chapter 4. In this chapter we'll focus on function, dysfunction, and our management of respiratory emergencies.

The job of the respiratory system is to take in air, which is conducted through the upper airways to the lungs, where oxygen is taken from the alveoli into the capillaries in exchange for carbon dioxide. The reverse takes place in the capillaries at the tissue levels throughout the body.

The active part of breathing is **inhalation**. The diaphragm and intercostal muscles contract, pulling the lungs into expansion. The passive part of breathing is **exhalation**—as the diaphragm and intercostal muscles relax, the lungs contract, and air leaves the chest.

Inadequate Breathing

Breathing efficiency is measured by rate, rhythm, and quality. Respiratory rates should be in these ranges:

- Adult—12–20 breaths per minute
- Child—15–30 breaths per minute
- Infant—25–50 breaths per minute

Any rates less or more may indicate inadequate breathing. The breathing must also have a steady regular rhythm; irregular breathing is indicative of inadequate breathing. The quality of respirations should also be assessed. Breath sounds should be present and equal and chest expansion and the depth of each breath should be adequate. Respiratory effort is a key assessment. Breathing should be effortless. Generally, if you think about it, you don't notice people are breathing unless they are in distress. Noisy breathing, use of accessory muscles (usually in children), or just a patient that appears to be working hard to breathe indicate inadequate breathing. The harder it looks for them, the more severe their distress. Inability to speak or speaking in short bursts is another indication of serious respiratory distress. The patient with difficulty will also use positioning to assist breathing. The tripod position (leaning forward on the arms), sitting upright with legs dangling, standing, or an inability to lie down on the back are common. Patients with long histories of COPD can develop a barrel chest appearance.

Noisy breathing is a sign of distress and it can give you an idea of where the problem is in the respiratory anatomy. Stridor, crowing, gurgling, and snoring are caused by obstruction of the upper airway (above the larynx). Wheezing or crackles are lower airway obstruction heard when auscultating the lungs with your stethoscope.

Inadequate respirations are unable to provide adequate oxygenation of the body's tissues and carbon dioxide levels will build. As this worsens, there will be observable changes in the patient's condition.

The earliest sign of inadequate respiration may be a change in the LOC (level of consciousness) or mental status of the patient. The patient becomes increasingly hypoxic the longer he or she is in respiratory distress. Early changes in LOC may be nervousness, agitation, or confusion. This will worsen along with increasing hypoxia, eventually causing a loss of consciousness if uncorrected.

Skin condition will also change as hypoxia worsens. The skin may be pale, blue, and/or clammy and can vary depending on the patient's race. The circulatory system will also respond to the lack of oxygen in the blood by speeding up the heart rate.

The respiratory rate may speed up in early phases of distress if the respiratory rate becomes gasping and sporadic; this is an indication that respiratory arrest is imminent.

Special considerations for the pediatric patient include anatomical differences. The airways are smaller and more easily obstructed and the head is larger, causing hyperflexion when the patient is supine. Infants' and children's tongues are proportionately larger than those of adults and take up more space in the airway. Their tracheas are narrower and softer, more flexible and more easily obstructed, and their cartilage is less developed and less rigid. Their chest walls are softer and they depend more on their diaphragm for breathing. Infants and children are subject to respiratory fatigue if they are in respiratory distress for too long. They can actually become "too tired to breathe."

Artificial Ventilation

If the EMT-B is providing adequate artificial ventilation, the chest should rise and fall with each ventilation at a sufficient rate of about 12 times per minute in the adult. Improving mental status, good skin color, and a heart rate that returns to normal are indications of adequate ventilation.

If the chest does not rise and fall at an adequate rate or if the rate is too fast, the artificial ventilations will be inadequate. Abnormal skin color and a heart rate that continues to be fast are indications of inadequate ventilation.

Scenarios

1. You are presented with a 70-year-old unresponsive male. Your partner tells you that his respirations are shallow at about 30 breaths per minute. How would you manage this patient?

Solution

These respirations are inadequate. Maintaining his airway in an open position, you should ventilate him with a bag-valve mask connected to an oxygen source at a rate of 12–20 breaths per minute.

2. You were called out for a patient with difficulty breathing. On your arrival you find a 16-year-old male who tells you that he is fine. You can hear audible wheezing and he is posturing but he says he is fine. Is the young man "fine" as he says?

Solution

Breathing is supposed to be effortless. Anytime breathing is remarkable because it is noisy or the patient is working hard to breathe, it is evidence of distress.

3. Is there any clue as to the origin of the respiratory distress a patient may be experiencing?

Solution

Noise or distress on inspiration indicates upper airway obstruction or obstruction above the larynx as with laryngeal edema or choking. Noise on expiration indicates lower airway obstructions in asthma or emphysema.

Review Questions

1. The voice box is also known as the

   (A) trachea.
   (B) larynx.
   (C) pharynx.
   (D) epiglottis.

2. The windpipe is also known as the

(A) trachea.
(B) larynx.
(C) pharynx.
(D) epiglottis.

3. The dome-shaped muscle(s) that participate(s) in breathing is/are the

(A) intercostals.
(B) gluteus.
(C) latisimus.
(D) diaphragm.

4. The muscles of respiration contract during inspiration.

(A) True.
(B) False.

5. The normal respiratory rate for an adult is

(A) 12–20.
(B) 15–30.
(C) 25–50.
(D) 30–60.

6. Inadequate breathing is indicated by

(A) the rate outside normal ranges.
(B) an irregular rhythm.
(C) shallow breathing.
(D) an increased effort to breathe.
(E) All of the above.

7. Special considerations in infant and child airways include

(A) smaller structures more easily obstructed.
(B) proportionately larger tongue and head.
(C) softer cartilage that is easily kinked if hyperflexed or extended.
(D) All of the above.

8. Using **OPQRST** (see Chapter 8) helps us remember the questions to answer in assessing respiratory emergencies. The **P** stands for

(A) pulse.
(B) provocation.
(C) palpation.
(D) peripheral.

9. Albuterol and Ventolin are names of

(A) inhalers.
(B) ventilator masks.
(C) airway devices.
(D) respiratory diseases.

10. If a patient exceeds the recommended total dose of any inhaler but remains in distress, an additional dose is

(A) recommended.
(B) optional.
(C) contraindicated.
(D) up to the patient.

Answers to Review Questions

1. **B** Objective 1
The voice box is the larynx, the trachea is the windpipe, the pharynx is that part of the digestive tract that connects the mouth cavity to the esophagus, and the epiglottis is the leaf-shaped muscle flap that moves to cover the trachea when one swallows and the esophagus when one breathes.

2. **A** Objective 1
The trachea is the windpipe, the larynx is the voice box, the pharynx connects the mouth cavity to the esophagus, and the epiglottis is a leaf-shaped muscle flap that covers the trachea when one swallows and the esophagus when one breathes.

3. **D** Objective 1
The diaphragm is the dome-shaped muscle that forms the base of the chest cavity and the upper limits of the abdomen. The intercostal muscles between the ribs also assist in breathing. The gluteus is the muscle that forms the buttock and the latisimus is a muscle on the superior aspect of the anterior chest.

4. **A** Objective 1
The muscles of respiration contract to pull the lungs open, causing air to enter the lungs during inspiration. When these muscles relax, the chest cavity shrinks and air leaves the lungs during expiration.

5. **A.** Objective 2
12–20 breaths per minute are normal for adults. Respiratory rates that are much slower or faster than these limits decrease the overall volume of air being exchanged, causing hypoxia, meaning that oxygen levels in the blood drop and the carbon dioxide levels rise.

6. **E** Objective 2
Breathing needs to have sufficient "tidal volume" to bring enough air into the lungs to accommodate and exchange oxygen for carbon dioxide. If the volumes are inadequate, hypoxia results, which is rising blood carbon dioxide levels and dropping oxygen levels. In order for breathing to be adequate, rate, rhythm, and volume breathed must be within normal ranges.

7. **D** Objective 10
Infants and children have anatomical differences that affect management of airway and respiratory problems. The head is larger and when they are supine, its size causes flexion and compression of the airway. The shoulders should be padded to maintain a neutral line with an open airway. The tongue is also proportionately larger compared to that of adults and can easily obstruct the airway, particularly if the neck is flexed. The airways are also shorter and narrower, hence more easily obstructed.

8. **B** Objective 3

OPQRST is a way of remembering the important points of obtaining a history from your patient:

O = Onset, or when did the problem start?

P = Provocation, or does anything make it worse or better?

Q = Quality, or how would you describe how it feels?

R = Radiation, or does it feel like the pain moves?

S = Severity, or on a scale of 1–5 or 1–10 how bad is this event?

T = Time, or how long has it been going on?

9. **A** Objective 8

Albuterol and Ventolin are examples of prescribed inhalers patients with asthma may use.

10. **C** Objective 8

Any time a patient exceeds the recommended dose of a medication, further doses are contraindicated. Prescription drugs are powerfully effective but more is not always better; in fact it can even be fatal. A higher dose may sometimes be called for but this will be up to medical control.

CHAPTER 13

Cardiac Emergencies

■ Objectives

1. Describe the structure and function of the cardiovascular system.

2. Describe the emergency medical care of the patient experiencing chest pain/discomfort.

3. List the indications for automated external defibrillation.

4. List the contraindications for automated external defibrillation.

5. Define the role of the EMT-B in emergency cardiac care.

6. Explain the impact of age and weight on defibrillation.

7. Discuss the position of comfort for patients in various cardiac emergencies.

8. Establish the relationship between airway management and the patient with cardiovascular compromise.

9. Predict the relationship between the patient experiencing cardiovascular compromise and basic life support.

10. Discuss the fundamentals of early defibrillation.

11. Explain the rationale for early defibrillation.

12. Explain that not all chest pain patients result in cardiac arrest and do not need to be attached to an automated external defibrillator.

13. Explain the importance of prehospital ACLS (Advanced Cardiac Life Support) intervention if it is available.

14. Explain the importance of urgent transportation to a facility with Advanced Cardiac Life Support if it is not available in the prehospital setting.

15. Discuss the various types of automated external defibrillators.

16. Differentiate between the fully automated and the semiautomated defibrillator.

17. Discuss the procedures that must be taken into consideration for standard operations of the various types of automated external defibrillators.

18. State the reasons for assuring that the patient is pulseless and apneic when using the automated external defibrillator.

19. Discuss the circumstances that may result in inappropriate shocks.

20. Explain the considerations for interruption of CPR, when using the automated external defibrillator.

21. Discuss the advantages and disadvantages of automatic external defibrillators.

22. Summarize the speed of operation of automatic external defibrillation.

23. Discuss the use of remote defibrillation through adhesive pads.

24. Discuss the special considerations for rhythm monitoring.

25. List the steps in the operation of the automated external defibrillator.

26. Discuss the standard of care that should be used to provide care to a patient with persistent ventricular fibrillation and no available ACLS.

27. Discuss the standard of care that should be used to provide care to a patient with recurrent ventricular fibrillation and no available ACLS.

28. Differentiate between the single rescuer and multirescuer care with an automated external defibrillator.

29. Explain the reason for pulses not being checked between shocks with an automated external defibrillator.

30. Discuss the importance of coordinating ACLS-trained providers with personnel using automated external defibrillators.

31. Discuss the importance of postresuscitation care.

32. List the components of postresuscitation care.

33. Explain the importance of frequent practice with the automated external defibrillators.

34. Discuss the need to complete the automated defibrillator: Operator's Shift Checklist.

35. Discuss the role of the American Heart Association (AHA) in the use of automated external defibrillation.

36. Explain the role medical direction plays in the use of automated external defibrillation.

37. State the reasons why a case review should be completed following the use of the automated external defibrillator.

38. Discuss the components that should be included in a case review.

39. Discuss the goal of quality improvement in automated defibrillation.

40. Recognize the need for medical direction protocols to assist in the emergency medical care of the patient with chest pain.

41. List the indications for the use of nitroglycerin.

42. State the contraindications and side effects for the use of nitroglycerin.

43. Define the function of all controls on an automated external defibrillator, and describe event documentation and battery defibrillator maintenance.

Review of Anatomy and Physiology (A and P)

✔ The heart is a four-chambered muscle that pumps blood to the lungs and out to the body. The right atrium receives blood from the vena cava and pumps it to the right ventricle. The right ventricle pumps the blood to the lungs through the pulmonary artery, the only artery that carries unoxygenated blood. The lungs exchange oxygen for carbon dioxide between the alveoli and capillary beds and return the oxygenated blood to the left atrium through the pulmonary veins, the only veins that carry oxygenated blood. The left atrium pumps the blood to the left ventricle, and the left ventricle pumps the oxygenated blood out to the body through the aorta.

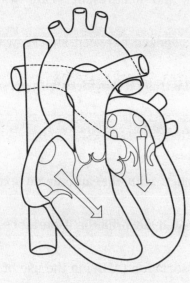

The right atrium receives blood from the vena cava and pumps it to the right ventricle, which pumps blood to the lungs from the pulmonary artery.

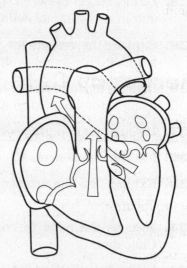

The left atrium pumps the blood to the left ventricle, which pumps the oxygenated blood to the body through the aorta.

✔ The heart muscle is also highly specialized in that it conducts its own electrical impulses that travel across the muscle causing the contractions that pump the blood out to the lungs and the body.

✔ The arteries carry oxygenated blood throughout the body, and the veins return the blood to the heart for return to the lungs to exchange carbon dioxide for oxygen.

✔ Capillaries exchange oxygen and nutrients for carbon dioxide and waste from tissue cells. Blood flows into the capillaries from arterioles and out through venules.

✔ Plasma carries the other parts of circulating blood. Red blood cells carry oxygen or carbon dioxide; white blood cells help to fight infection; and platelets help to form clots.

✔ Obtainable pulses can be felt when an artery runs over muscle and/or bone and close to the surface of the skin. Easily palpable pulses are carotid (neck) and femoral (groin). Important peripheral pulses are brachial (anticubital fossa), radial (wrists), posterior tibial (ankle), and dorsalis pedis (top of foot).

✔ The blood pressure consists of the systolic pressure and the diastolic pressure. The systolic is the sound heard or auscultated, brought about by the pressure exerted against the walls of the artery when the ventricle contracts. The diastolic is the last sound auscultated and represents the pressure in the arteries during the relaxation of the ventricles.

✔ Inadequate circulation brings about shock or hypoperfusion and depresses the vital functions of the body. This inadequate circulation can be recognized as pale, cyanotic, cool and clammy skin, rapid weak pulses, rapid shallow breathing, restlessness and anxiety, nausea and/or vomiting.

Cardiac problems may be evidenced by patients experiencing chest pain, difficulty breathing, or changes in their mental status. Signs and symptoms of shock may also be present; irregular pulses and complaints of a feeling of impending doom are also common.

Emergency Care for Cardiac Patients

Emergency care for cardiac patients includes position of comfort, oxygen, a full assessment, and baseline vital signs. Any complaint of pain or breathing difficulty can be assessed using **OPQRST**.

O = Onset

P = Provocation

Q = Quality

R = Radiation

S = Severity

T = Time

Nitroglycerin is a medication the cardiac patient may already have and require the EMT-B's assistance with. It is a medication that relaxes blood vessels and in a patient with chest pain, it may open the blood vessels to better perfuse the heart muscle. The EMT-B may give one dose to the patient with chest pain if it has been prescribed to the patient and if the systolic pressure is over 100. It can be given every three to five minutes up to three doses, and vital signs should be assessed before and after each dose. Side effects include headaches, hypotension, and pulse rate changes.

Cardiac patients who go into full cardiopulmonary arrest will be supported by the EMT-B performing CPR. EMT-Bs should be familiar with both one- and two-rescuer CPR. They should also be familiar with the use of automatic external defibrillators (AEDs) and they should not use them if the patient is less than 12 years old, weighs less than 90 pounds, or is awake. EMT-Bs should also know when ALS backup might be beneficial. They must be familiar with the use of airway adjuncts, bag-valve masks, suction, and other airway devices used to keep the airway open and ventilate the patient.

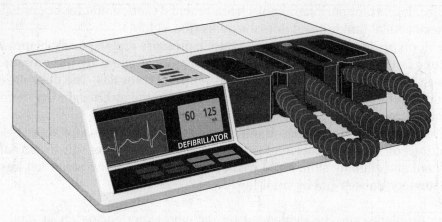

The EMT-B should be completely familiar with the automatic external defibrillator, including when not to use it.

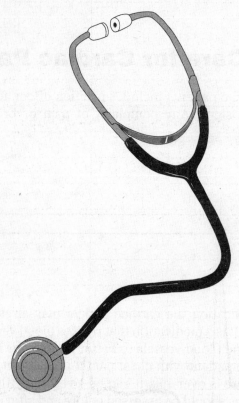

Using a stethoscope soon becomes second nature to the EMT-B.

Scenarios

1. You have arrived at the scene where a 49-year-old male is complaining of chest pain. After you've determined the scene to be safe, and donned personal protection equipment (PPE), what should you do for this patient?

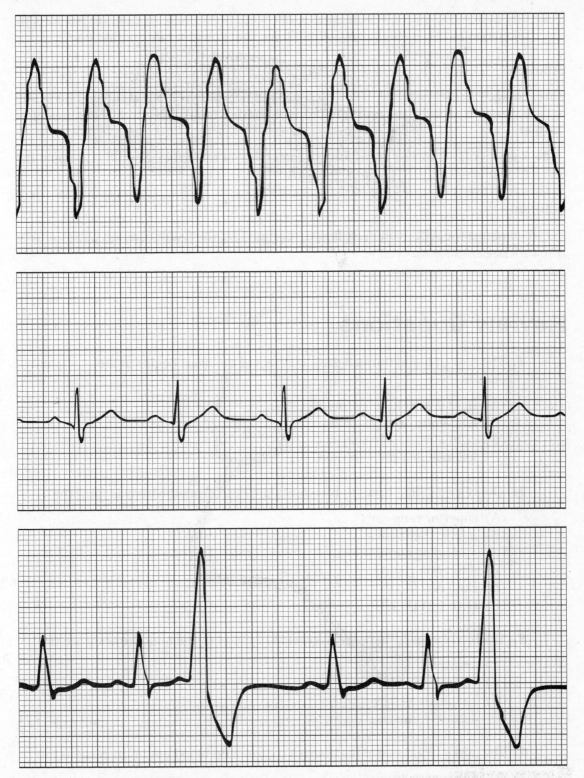

Every EMT-B should have the ability to accurately interpret EKG readings.

Solution

After performing your assessments, you should place the patient in a position of comfort and provide oxygen. Further history should be done to determine the **OPQRST** or the Onset, Provocation, Quality, Radiation, Severity, and Time of the patient's complaints.

2. The patient has nitroglycerin tablets that were prescribed for him. He has already taken one but he is still having a lot of pain. Can you give him another one?

Solution

First, contact medical control. If his pressure remains above 100 systolic and he is still in pain, you will probably be instructed to give another tablet three to five minutes after the first.

3. You've come upon an unresponsive man lying in the street. Should you apply the AED immediately?

Solution

Before applying the AED, you must first determine that the patient has no pulses and/or respirations.

Review Questions

1. The flow of blood through the chambers of the heart begins in the _____ and ends in the _____.

    (A) right ventricle, left atrium.
    (B) left ventricle, right atrium.
    (C) right atrium, left ventricle.
    (D) left atrium, right ventricle.

2. The vessel(s) that bring(s) blood into the heart from the body is (are) the

    (A) superior vena cava.
    (B) inferior vena cava.
    (C) ascending aorta.
    (D) descending aorta.
    (E) Both A & B.
    (F) Both C & D.

3. The blood vessels that carry oxygenated blood throughout the body are the

    (A) arteries.
    (B) veins.
    (C) lymphatic vessels.
    (D) digestive vessels.

4. The major blood vessel that carries oxygenated blood out of the heart is the

    (A) pulmonary artery.
    (B) aorta.
    (C) vena cava.
    (D) pulmonary vein.

5. The arteries that carry blood to the brain are the

    (A) radial arteries.
    (B) brachial arteries.
    (C) carotid arteries.
    (D) femoral arteries.

6. Red blood cells

    (A) help fight infection.
    (B) help to form clots.
    (C) carry oxygen and carbon dioxide.
    (D) are the fluid that carries the cells and nutrients.

7. Plasma

    (A) helps fight infection.
    (B) helps form clots.
    (C) carries oxygen and carbon dioxide.
    (D) is the fluid that carries the cells and nutrients.

8. OPQRST can also be used to assist in assessing chest pain. **R** stands for

    (A) rate.
    (B) rhythm.
    (C) radiation.
    (D) risks.

9. A fully automatic defibrillator

    (A) requires only that the EMT-B apply it to the patient and turn it on.
    (B) requires that the EMT-B apply paddles to the chest and fire the paddles.
    (C) requires that the EMT-B follow the synthesized voice commands.
    (D) requires the EMT-B to be able to read ECG strips.

10. AEDs should not be used if

    (A) a patient weighs less than 90 pounds.
    (B) a patient is under 12 years of age.
    (C) the patient is awake.
    (D) All of the above.

Answers to Review Questions

1. **C** Objective 1
Oxygen-poor blood enters the heart at the right atrium, flows into the right ventricle, and is pumped to the lungs to exchange carbon dioxide for oxygen. The blood reenters the heart from the lungs at the left atrium where it flows to the left ventricle. From there the oxygenated blood is pumped to the body through the aorta.

2. **E** Objective 1
The superior vena cava brings blood to the heart from the head and upper extremities and the inferior vena cava brings the blood to the heart from the rest of the body.

3. **A** Objective 1

The arteries are double-walled blood vessels that contract along with the heart to push the blood throughout the body to deliver oxygen and nutrients to the body's cells.

4. **B** Objective 1

The largest artery in the body is the aorta, which leaves the left ventricle and divides into the ascending aorta, which takes blood to the head and upper extremities, and the descending aorta, which delivers blood-carrying oxygen and nutrients to the rest of the body.

5. **C** Objective 1

The carotid arteries, one on each side of the neck, carry blood to the brain. The radial arteries are located in the forearms and can be located on the thumb side of each wrist. The brachial arteries are in the upper arms and can be located at the medial antecubital fossa (inside the elbow) on each arm.

6. **C** Objective 1

The blood is composed of red blood cells, which carry oxygen or carbon dioxide, white blood cells that fight infection and foreign material in the blood, and platelets that assist in forming clots and plasma, which is the fluid or medium that carries the components throughout the body.

7. **D** Objective 1

Plasma is the fluid that carries all of the other components of the blood around. It also contains a collection of elements such as potassium, sodium, and calcium, which provide and must maintain a critical chemical balance throughout the body.

8. **C** Objective 2

As discussed earlier, **OPQRST** is an acronym that will assist you in remembering the points to cover during history taking:

O = Onset, or when did the pain begin?

P = Provocation, or does anything make the pain better or worse?

Q = Quality, or how would you describe the pain? Examples would be crushing or sharp.

R = Radiation, or does the pain radiate or move to another part of the body?

S = Severity, or how bad is the pain on a scale of 1–5 or 1–10?

T = Time, or how long have you been in pain?

9. **A** Objective 10

A fully automatic AED or Automatic External Defibrillator does not require the EMT to do anything but attach and turn it on. Many of the AEDs in use require the EMT to approve defibrillation by pressing another button.

10. **D** Objective 10

Patients who weigh less than 90 pounds, patients who are under 12 years of age, and awake patients would all be contraindicated, or reasons not to use an AED.

CHAPTER 14

Diabetes/Altered Mental Status

Objectives

1. Identify the patient taking diabetic medications with altered mental status and the implications of a diabetes history.

2. State the steps in the emergency medical care of the patient taking diabetic medicine with an altered mental status and a history of diabetes.

3. Establish the relationship between airway management and the patient with altered mental status.

4. State the generic and trade names, medication forms, dose, administration, action, and concentrations for oral glucose.

5. Evaluate the need for medical direction in the emergency medical care of the diabetic patient.

Signs and Symptoms

Other than head injuries, diabetes is the most common cause of unconsciousness. Patients with histories of diabetes who experience rapid onset altered mental status should be evaluated to determine if meals were missed or insulin given, and if the patient is vomiting, or has a history of unusual work, exercise, or stress. Hypoglycemic patients can appear intoxicated with elevated heart rate, cold clammy skin, hunger, or seizures.

You may find Diabenase, Orinase, or Micronase in the patient's home (often in the refrigerator). Uncharacteristic, anxious, or combative behavior is possible.

When confronted with a known insulin-dependent diabetic patient with sudden onset altered mental status, the EMT-B may administer glucose gel between the cheek and gum.

Seizures

Another frequent cause of altered mental status is seizures. While chronic seizure disorders are rarely fatal, all seizures, including febrile seizures in children, should be considered life-threatening. The key thing to remember in treating seizure disorders is to protect and not to restrain. In general, the seizure activity will stop and the EMT-B can then clear and maintain the airway, deliver oxygen, and transport.

The preferred position in which to place patients with altered mental status is the recovery position. This allows saliva and other material to drain from the airway and allows for free and easy breathing.

Scenarios

1. A patient is presented to you with slurred speech, a staggering gait, and a fruity acetone odor to his breath. Your partner thinks the patient is intoxicated, but what else might it be?

Solution

This is a classic presentation of an acute diabetic patient. Specifically, this patient is hyperglycemic.

2. A patient complains of a sudden onset of weakness and nausea. During your history, the patient tells you that he is an insulin-dependent diabetic and while he took his insulin today, he hasn't eaten since last night. What should you do for this patient?

Solution

Your protocols call for you to administer glucose gel to any medication-dependent diabetic patient with an altered mental status, as long as the patient is able to swallow and you keep an eye on the airway. The patient is presenting a classic history and symptoms of hypoglycemia and should respond quickly to the glucose.

3. You arrive on the scene where a group of friends are holding down a patient who appears to be having a seizure, and trying to insert a spoon into his mouth. Are they treating him appropriately?

Solution

Many people are under the mistaken impression that they must restrain the patient and jam something/anything between his or her teeth. This is not true. Your priority is to protect, not restrain. The seizure will end after a few moments; just get everything out of the patient's way so he or she doesn't get hurt during the seizure by striking something.

Review Questions

1. The most common cause of unconsciousness, other than head injuries is

(A) diabetes.
(B) a heart attack.
(C) seizures.
(D) a stroke.

2. Not eating or too much insulin can cause

(A) hypertension.
(B) hypotension.
(C) hyperglycemia.
(D) hypoglycemia.

3. A seizing patient should

(A) be restrained to prevent injury.
(B) be protected from injury by having things moved out of the way.
(C) have an oral airway inserted.
(D) have a tongue blade inserted.

4. Orinase, Diabenase, and Micronase are examples of

(A) insulin.
(B) sugar pills.
(C) pancreatic stimulants.
(D) vitamins.

5. Important history to obtain from a seizure patient or family member includes

(A) a history of previous seizures.
(B) a recent or remote history of head injury.
(C) medications.
(D) a child with a history of fever.
(E) All of the above.

6. Signs and symptoms consistent with hyperglycemia are

(A) an appearance of intoxication.
(B) fruity or acetone breath.
(C) unconsciousness.
(D) All of the above.

7. Signs and symptoms consistent with hypoglycemia include

(A) rapid onset.
(B) diaphoresis.
(C) cool, clammy skin.
(D) seizures.
(E) All of the above.

8. The hormone that facilitates the transport of glucose into the cells to enable metabolism is

(A) insulin.
(B) epinephrine.
(C) norepinephrine.
(D) testosterone.

9. The hormone defined in question number 8 is secreted by the

(A) spleen.
(B) pancreas.
(C) liver.
(D) colon.

10. Type I diabetics are

(A) insulin-dependent.
(B) noninsulin-dependent.
(C) under the age of 14.
(D) over the age of 14.

Answers to Review Questions

1. **A** Objective 1
Outside of head injuries, the most common cause of unconsciousness is diabetes. Diabetes should be suspected in all unconscious patients until proven otherwise.

2. **D** Objective 1
The glucose we need for cellular metabolism and the production of energy is provided by the food we eat. If we do not eat, the glucose will be consumed and hypoglycemia results.

3. **B** Objective 3
Patients experiencing seizures are often injured during restraint or by objects too close to them during the seizure. The seizure will run its course and the EMT-B should protect the patient by getting everything out of the way.

4. **C** Objective 4
Type II or noninsulin-dependent diabetics may use medications that stimulate the pancreas to produce insulin. Orinase, Diabenase, and Micronase are examples of this type of medication.

5. **E** Objective 3
Seizure patients most often have a history of seizure activity. Life-threatening conditions such as subdural hematomas can happen even days after head injuries so it's important to determine if a seizure patient with no history of seizure activity might have a history of head injury. Fever is the most common cause of seizures in children. Medications such as Dilantin and Tegretol are prescribed to seizure patients, so they are another clue to a history of seizures.

6. **D** Objective 1
In the absence of insulin, sugar will build up in the bloodstream, creating acidosis. The body breaks the acid down into water and carbon dioxide. The water is secreted as urine and the carbon dioxide is exhaled with ventilations. This can cause patients to be thirsty and find themselves urinating often, and they may have a fruity or acetone odor to their breath. As the condition worsens, they may appear inebriated before losing consciousness.

7. E Objective 1
Hypoglycemia is a lot like a car running out of gas. The patient may become weak, dizzy, and tired, and the skin may be cool and clammy, as though the patient were in shock. This condition has a rapid onset and can rapidly cause the loss of consciousness and seizures.

8. A Objective 1
In order for glucose to make it into the cell for combustion, it must be accompanied by the hormone insulin, which is secreted in the islets of Langerhans in the pancreas.

9. B Objective 1
Insulin is secreted by the islets of Langerhans in the pancreas.

10. A Objective 1
Type I diabetics are insulin-dependent; Type II diabetics are noninsulin-dependent.

CHAPTER 15

Allergies

SECTION 1—ALLERGIC REACTIONS

Objectives

1. Recognize the patient experiencing an allergic reaction.

2. Describe the emergency medical care of the patient with an allergic reaction.

3. Establish a relationship between the patient with an allergic reaction and airway management.

4. Describe the mechanisms of allergic response and the implications for airway management.

5. State the generic and trade names, medication forms, dose, administration, action, and contraindications for the epinephrine auto-injector.

6. Evaluate the need for medical direction in the emergency medical care of the patient with an allergic reaction.

7. Differentiate between the general category of those patients having an allergic reaction and those patients having an allergic reaction and requiring immediate medical care, including the immediate use of the epinephrine auto-injector.

Symptoms and Treatment

Allergic reactions are a frequent cause of medical emergencies. People can have reactions to almost anything. Insect bites, food, plants, and medications can cause even fatal reactions. The typical allergic response ranges from itching, hives, flushed, abnormally-colored skin, and swelling in the face and hands. A serious allergic response can result in difficulty breathing due to swelling and inflammation of the airways. A coughing, wheezing patient with noisy respirations or a hoarse voice who has been exposed to a possible allergen is suspect. Other symptoms can include an increase in heart rate, itchy, watery eyes, headache, and a runny nose. As the reaction advances without intervention, mental status can decrease and hypoperfusion (shock) can result.

The treatment of allergic reactions consists of early recognition, airway and oxygen therapy, and, if the patient has a history and an Epipen auto-injector, administration of epinephrine. Side effects of epinephrine include increased heart rate, pallor, dizziness, chest pain, and headaches.

SECTION 2—POISONING/OVERDOSE

▇ Objectives

1. List various ways that poisons enter the body.

2. List signs/symptoms associated with poisoning.

3. Discuss the emergency medical care for the patient with a possible overdose.

4. Describe the steps in the emergency medical care for the patient with suspected poisoning.

5. Establish the relationship between the patient suffering from poisoning or overdose and airway management.

6. State the generic and trade names, indications, contraindications, medication form, dose, administration, actions, side effects, and reassessment strategies for activated charcoal.

7. Recognize the need for medical direction in caring for the patient with poisoning or overdose.

Determining the Poison Taken and Treatment

Poisonings and overdoses are common causes of medical emergencies. The EMT-B needs to determine what substance the patient took or was exposed to, when it was taken or exposed to, over what time it was taken or exposed to, what, if any, interventions were taken, and what the patient's weight is.

Poison can enter the body via ingestion, injection, inhalation, or absorption. Emergency medical care includes maintaining airway and breathing and identifying the substance.

Activated charcoal can be administered to patients who have ingested poisons. Adults and children can be given 1 gram/kg with the usual adult dose being 25–50 grams and the usual infant or child dose being 12.5–25 grams. Activated charcoal prevents poisons from being absorbed into the body. Side effects include black stools and possibly nausea and vomiting. The dose should be repeated if the patient vomits after administration.

▇ Scenarios

1. You are called to evaluate a 25-year-old female complaining of "feeling funny." On arrival, you find the patient to have flushed skin and be complaining of itching and tingling sensations all over her body. She also says that it started not long after a wasp stung her. What do you suspect is the nature of her problem?

Solution

The patient seems to be having an allergic reaction. The fact that her complaints came on not long after the sting makes it likely.

2. Hives, itching, and swelling may not be life-threatening but if the reaction progresses it can become a life threat. What should the EMT-B be watching for?

Solution

One of the most common allergic responses is difficulty breathing in the form of asthma-like presentation. The patient will wheeze and possibly present with stridor if the edema settles into the upper airways. The EMT-B should monitor the patient's airway and breathing closely.

3. You are caring for a patient who claims to have taken numerous pills and the hospital has ordered activated charcoal. How much should you give to this 150-pound male?

Solution

Activated charcoal is dosed at 1 gm/kg body weight. The typical adult dose is 25–50 grams. This patient weighs 150 pounds so the full 50 grams should be given.

■ Review Questions

1. Signs and symptoms of allergic reactions include

(A) flushed skin, itching, labored breathing.
(B) swelling of the face, neck, and hands.
(C) hoarseness and cough.
(D) All of the above.

2. Epipen auto-injectors

(A) are prescribed to people who've had previous allergic reactions.
(B) are designed to allow the patient to self-administer adrenalin in case of a reaction.
(C) A & B.
(D) are available over the counter.

3. In administering the auto-injector, it should be positioned on the

(A) lateral portion of the thigh midway between the waist and knee.
(B) medial portion of the thigh midway between the waist and knee.
(C) lateral portion of the thigh near the hip.
(D) medial portion of the thigh near the groin.

4. In the case of severe allergic reactions the patient may become hypotensive.

(A) True.
(B) False.

5. The Epipen auto-injector works by

(A) dilating the bronchioles and blood vessels.
(B) constricting the bronchioles and blood vessels.
(C) dilating the bronchioles and constricting the blood vessels.
(D) constricting the bronchioles and dilating the blood vessels.

6. Poisons can enter the body through

(A) absorption.
(B) inhalation.
(C) ingestion.
(D) injection.
(E) All of the above.

7. In the case of ingested poisons the EMT-B should consider

(A) administering ipecac.
(B) inducing vomiting.
(C) administering activated charcoal.
(D) All of the above.

8. The pediatric dose of activated charcoal is typically

(A) 5–12.5 grams.
(B) 12.5–25 grams.
(C) 25–50 grams.
(D) 50–100 grams.

9. Activated charcoal works by

(A) binding to certain poisons, preventing them from being absorbed.
(B) inducing vomiting.
(C) Both A & B.
(D) None of the above.

10. Black stools are a _____ of activated charcoal administration:

(A) side effect
(B) complication
(C) contraindication
(D) desired effect

■ Answers to Review Questions

1. **D** Section 1, Objective 1
Signs and symptoms of allergic reaction can include itching, hives, swelling of the hands and face, congestion and/or spasm of the airways, and respiratory distress.

2. **C** Section 1, Objective 5
People who have had allergic reactions requiring medical attention are usually given prescriptions for epinephrine auto-injectors. These are designed so that a patient experiencing a reaction can self-administer a dose of epinephrine in the hopes that he or she will be able to ward off any serious consequences before receiving medical treatment.

3. **A** Section 1, Objective 5
The auto-injector should be administered on either lateral thigh midway between the waist and the knee.

4. **A** Section 1, Objective 2
A severe allergic reaction is called anaphylactic shock. The patient becomes hypotensive and the condition can be fatal if not aggressively treated.

5. **C** Section 1, Objective 5
The individual having the allergic reaction can be suffering from constriction of the airways and dilation of the blood vessels. Epinephrine causes dilation of the airways and constriction of the blood vessels, counteracting the effects of the reaction.

6. **E** Section 2, Objective 1
Poisons can be absorbed through the skin, inhaled into the respiratory system, ingested into the digestive system, or injected, as with a needle and syringe or by an insect.

7. **C** Section 2, Objective 6
Administering activated charcoal to someone who has ingested poison can limit the absorption of the poison and its effects.

8. **B** Section 2, Objective 6
The pediatric dose for activated charcoal is 12.5–25 grams.

9. **A** Section 2, Objective 6
The action of activated charcoal is to bind to the ingested toxins, preventing them from being absorbed. They can then be removed by external suction or passed through the digestive tract.

10. **A** Section 2, Objective 6
Black stools are evidence that the charcoal has passed through the digestive tract.

CHAPTER 16

Environmental Emergencies

Objectives

1. Describe the various ways in which the body loses heat.

2. List the signs and symptoms of exposure to cold.

3. Explain the steps in providing emergency medical care to a patient exposed to cold.

4. List the signs and symptoms of exposure to heat.

5. Explain the steps in providing emergency care to a patient exposed to heat.

6. Recognize the signs and symptoms of water-related emergencies.

7. Describe the complications of near drowning.

8. Discuss the emergency medical care of bites and stings.

Types of Environmental Emergencies

Environmental emergencies include exposure to heat and cold. The body can lose heat via radiation, convection, conduction, evaporation, and breathing or respiration, creating hypothermia. If the heat gained by the body exceeds the heat lost by the body, hyperthermia can occur.

Any environmental exposure calls for the EMT-B to determine the source and the environment and determine, in the case of a loss of consciousness, if the effects are general or local.

Generalized hypothermia can be caused by immersion (soaked, as in a rain) or submersion (as in being underwater). Infants and children might actually be at greater risk as they have a larger surface area relative to their overall mass, making them more susceptible. Less body fat also places them at risk.

People who are compromised by other problems such as shock, injury, burns, infection, diabetes, or other disease or injury are also more susceptible.

Treatment of Generalized Hypothermia

Generalized hypothermia is treated first with removal from the environment. Remove wet or restrictive clothing. Don't let the patient walk or exert himself or herself, and if hypothermia is profound, administer warm humidified oxygen, if available.

Cold Injuries

Local cold injuries include:

✔ Superficial injury exposure that can be recognized by blanching of the skin with palpation and the fact that normal color does not return.
✔ Loss of feeling and sensation, skin that remains soft, and tingling with rewarming.
✔ Late or deep injury, discolored waxy skin, firm to frozen feeling, blisters, mottled skin with rewarming.

Care includes removal of the patient from the environment, protection from further injury, removal of wet or restrictive clothing, and administration of oxygen.

After removing the clothing and jewelry, keep the patient warm and dry; if transport is exceedingly long, immerse the patient in warm water until color returns, then dress the injuries with dry, sterile dressings.

Heat Exposure

Climate, exercise, and activity, and the age and general physical condition of an individual can contribute to the potential for problems associated with heat exposure. Muscle cramps, weakness and exhaustion, dizziness or faintness, and moist skin, with normal to cool temperature and rapid heart rate, are examples of heat exhaustion, while hot, dry skin and altered mental status are signs of heatstroke or severe heat exposure.

Exposed to heat, the body can rapidly lose fluid, causing heat exhaustion, progressing to heatstroke or shock. The body can lose up to a liter of sweat per hour.

Quick action by the EMT-B often makes the difference between success and failure in treating exposure patients.

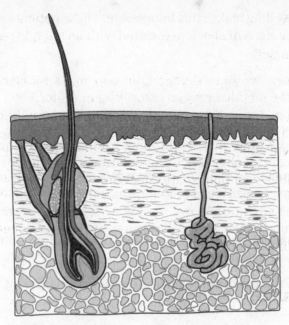

A cross-section of a subcutaneous view of the skin
showing a hair follicle and sweat gland.

Patients with heat exposure should be removed from the environment, given oxygen, have clothing loosened or removed, and cooled by fanning. If the patient is alert and not nauseated, cool liquids can be administered. If the patient is vomiting, transport the patient to the hospital.

Cool packs to the neck and groin are appropriate for the patient with hot, dry skin and altered mental status.

Drowning

Drowning or near drowning victims should be removed from the water with attention to the potential for spinal injuries once safety of the rescuers is assured. Contrary to what is generally supposed, drowning victims don't take a large amount of water into the lungs. What actually happens is that the water entering the airway stimulates the gag reflex, closing the airway and causing the patient to suffocate. The water temperature also causes the patient to become hypothermic. Treatment of the drowning victim centers on creating and protecting an airway and considering that the patient will need to be warmed and ventilated for a time before resuscitation can be successful. CPR should be performed if the patient is without a pulse and is not breathing. The EMT-B should also consider head and neck injuries. Often, such injuries cause the patient to sink under the water. This further explains why many drowning victims succumb in less than five feet of water.

Bites and Stings

Bites and stings are included in environmental injuries. Pain, redness, swelling, and associated weakness, dizziness, chills, fever, nausea, and vomiting can indicate a possible serious reaction to the bite or sting. If the stinger is visible, it can/should be removed by brushing along its length with the edge of a card. Jewelry and restrictive clothing should be removed before swelling makes this impossible. These patients should be observed for respiratory distress or signs of shock associated with an allergic response.

Scenarios

1. You are called out for a "man down" on a cold, damp evening and find a man in his underwear lying in an alley. Once you determine whether the man is breathing and has pulses, what is your immediate concern?

Solution

Hypothermia. The patient should be removed from the environment that led to the hypothermia as soon as possible.

2. Once moved to the warm ambulance, how else can you treat the hypothermia?

Solution

Remove any wet clothing and cover the patient with warm, dry blankets.

3. You are working with an unresponsive heat exposure patient. She is breathing and has a rapid, shallow respiratory rate. Her skin is hot and dry to the touch. What treatments are you considering for this patient?

Solution

Remove restrictive clothing, administer oxygen, apply cool packs to the neck, groin, and armpits, and keep the skin moist with a sponge or wet towels.

Review Questions

1. Losing heat from an uncovered head is an example of

   (A) conduction.
   (B) convection.
   (C) radiation.
   (D) evaporation.

2. Heat loss through wet clothing is

   (A) conduction.
   (B) convection.
   (C) radiation.
   (D) evaporation.

3. Hypothermia due to being underwater is called

(A) inundation.
(B) covering.
(C) submersion.
(D) immersion.

4. To assess the general body temperature of the patient, the EMT-B should

(A) place the back of the hand on the patient's forehead.
(B) place the back of the hand between the patient's clothing and his or her abdomen.
(C) place the back of the hand in the patient's palm.
(D) place the back of the hand in the small of the patient's back.

5. Which of the following is true of treating cold injuries to the extremities?

(A) Fingers and toes should be rubbed vigorously.
(B) Cold water should be run over the extremity.
(C) The patient should be encouraged to walk on cold, injured feet.
(D) The patient should be handled gently.

6. Early or superficial cold injury is evidenced by

(A) a tingling sensation when rewarmed.
(B) blisters.
(C) flushed skin.
(D) pale, waxy skin.

7. Rewarming affected parts by immersing in warm water should only be done

(A) if there is a late or deep cold injury.
(B) if the injury is superficial.
(C) if transport is long or delayed.
(D) by physicians.

8. Exercise and heat can work together to cause the loss of

(A) 50 cc of sweat per hour.
(B) 500 cc of sweat per hour.
(C) 1 liter of sweat per hour.
(D) 2 liters of sweat per hour.

9. The progression of responses due to heat exposure is

(A) heat cramps, heat exhaustion, heatstroke.
(B) heat exhaustion, heatstroke, heat cramps.
(C) heatstroke, heat cramps, heat exhaustion.
(D) heat cramps, heatstroke, heat exhaustion.

10. A heat exposure patient complaining of weakness and nausea with pale, cool, clammy skin and a rapid heart rate is suffering from

   (A) heat cramps.
   (B) heat exhaustion.
   (C) heatstroke.
   (D) a heat rash.

Answers to Review Questions

1. C Objective 1
Heat can be transferred by several mechanisms. Conduction is by direct contact as from the elements on an electric stove to the pan sitting on it. Convection is warming something by heating the air around it. Radiation is passing the heat directly across a space, which is how "radiators" work or how we receive the heat from the sun. Evaporation is the transfer of heat from the surface of the skin by the evaporation of water (sweat).

2. A Objective 1
As in the previous explanation, conduction is direct contact. Another example is your hand getting cold while holding a cold can of soda.

3. C Objective 2
There are two types of hypothermia involving water. Submersion means that the face and head actually were underwater; immersion is getting soaked, as in the rain.

4. B Objective 3
The best way to differentiate the temperature of another body from the temperature of your own body is to place the back of your hand on the patient's abdomen. The back of your hand will be sensitive, as the skin is thin there and the abdomen is close to the body's core or central temperature.

5. D Objective 3
Patients who have been exposed to extreme cold may have brittle tissues so they should be handled carefully. Frozen soft tissue can be easily damaged, causing internal fluid loss when the patient warms up.

6. A Objective 3
Superficial frostbite recovers quickly and is evidenced by tingling, maybe even a painful stinging sensation as the tissue warms and the nerve endings respond to the superficial soft tissue damage.

7. C Objective 3
Rewarming cold exposure extremities should be done only in situations where transport is delayed. This is done by placing the extremities in water maintained at a warm temperature.

8. **C** Objective 4

Dehydration and shock due to heat exposure can happen rapidly if fluids aren't maintained. The body loses much of the fluid through perspiration. As much as 1 liter per hour can be lost through sweating.

9. **A** Objective 4

The progression of responses due to heat exposure is: First, heat cramps, as the dehydration and loss of salts causes muscle spasms. Second, heat exhaustion, where the patient is diaphoretic, pale, clammy, dizzy, and nauseated. Third, heatstroke where all of the body's heat regulating mechanisms are overwhelmed and the body temperature rises. The patient loses consciousness and may have seizures. The skin will be hot and dry at this point.

10. **B** Objective 4

Weakness, nausea, pale, cool, and clammy skin, and tachycardia are all signs and symptoms of heat exhaustion.

CHAPTER 17

Behavioral Emergencies

◼ Objectives

1. Define behavioral emergencies.

2. Discuss the general factors that may cause an alteration in a patient's behavior.

3. State the various reasons for psychological crises.

4. Discuss the characteristics of an individual's behavior that suggest that the patient is at risk for suicide.

5. Discuss special medical/legal considerations for managing behavioral emergencies.

6. Discuss the special considerations for assessing a patient with behavioral problems.

7. Discuss the general principles of an individual's behavior that suggest that he or she is at risk for violence.

8. Discuss methods to calm behavioral emergency patients.

◼ Behavior

The manner in which a person acts or performs is called behavior. A behavioral emergency is a situation in which a person's behavior is unacceptable to the patient, family, or community. This behavior can be due to emotional extremes or psychological or physical conditions.

Factors that can cause changes in behavior include stress, illness, psychiatric problems, or drugs. Low blood sugar, hypoxia, poor cerebral blood flow, head injuries, or environmental extremes of heat or cold can also cause changes in behavior.

Psychological crises include panic, agitation, bizarre thinking and behavior, danger to self and self-destructive behavior, suicide, danger to others, threatening behavior, and violence.

Assessing for Suicide Risk

Assessing for suicide risk includes recognizing depression, as in sad, tearful people with thoughts of death or taking their life. Risk factors for suicidal gestures include individuals over 40, single, widowed, or divorced, alcoholic, or depressed; also present may be a defined lethal plan of action that has been verbalized. An unusual collection of things can cause death, such as guns, pills, etc.; a previous history of suicide attempts; a recent diagnosis of a serious illness; loss of a loved one; arrest; or job loss. Look for patients in unsafe surroundings, with self-destructive behavior.

The EMT-B should size up the scene, determine safety and perform a patient assessment.

Calm the patient and do not leave the patient alone. These patients must be restrained, if necessary. Police should help and can provide legal support as well as physical support. If drugs or poisons are used, bring them along to the hospital.

Remember that if you are treating and transporting against a disturbed patient's will, you must be able to describe a risk to the patient or others. When in doubt seek advice from medical control. It is also important to accurately document your assessments and justifications for your treatment.

Communication is important when dealing with disturbed patients. Identify yourself and show a willingness to listen and help. Use a calm, reassuring voice. Do not judge but accept what the patient tells you without scolding. You can show that you are listening by repeating what the patient says. Acknowledge the patient's feelings and observe his or her mental status by assessing appearance, speech, activity, and orientation to time, person, and place.

Scenarios

1. You are called to assist a suicidal patient. What is your first concern?

Solution

Determining scene safety. If police are not yet on the scene, you should stage at a safe distance until the scene has been made safe.

2. In addressing the patient, what can you do in your approach to help set the patient at ease and gain his or her trust?

Solution

Maintain a passive stance, palms open and facing forward at a safe distance, out of the patient's personal space. Speak slowly and in a calm, reassuring voice, listen carefully to the patient, and occasionally repeat what he or she says to show that you are listening.

3. If the patient is unwilling to go to the hospital, can you allow a suicidal patient to refuse care?

Solution

This is one of the few situations where restraining the patient is advisable. With the advice and consent of medical control and the assistance of police, the patient should be restrained and transported, even if against his or her will.

Review Questions

1. When behavioral changes occur in trauma patients, you should assume

   (A) that there is a psychological disorder.
   (B) that the patient may be suffering from hypoxia.
   (C) that the patient may be a violent sociopath.
   (D) that the patient is suicidal.

2. A special risk group for suicidal tendencies is

   (A) males over 40.
   (B) a single person.
   (C) widowed or divorced individuals.
   (D) All of the above.

3. In dealing with a disturbed patient you should

   (A) identify yourself and let him or her know you're there to help.
   (B) sneak up and subdue the patient before speaking.
   (C) have the police restrain the patient and avoid communicating with him or her.
   (D) refuse to treat the patient unless the patient consents.

4. When disturbed patients express hallucinatory thoughts, you should

   (A) tell them that the thoughts are crazy.
   (B) tell them that the thoughts are not real and convince them that they need help.
   (C) listen carefully and repeat their thoughts to show you are listening and concerned.
   (D) ignore what they say.

5. With suicidal or disturbed patients

   (A) consent is not necessary.
   (B) restraining the patient is the only option.
   (C) getting patient consent is preferred.
   (D) you can allow the patient to refuse care.

6. The definition of behavioral emergency is:

   (A) any reaction to events that interferes with activities of daily living (ADL).
   (B) any patient posing a threat of harm to himself or herself or others.
   (C) any patient showing signs of mental illness.
   (D) an injury to a patient with a history of mental illness.

7. Patients who are at risk for violent behavior may

   (A) exhibit signs of poor impulse control.
   (B) have a history of unstable family life.
   (C) have a history of substance abuse.
   (D) describe hearing voices telling them to do violent things.
   (E) All of the above.

8. Restraining a patient against his or her will

(A) requires an order from medical direction.
(B) should be done only with police assistance.
(C) needs only the EMT's assessment that the patient is not competent.
(D) All of the above.
(E) A & B.

9. If a patient is a danger to himself or herself or others, the EMT should

(A) get direction from medical control.
(B) seek the assistance of family.
(C) seek the assistance of law enforcement.
(D) All of the above.

10. Distrust, jealousy, seclusiveness, and hostile, uncooperative behavior are all signs of

(A) suicidal patients.
(B) paranoid patients.
(C) depressed patients.
(D) phobic patients.

Answers to Review Questions

1. **B** Objective 1
The first consideration when confronting someone with an altered level of consciousness or inappropriate behavior is that he or she is suffering from hypoxia due to a potentially life-threatening condition.

2. **D** Objective 2
Middle-aged men with unstable or a nonexistent family and/or social lives are one of the most typical suicide potential profiles.

3. **A** Objective 6
In treating a disturbed patient it is important to establish trust. Identifying yourself and making it clear that you are prepared to listen and that you don't pose a threat are key.

4. **C** Objective 6
It is important to let the patient know you are listening by rephrasing things he or she expresses, but it is important not to encourage or make light of his or her hallucinations.

5. **C** Objective 6
Getting the patient's consent is crucial. Treating or transporting without consent is tricky at best and requires medical control's order and probably assistance from law enforcement.

6. **A** Objective 1
By definition, a "behavioral emergency" is "Any event that interferes with the Activities of Daily Living (ADL)."

7. **E** Objective 7
The potential for violence should be considered when patients exhibit or describe poor impulse control, have histories of unstable or nonexistent family and social lives, wear tattoos (especially gang insignia), suffer substance abuse, are hearing voices telling them to do things, or suffer depression.

8. **E** Objective 5
Restraining a patient is a very controversial action; however, it may need to be done and if it is, it must be with medical control's order and with the assistance of law enforcement.

9. **D** Objective 5
People who present a danger to themselves or others need to be brought to the hospital. When this happens, though, an order from medical control and the assistance of law enforcement will be needed and the assistance of family members should be encouraged.

10. **B** Objective 3
Paranoid patients show distrust, are seclusive, jealous, and often uncooperative.

CHAPTER 18

Obstetrics/Gynecology

Objectives

1. Identify the following structures: uterus, vagina, fetus, placenta, umbilical cord, amniotic sac, and perineum.

2. Identify and explain the use of the contents of an obstetric kit.

3. Identify predelivery emergencies.

4. State indications of an imminent delivery.

5. Differentiate the emergency medical care provided to a patient with predelivery emergencies and a normal delivery.

6. State the steps in the predelivery preparation of the mother.

7. Establish the relationship between body substance isolation and childbirth.

8. State the steps to assist in the delivery.

9. Describe care of the baby as the head appears.

10. Describe how and when to cut the umbilical cord.

11. Discuss the steps in the delivery of the placenta.

12. List the steps in the emergency medical care of the mother post-delivery.

13. Summarize neonatal resuscitation procedures.

14. Describe the procedures for the following abnormal deliveries: breech birth, prolapsed cord, and limb presentation.

15. Differentiate the special considerations for multiple births.

16. Describe special considerations of meconium.

17. Describe special considerations of a premature baby.

18. Discuss the emergency medical care of a patient with a gynecological emergency.

Anatomy

The fetus grows in the **uterus**, getting its life-giving nutrients through the umbilical cord from the **placenta**. To be born, it must move down the birth canal. When the child is born, emerging from the vagina, it may be covered by the **amniotic sac** that protected it while in the uterus. Deliveries can expose the EMT-B to lots of blood and body fluids, so gloves, eye protection, a mask, and even a gown should be worn to protect from the fluids.

Delivery

As the baby's head emerges, the face should be cleaned and the airway suctioned before the baby breathes and inhales fluids and debris that came out with it. When the rest of the baby is delivered, hold the baby below the vaginal opening to prevent blood from the baby from flowing back into the placenta, which has probably detached from the uterine wall. After drying and warming the baby, and after the cord stops pulsating, the cord should be clamped four finger widths from the infant and again a couple of inches beyond that. The cord can be cut between the clamps. Wrap the baby in dry towels and allow the mother to hold the baby to her chest. The baby may be able to hear her heartbeat, which can soothe the baby. If the baby suckles to the mother's breast, it may assist in creating contractions that will control bleeding in the mother and deliver the placenta. If the placenta delivers, wrap it in a towel and bring it to the hospital. If it doesn't deliver within a few minutes, transport.

Complications

✔ If the baby is breech, and the head is undelivered, insert a gloved hand into the vaginal opening and create an airway in case the baby tries to breathe before the head is delivered. Be prepared, as inserting your hand may stimulate a contraction to expel the baby the rest of the way out of the mother.

✔ If an arm or a leg presents first, the baby cannot be delivered in the field and you should elevate the mother's hips and expedite transport.

✔ The APGAR score is a method of determining the baby's condition. It should be done at one minute and five minutes in the field and it will be repeated at the hospital to determine the infant's development after birth. A number is assigned for each of five assessments.

Sign	0	1	2
Appearance Skin color	Blue, Pale	Normal body,* Blue Extremities	Normal*
Pulse (Heart) Rate	Absent	<100 per minute	>100 per minute
Grimace Irritability	No Response	Grimace	Cough, Sneeze, Cry
Activity Muscle tone	Limp	Some Flexion	Active Motion
Respirations Respiratory Effort	Absent	Slow, Irregular	Good, Crying

*Based on race.

✔ If the baby does not breathe spontaneously, open and clear the airway and begin artificial ventilations. After 30 seconds, reassess. If the baby's heart rate is less than 100, continue ventilations; if it is less than 60, begin compressions. Reassess and adjust resuscitation every 30 seconds.

✔ Some bleeding is normal after delivery. Up to 500 cc is common without creating a danger to the mother. Fundal massage (massaging the abdomen over the uterus) and allowing the baby to suckle at the mother's breast can encourage uterine contraction to control bleeding from the mother. The EMT-B should never pack the vagina but should place dressings over the vagina and transport. Consider the need for psychological care in assault patients and using female technicians when possible; be reassuring and considerate when it's not possible.

✔ A prolapsed cord is another situation in which you cannot deliver in the field. Insert a gloved hand to keep the baby's head from pressing on the cord, elevate the mother's hips, and transport.

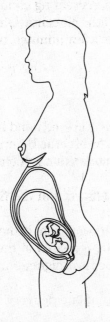

In the normal position, the fetus will lie head down in the uterus.

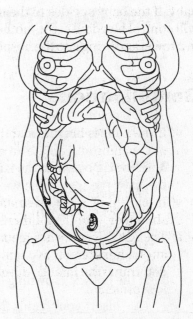

Even with normal presentations, complication can result from the position of the umbilical cord during the birth process.

▨ Scenarios

1. You are called to assist a 22-year-old female with abdominal pain in the pelvis area. Upon examination you notice that she is crowning. What should the EMT-B do at this point?

Solution

Address BSI and prepare for the birth of the baby.

2. After preparing for the birth of the child, you notice that the cord is prolapsed. What should the EMT-B do at this point?

Solution

Elevate the mother's hips and transport. You cannot deliver a prolapsed cord birth in the field.

3. You've cleared the baby's airway, dried and rewarmed the baby, and the heart rate is less than 100. What should you do next?

Solution

Begin artificial respirations and recheck the heart rate in 30 seconds.

Review Questions

1. The organ that the fetus grows in is the

  (A) uterus.
  (B) pancreas.
  (C) colon.
  (D) fallopian tubes.

2. The skin between the vagina and the anus that often tears during delivery is the

  (A) peritoneum.
  (B) perineum.
  (C) amniocentesis.
  (D) uvula.

3. If the baby is crowning but undelivered after 10 minutes

  (A) insert your hands into the vaginal opening to stimulate delivery.
  (B) try to pull the baby from the vagina.
  (C) contact medical control for permission to transport.
  (D) continue to wait for the delivery to progress.

4. After delivery of the child, the cord should be clamped

  (A) as close to the baby as possible.
  (B) as close to the mother as possible.
  (C) four finger widths from the baby.
  (D) two finger widths from the baby.

5. Bleeding of up to _____ is normal following delivery.

  (A) 100 cc
  (B) 500 cc
  (C) 1 liter
  (D) 1,500 cc

6. With excessive blood loss after delivery, the EMT-B should

   (A) pack the vagina with gauze.
   (B) massage the uterus.
   (C) apply loose dressings over the vagina.
   (D) B & C.

7. The APGAR score measures

   (A) appearance, pulse, grimace, activity, and respirations.
   (B) appearance, pupils, gait, activity, and respirations.
   (C) appearance, pallor, grimace, activity, and respirations.
   (D) appearance, pulse, gait, activity, and respirations.

8. The newborn's heart rate should be at least

   (A) 60.
   (B) 70.
   (C) 80.
   (D) 100.

9. When resuscitating a newborn, heart rate should be reassessed every

   (A) 5 minutes.
   (B) 2 minutes.
   (C) minute.
   (D) 30 seconds.

10. Greenish or brownish amniotic fluid

   (A) is normal.
   (B) indicates meconium and the need for aggressive suctioning.
   (C) indicates serious infection.
   (D) indicates foreign bodies in the uterus.

Answers to Review Questions

1. **A** Objective 1
The fetus grows in the uterus, nourished by the placenta, which grows along with the fetus.

2. **B** Objective 1
Often during delivery, the force of the baby's delivery tears the perineum. Pressure may need to be applied externally to control bleeding and sutures will probably be required at the hospital.

3. **C** Objective 4
The baby's birth should be continuous. Any delay may indicate difficulties that can only be managed at the hospital.

4. **C** Objective 10

After the baby is delivered and the cord stops pulsating, it should be clamped the width of four fingers from the baby, and three to four inches beyond that and cut between. This allows for some of the cord to be available in case an intravenous is needed to be started there, and also allows room for reclamping should there be bleeding after the cord is cut. In that event, another clamp should be applied behind the first clamp, without removing the first.

5. **B** Objective 12

There will be bleeding during and following the delivery. Up to 500 cc is normal.

6. **D** Objective 12

When bleeding is excessive, it is important to never pack dressings into the vagina but to apply them in a diaper-like fashion on the outside. Massaging the abdomen over the uterus and allowing the baby to suckle may result in contractions and so control bleeding.

7. **A** Objective 13

The APGAR score measures appearance, pulse, grimace, activity, and respirations. It should be done at one and five minutes in the field and will be repeated at the hospital.

8. **D** Objective 13

If the newborn's heart rate is less than 100, supplementary ventilations should be given.

9. **D** Objective 13

Newborns should improve rapidly after birth so they should be reassessed every 15 to 30 seconds. Even newborns in distress should improve rapidly with ventilations and oxygen.

10. **B** Objective 13

Greenish brown, greasy material in the fluid or on the baby is evidence that the baby may have been stressed during delivery and moved its bowels while in utero. The only danger is that the baby may inhale this material in those first few breaths so immediate suction is important.

CHAPTER 19

Bleeding and Shock

■ Objectives

1. List the structure and function of the circulatory system.

2. Differentiate between arterial, venous, and capillary bleeding.

3. State methods of emergency medical care of external bleeding.

4. Establish the relationship between body substance isolation and bleeding.

5. Establish the relationship between airway management and the trauma patient.

6. Establish the relationship between the mechanism of injury and internal bleeding.

7. List the sign of internal bleeding.

8. List the steps in the emergency medical care of the patient with signs and symptoms of internal bleeding.

9. List signs and symptoms of shock (hyperperfusion).

10. State the steps in the emergency medical care of the patient with signs and symptoms of shock (hypoperfusion).

■ The Circulatory System

The circulatory system consists of the heart, which pumps blood throughout into the arteries and out to the capillaries where oxygen and nutrients are exchanged for carbon dioxide and waste. The blood then returns through the veins to the heart where it is pumped to the lungs. In the lungs the carbon dioxide is exchanged for oxygen between the capillaries and alveoli.

The EMT-B must protect himself or herself from exposure to blood and body fluids by practicing BSI, or body substance isolation. This includes gloves, eye protection, gowns, masks, and hand washing between patient contacts.

The sudden loss of a liter of blood in the adult, 500 cc in a child, or 100–200 cc in an infant constitutes serious bleeding. The patient's signs and symptoms will illustrate the severity of the blood loss.

Bleeding

While clotting is the body's natural response to minimize bleeding, serious injury may prevent clotting from being effective. Uncontrolled bleeding leads to hypoperfusion, or shock and death.

✔ **Arterial bleeding** is bright red in color (oxygen) and spurts or pulses.
✔ **Venous bleeding** is darker red (low in oxygen) and flows.
✔ **Capillary bleeding** is dark red and oozing.

To control external bleeding, after BSI, the EMT-B should apply direct pressure followed by a pressure dressing. Pressure points or compression of the artery above the wound may assist in slowing the bleeding while the dressings are applied. Splints may also be effective in helping to control bleeding by limiting motion that might encourage it.

Tourniquets

Tourniquets are a last resort and should never be used below the elbow or knee and seldom used elsewhere. Tourniquets should be at least four inches wide and wrapped around the extremity twice, proximal to the bleeding site, but as close to the wound as possible. Tie a knot in the bandage being used as a tourniquet, place a stick over the knot, and tie a knot over the stick. Turn the stick until the bleeding stops and secure the stick in place. Leaving a blood pressure cuff inflated in place may also work as a tourniquet until bleeding stops. Once in place, a tourniquet should not be removed and the EMT-B must be certain to alert medical staff as to its existence.

Bleeding in the face and head is a special problem. The EMT-B should not attempt to stop the flow of blood from the ears or nose if it is the result of trauma. Loose dressings should collect the blood. To treat nosebleeds, place the patient in a sitting position leaning slightly forward. Apply pressure by pinching the fleshy portion of the nostrils together.

Internal bleeding can result in hidden, severe, and deadly blood loss from large blood vessels or internal organs. Knowledge of the mechanism of injury or illness along with the patient's signs and symptoms will be the clue to internal bleeding. Pain, tenderness, swelling, discoloration, bleeding from the mouth, rectum, or vagina, vomiting bright red or coffee ground-colored blood, dark, tarry, or bright flecked stools, tender or rigid abdomen are all signs of possible internal bleeding. Early on in the bleeding patient, nervousness or agitation may reflect developing hypoxia. As the condition worsens the mental status will also worsen. As the bleeding continues or worsens, the patient's condition will deteriorate and the vital signs will begin to reflect that. Pale, cool, and clammy skin, rapid breathing and heart rate, and ultimately a falling blood pressure and shock will result. In infants and children, capillary refill of greater than two seconds is also a sign of developing shock.

In some cases of internal bleeding, as in bleeds below the diaphragm in the abdomen and pelvis, the pneumatic antishock garment (PASG) may be indicated to limit the bleeding.

Scenarios

1. You are called to the scene of a stabbing. After staging, until the scene is made safe, you ensure BSI and approach the patient and find that bright red blood is spurting from a wound in his right upper arm. How would you manage this patient?

Solution

After ensuring that there are no more serious life threats, the EMT-B should apply direct pressure to the wound followed by a pressure dressing. Before and after placing the dressing, pulses and sensations below the dressing should be checked. Before transport, splinting the arm will limit the possibility of the dressing coming loose and increased bleeding.

2. You are called to the scene to evaluate a patient who was struck in the abdomen by a 55-gallon drum. After determining that the scene is safe and donning PPE, you find a drowsy man with cold, clammy skin, rapid pulse and respirations, clutching his abdomen. What do you think might be going on here and what will you do for this patient?

Solution

Your initial evaluation should already be telling you that this patient is in critical condition and expedited transport is going to be a goal of your treatment. The skin condition, altered mental status, and rapid heart and respiratory rate all indicate hypoperfusion and developing shock. You will need to do a quick trauma assessment and get this patient to the hospital as quickly as possible.

3. Your focused rapid trauma assessment shows a rigid, tender abdomen, with abrasions from the 55-gallon drum. The patient is responding only to pain now. What will you do in preparing this patient for transport?

Solution

Provide 15 liters of oxygen via a nonrebreather and monitoring airway and ventilations as your first priority. Placing the patient on a trauma board and securing him to prevent further injury and worsening the bleeding are also important. You may also use the PASG to manage the internal bleeding.

Review Questions

1. In an adult patient, the loss of _____ of blood is considered serious.

(A) 500 cc
(B) 1 liter
(C) 1,500 cc
(D) 2 liters

2. The possibility of internal bleeding is indicated by

(A) the patient's condition.
(B) the mechanism of injury or illness.
(C) vital signs.
(D) All of the above.

3. Bright red spurting blood is typical of _____ bleeding.

    (A) arterial
    (B) venous
    (C) capillary
    (D) All of the above.

4. The primary method of bleeding control is

    (A) a tourniquet.
    (B) a pressure point.
    (C) direct pressure.
    (D) clamps.

5. Tourniquets

    (A) should never be used.
    (B) should never be used below the knee or elbow.
    (C) should be used for all arterial bleeding.
    (D) should be used for all gunshots.

6. When treating a patient with head trauma, bleeding from the ears or nose

    (A) should be allowed to collect onto loose dressings.
    (B) should be packed with gauze to stop the bleeding.
    (C) should be treated with direct pressure.
    (D) All of the above.

7. The earliest signs of shock (hypoperfusion) are

    (A) nervousness and agitation.
    (B) a loss of consciousness.
    (C) a drop in blood pressure.
    (D) a slow pulse rate.

8. As the blood loss continues, the body tries to compensate for the developing hypoxia by

    (A) increasing the heart rate.
    (B) increasing the respiratory rate.
    (C) constricting peripheral blood vessels.
    (D) All of the above.

9. A falling blood pressure is a late sign of hypoperfusion (shock).

    (A) True.
    (B) False.

10. Capillary refill is evaluated in

    (A) all suspected shock patients.
    (B) infants.
    (C) children.
    (D) adults.
    (E) B & C.

■ Answers to Review Questions

1. **B** Objective 2
The loss of a liter of blood is considered serious.

2. **D** Objective 6
If the patient seems to be getting worse and you can't determine why, the mechanism of injury or worsening vital signs in the absence of any other explanation indicates possible internal bleeding.

3. **A** Objective 2
Arterial bleeding is bright red and spurts, venous bleeding is dark red and flows, and capillary bleeding is dark red and oozes.

4. **C** Objective 3
Bleeding should always first be controlled by direct pressure. If needed following that, pressure points can be used. Tourniquets should be used only as a last resort and never below the elbow or knee.

5. **B** Objective 3
As in the previous question, tourniquets should be used only as a last resort and then never below the elbow or knee.

6. **A** Objective 3
Bleeding from the nose or ears should be dressed loosely, collecting the blood but not binding the nose or ears.

7. **A** Objective 9
The earliest signs of hypoperfusion are nervousness and agitation caused by the hypoxia.

8. **D** Objective 9
The body attempts to compensate for a loss of blood. The first effect is a constriction of the body's blood vessels. As bleeding continues, pulse and respiratory rates rise. This is a temporary compensation, however, and when it fails, the vital signs will crash and the patient along with them.

9. **A** Objective 9
The last sign of developing shock is a drop in the blood pressure. This is a late sign of shock.

10. **E** Objective 9
Capillary refill is less relevant in adults for many reasons but is still used in evaluating infants and children.

CHAPTER 20

Dealing with Injuries

SECTION 1—SOFT TISSUE INJURIES

▮▮ Objectives

1. State the major functions of the skin.
2. List the layers of the skin.
3. Establish the relationship between body substance isolation (BSI) and soft tissue injuries.
4. List the types of closed soft tissue injuries.
5. Describe the emergency medical care of the patient with a closed soft tissue injury.
6. State the types of open soft tissue injuries.
7. Describe the emergency medical care of the patient with an open soft tissue injury.
8. Discuss the emergency medical care considerations for a patient with a penetrating chest injury.
9. State the emergency medical care considerations for a patient with an open wound to the abdomen.
10. Differentiate the care of an open wound to the chest from an open wound to the abdomen.
11. List the classifications of burns.
12. Define a superficial burn.
13. List the characteristics of a superficial burn.
14. Define a partial thickness burn.
15. List the characteristics of a partial thickness burn.
16. Define a full thickness burn.
17. List the characteristics of a full thickness burn.
18. Describe the emergency medical care of a patient with a superficial burn.
19. Describe the emergency medical care of a patient with a partial thickness burn.

20. Describe the emergency medical care of a patient with a full thickness burn.

21. List the functions of dressing and bandaging.

22. Describe the purpose of a bandage.

23. Describe the steps in applying a pressure dressing.

24. Establish the relationship between airway management and the patient with a chest injury, burns, and blunt and penetrating injuries.

25. Describe the effects of improperly applied dressings, splints, and tourniquets.

26. Describe the emergency medical care of a patient with an impaled object.

27. Describe the emergency medical care of a patient with an amputation.

28. Describe the emergency care for a chemical burn.

29. Describe the emergency care for an electrical burn.

The Skin

The skin serves us by keeping fluids in, regulating body temperature, and keeping bacteria out. Any significant disruption in the skin will cause possible loss of temperature regulation, infection, and loss of fluids. The skin's layers are the **epidermis** (outer) and the **dermis** (inner).

Soft Tissue Injuries

✔ Soft tissue injuries can be open or closed. Closed soft tissue injuries include contusions, hematoma, and crushing injuries. Open soft tissue injuries include abrasions, lacerations, avulsions, puncture/penetrations, amputations, and some crush injuries.

✔ Bleeding control is first provided with direct pressure, holding gauze to the wound with firm pressure. Pressure dressings can be used if the bleeding persists, and using pressure points, or applying pressure to a blood vessel above the wound, can help control the bleeding while you apply the dressing. Tourniquets are only a last resort and should never be used below the elbows or knees.

✔ Impaled objects should be secured in place unless they are in the face and are obstructing the airway.

✔ Treatment will center on bleeding control and immobilization.

Burns

Burns are classified as superficial, partial, or full thickness. The severity of a burn is determined evaluating the depth, total body surface area, and the location of the burn, along with the age and general physical condition of the patient. The rule of nines is used to determine the total percentage of body surface area affected by a burn, by using multiples of nine.

✔ In treating chemical burns, after the safety of the rescuer is assured, the chemical needs to be removed from the body to stop the burning. Dry chemicals should first be brushed off, then rinsed off. The patient will also need to be treated for toxic effects of the chemical.

✔ Electrical burns cause deep tissue death and there is generally more damage than is apparent on the surface.

✔ The biggest concern with electrical burns is cardiac arrest.

✔ In general, after some initial cooling, burns should be dressed in clean dry dressings.

SECTION 2—MUSCULOSKELETAL INJURIES

Objectives

1. Describe the function of the muscular system.

2. Describe the function of the skeletal system.

3. List the major bones or bone groupings of the spinal column, the thorax, the upper extremities, the lower extremities.

4. Differentiate between an open and a closed painful, swollen, deformed extremity.

5. State the reasons for splinting.

6. List the general rules of splinting.

7. List the complications of splinting.

8. List the emergency medical care for a patient with a painful, swollen, deformed extremity.

Mechanisms that can cause musculoskeletal injuries include direct, indirect, or twisting forces. A direct force would be injury to the knee when it strikes the dashboard of the car. Injury to the pelvis when the knee strikes the dashboard would be an example of an indirect injury caused when the energy is transmitted from the knee, through the femur, to the pelvis. Treatment includes BSI, ice, splinting, and elevation.

Proper splinting should prevent movement of bone fragments to limit further injury to nerves, blood vessels, and soft tissues and should be done before the patient is moved, if hazards permit. Before and after splints are applied, pulses and sensation should be checked distal to the injury. Splints include rigid, traction, pneumatic, improvised (pillows and blankets), and PASG (for pelvic injuries). When splinting joints, the bone above and below should be immobilized, and when splinting bones, the joint above and below the injury should be immobilized. Traction splints are indicated only for mid-shaft femur fractures (Thomas, Hare, or Sager).

▣ Scenarios

1. You've arrived at the scene of a motorcycle collision and the man you are looking at has extensive abrasions over much of his body. How would you tend to these wounds?

Solution

After rinsing the debris out of the wounds with saline, dress the wounds in dry sterile dressings. Keep in mind that hypothermia due to the loss of skin and exposure to the elements is a possibility.

2. Your patient has burns to his face and hands. He is able to speak and walk but is in a great deal of pain. How serious are these burns and how would you treat them?

Solution

These burns should be considered critical because of the possible airway involvement and the burns to the hands and feet. After light initial cooling, dry sterile dressings, oxygen delivered at 15 liters via a nonrebreather mask, you would transport to the appropriate facility as directed by medical control.

3. You have arrived on the scene where a young man has severed the index finger of his right hand. How would you care for this patient?

Solution

Apply a pressure dressing to the hand, locate the severed finger, wrap it in a sterile dressing, wrap or bag it in plastic, and keep it cool. Transport the finger along with the patient to the appropriate facility as directed by medical control.

4. You are on the scene with a young woman complaining of a painful, swollen right forearm. How would you treat her?

Solution

After BSI and checking distal pulses and sensation, you should splint the injury to include the wrist and elbow. The addition of a sling will further protect and relieve some of the discomfort of this injury.

5. While examining the pelvis of a trauma patient, you compress the pelvic wings together and notice a grating sensation (crepitus) and an increase in pain for the patient. What do you suspect and how will you treat it?

Solution

Your patient may have a pelvic fracture. The patient should be immobilized to a spine board. Using the PASG will help to immobilize the broken pelvis and could help to control the bleeding that accompanies this type of life-threatening fracture.

6. You are preparing to splint a deformed right forearm injury. While checking the arm distal to the injury you notice that it appears cyanotic and swollen, the patient has decreased sensation, and you don't feel pulses distal to the injury. How should the EMT-B address this?

Solution

While splinting this extremity, the EMT-B should apply gentle traction while trying to re-align the deformity in an attempt to return circulation distal to the injury.

▆ **Review Questions**

1. The function of the skin is to

   (A) hold in fluids.
   (B) regulate body temperature.
   (C) keep bacteria out.
   (D) All of the above.

2. When applying the traction splint on the leg, pulses should be checked

   (A) before and after the splint is applied.
   (B) before manual traction is applied and after manual traction is applied.
   (C) after the leg is placed in the splint and after traction is turned over to the splint.
   (D) B & C.

3. A large collection of blood beneath the skin is called

   (A) a contusion.
   (B) a laceration.
   (C) a hematoma.
   (D) an abrasion.

4. Flaps of skin or tissue torn loose or torn off are called

   (A) avulsions.
   (B) abrasions.
   (C) contusions.
   (D) lacerations.

5. In open fractures with bone protruding from the wound, the EMT-B should

   (A) push the bone back in.
   (B) pull on the extremity until the bone drops back into place.
   (C) splint the injury in a way that protects the bone end.
   (D) cover the bone end but do not splint.

6. Impaled objects

   (A) should never be removed.
   (B) should be removed only if interfering with airway.
   (C) should always be removed.
   (D) should only be removed from extremities.

7. A hip injury caused when a knee strikes the dashboard of a car is an example of

    (A) direct forces.
    (B) indirect forces.
    (C) twisting forces.
    (D) None of the above.

8. A burn that involves only the epidermis is considered a

    (A) full thickness burn.
    (B) partial thickness burn.
    (C) superficial burn.
    (D) critical burn.

9. A burn of the anterior surface of the chest and the anterior surface of one arm would be what total body surface area according to the rule of nines?

    (A) 9%
    (B) 13.5%
    (C) 18%
    (D) 27%

10. Traction splints are indicated for

    (A) mid-shaft femur fractures.
    (B) mid-shaft humerus fractures.
    (C) hip fractures.
    (D) All of the above.

▦ Answers to Review Questions

1. **D** Section 1, Objective 1
The skin is the largest organ of the body and it holds in fluids, regulates body temperature, keeps bacteria out, and is a sensory organ.

2. **D** Section 2, Objective 6
There are four pulse checks when using traction on the leg. On initial exam, after manual traction is applied, after the splint is placed, and finally, after traction is turned over to the splint.

3. **C** Section 1, Objective 4
A hematoma is a closed soft tissue injury in which blood accumulates in a space, causing a lump.

4. **A** Section 1, Objective 6
An avulsion is an open soft tissue injury in which the skin is gouged, creating a skin flap that may be hinged to the skin or torn loose.

5. **C** Section 1, Objective 6
In the case of an open fracture where bone ends are sticking out, secure the extremity to prevent the bone ends from retreating beneath the skin, and cover the bone and wound.

6. **B** Section 1, Objective 24
Impaled objects should always be immobilized in place unless they are in the face and interfere with the airway.

7. **B** Section 2, Objective 1
Indirect forces are at work when the energy is applied to a point and travels along it, causing injury somewhere else along the line of transfer.

8. **C** Section 1, Objective 18
Burns are classified as superficial involving only the epidermis, partial thickness involving the epidermis and dermis, and full thickness involving all three layers of the skin including the subcutaneous layer.

9. **B** Section 1, Objective 11
Using the rule of nines, the anterior chest accounts for 9%, and the anterior surface of a single arm would be 4.5%, for a total of 13.5%.

10. **A** Section 2, Objective 6
Traction splints are indicated only for mid-shaft femur fractures. Anatomical splinting should be used if the injury is near the hip or knee.

CHAPTER 21

Injuries to the Head and Spine

▇▇ Objectives

1. State the components of the nervous system.

2. List the functions of the central nervous system.

3. Define the structure of the skeletal system as it relates to the nervous system.

4. Relate the mechanism of injury to potential injuries of the head and spine.

5. Describe the implications of not properly caring for potential spine injuries.

6. State the signs and symptoms of a potential spine injury.

7. Describe the method of determining if a responsive patient may have a spine injury.

8. Relate the airway emergency medical care techniques to the patient with a suspected spine injury.

9. Describe how to stabilize the cervical spine immobilization device.

10. Discuss indications for sizing and using cervical spine immobilization.

11. Establish the relationship between airway management and the patient with head and spine injuries.

12. Describe a method for sizing a cervical spine immobilization device.

13. Describe how to logroll a patient with a suspected spine injury.

14. Describe how to secure a patient to a long spine board.

15. List instances when a short spine board should be used.

16. Describe how to immobilize a patient using a short spine board.

17. Describe the indications for the use of rapid extrication.

18. List the steps in performing rapid extrication.

19. State the circumstances when a helmet should be left on the patient.

20. Discuss the circumstances when a helmet should be removed.

21. Identify different types of helmets.

22. Describe the unique characteristics of sports helmets.

23. Explain the preferred methods to remove a helmet.

24. Discuss alternative methods to remove a helmet.

25. Describe how the patient's head is stabilized to remove the helmet.

26. Describe how the patient's head is stabilized with a helmet compared to without a helmet.

The Nervous System

The nervous system consists of the **central** (brain) and **peripheral** (motor and sensory) systems. The **cranium** and the **spinal column** protect these systems. The spine is made up of 33 vertebrae: 7 cervical, 12 thoracic, 5 lumbar, 5 sacral, and 4 coccyx.

Injuries to the Spine

Injuries to the spine can be compression, flexion, extension, lateral bending, or distraction type. Any injury of the nervous system will be evidenced by some dysfunction in mental status, ability to move, or sensation. Injuries to the vertebrae should be suspected when there is mechanism of injury with tenderness, deformity, pain with movement, loss of sensation or ability to move. High cord injuries can disrupt the patient's ability to breathe and respiratory arrest should be anticipated with possible neck injuries.

When spine injuries are suspected, patients should be manually immobilized, then have cervical collars applied and be logrolled onto a spine board. If patients are in a sitting position, then short board or a Kendrick-type device (KED) should be used to immobilize them as much as possible before bringing them down onto a long board.

If the patient is critical or the scene is hazardous, the patient can be moved urgently without the short board device using the rapid extrication technique.

Injuries to the Head

Injuries to the head can bleed severely. Gentle pressure should be applied to control the bleeding but care should be given in the event there is a skull fracture associated with the wound. Injury to the brain should be suspected with any head injury.

Changes in mental status and/or fluid coming from the ears or nose, and unequal pupils are indicators of head injury.

Helmets should be removed if you are unable to assess the patent with the helmet in place, if the helmet does not fit properly, or if you are unable to immobilize the patient with the helmet in place.

When immobilizing infants, children, the elderly, or any other individual who might not fit onto the board uniformly or has misshapen spines, it should be padded to maintain in-line and neutral positioning.

The spine can be the source of serious problems while handling injured patients.

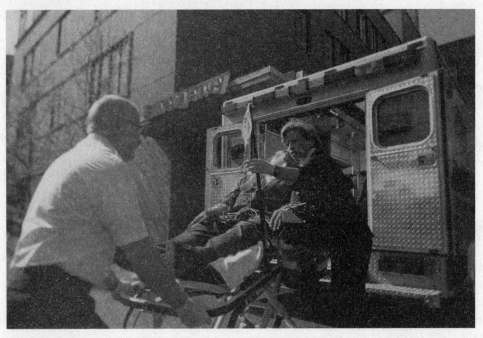

If circumstances warrant, padding on the stretcher might be needed for a patient with a misshapen spine.

▆ Scenarios

1. A patient walks up to you at the scene of a motor vehicle accident, says he was in one of the vehicles, and complains of neck pain. How should you treat this person?

Solution

Immediately provide manual cervical immobilization, apply a cervical collar, and do a standing board maneuver to get this person onto a backboard and immobilized.

2. You are called to assist with an unresponsive man who was pulled from a shallow pool. Besides beginning to resuscitate this patient, what do you think may have happened before he became unresponsive?

Solution

The EMT-B should always suspect head and neck injuries in unconscious patients, particularly in shallow pools, as there might have been a diving accident prior to the patient becoming unresponsive.

3. You are preparing to immobilize a child onto a long board. What special consideration do you need to address in children and spinal immobilization?

Solution

Because the head is proportionately larger in many children, you should check positioning on the board to maintain neutral and inline position and be prepared to pad the child's shoulders to prevent hyperflexion of the neck.

Review Questions

1. Falls are likely to cause what type of spinal fractures?

(A) Compression.
(B) Distraction.
(C) Flexion.
(D) Extension.

2. A face striking the windshield of a car is likely to cause what type of spinal injury?

(A) Compression.
(B) Distraction.
(C) Flexion.
(D) Extension.

3. All unconscious patients with no history to prove otherwise

(A) should be assumed to have a head injury.
(B) should be assumed to have a neck injury.
(C) Both A & B.
(D) None of the above.

4. Interruption of respirations is a possible complication of injuries to

(A) the cervical vertebrae.
(B) the thoracic vertebrae.
(C) the lumbar vertebrae.
(D) the sacral vertebrae.

5. An unconscious person in the front seat of a vehicle involved in a motor vehicle collision with rapid and weak ventilations and pulses should be

   (A) immobilized to a short board device and brought out onto a long board.
   (B) brought out via rapid extrication.
   (C) be worked on in the car before moving.
   (D) None of the above.

6. The nervous system is divided into two parts. The central nervous system consists of

   (A) the brain.
   (B) the spinal cord.
   (C) motor nerves.
   (D) sensory nerves.
   (E) A & B.
   (F) C & D.

7. Manual immobilization must be maintained in the spine injured patient until

   (A) the cervical collar is in place.
   (B) the patient is placed on the backboard.
   (C) the head blocks are in place.
   (D) the patient is completely secured to the spine board.

8. Once placed on the spine board, the order that the straps should be applied is

   (A) torso, feet, head.
   (B) feet, torso, head.
   (C) head, torso, feet.
   (D) head, feet, torso.

9. Signs and symptoms of a possible injury to the spinal cord include

   (A) loss of feeling in the arms or legs.
   (B) inability to move any extremity.
   (C) pain over the spine.
   (D) All or any of the above.

10. According to most protocols, helmets should be

   (A) left on and used to immobilize the head and neck.
   (B) removed if the helmet prevents airway management.
   (C) removed if it impairs the ability to immobilize the head and neck.
   (D) Any or all of the above.

▆▆ Answers to Review Questions

1. **A** Objective 4
Falls are likely to cause compression injuries in which bones are compressed together, crushing the tissues between them and shattering the bones. In this type of injury one bone end may also be imbedded into another.

2. **D** Objective 4

The part of the head that strikes the windshield can indicate the position of the neck on impact. If the face strikes the windshield, the neck was extended. If the forehead strikes the windshield, the neck was in a more neutral position, and if the top of the head strikes the windshield, the neck was flexed on impact.

3. **C** Objective 4

Head injury is a common cause of unconsciousness. Neck injuries are common with head injuries. Due to this potential, all unconscious patients should be assumed to have head injuries and all head-injured patients should be assumed to have neck injuries.

4. **A** Objective 11

The nerves that power the muscles that allow us to breathe come out of the spinal cord in the cervical region. Because of this, injuries to the cervical spine have the potential to disrupt the patient's ability to breathe.

5. **B** Objective 17

Rapid extrication is an urgent move to be used when the patient's condition is critical. The patient described here is in critical condition and should be removed using rapid extrication.

6. **E** Objective 1

The nervous system is divided into the central and peripheral nervous system. The central nervous system includes the brain and spinal cord. The peripheral nervous system is made up of motor and sensory nerves running between the rest of the body and the spinal cord.

7. **D** Objective 10

Manual immobilization must be maintained during the entire process of extricating or moving the patient to the spine board. Until the patient is completely secured to the board manual control of the head and cervical spine must be maintained.

8. **A** Objective 10

The head should be secured last to ensure that patient movement is contained before the head is finally secured. By securing the head last, the EMT-B ensures that the patient is completely secured before manual immobilization is released.

9. **D** Objective 6

Signs and symptoms of an injury to the spinal cord are related to the area damaged. Injury to the cervical spine can cause respiratory arrest by disrupting the nerves that control breathing. Further down the cord, injury can disrupt nervous communication with the internal organs or the extremities, causing loss of function and sensation.

10. **D** Objectives 19 and 20

There is some controversy as to whether helmets should be removed in the field. This includes sports and motorcycle helmets. In general, the standard of care is that if the helmet can be included in the immobilization of the patient and the EMT-B can complete an assessment with clear access to the airway, the helmet can remain in place. On the other hand, if the helmet needs to be removed to gain access to the airway, or to immobilize or assess the injuries, the helmet should be removed.

CHAPTER 22

Infants and Children

◼ Objectives

1. Identify the developmental considerations for the following age groups:
   - Infants
   - Toddlers
   - Preschool
   - School age
   - Adolescent

2. Describe the differences in anatomy and physiology of the infant, child, and adult.

3. Differentiate the response of the ill or injured infant or child (age specific) from that of an adult.

4. Indicate various causes of respiratory emergencies.

5. Differentiate between respiratory distress and respiratory failure.

6. List the steps in the management of foreign body airway obstruction.

7. Summarize emergency medical care strategies for respiratory distress and respiratory failure.

8. Identify the signs and symptoms of shock (hypoperfusion) in the infant and child.

9. Describe the methods of determining end organ perfusion in the infant and child.

10. State the usual cause of cardiac arrest in infants and children versus adults.

11. List the common causes of seizures in the infant and child.

12. Describe the management of seizures in the infant and child.

13. Differentiate between the injury patterns in adults, infants, and children.

14. Discuss the field management of the infant and child trauma patient.

15. Summarize the indicators of possible child abuse and neglect.

16. Describe the medical-legal responsibilities in suspected child abuse.

17. Recognize the need for EMT-Basic debriefing following a difficult infant or child transport.

Developmental Phases

In order to assess infants and children effectively, the EMT-B needs to understand the developmental phases. These are broken down into:

- ✔ birth to 1 year (newborn)
- ✔ 1 to 3 years (toddlers)
- ✔ 3 to 6 years (preschool)
- ✔ 6 to 12 years (school age)
- ✔ 12 to 18 years (adolescent)

The way infants and children respond to the EMT-B will change at each of these phases. Determining the mental status of a child too young to speak will depend on your assessment of their activity levels.

There are physical differences to remember as well. The smaller, shorter airways and proportionately larger head and tongue of the infant create airway obstruction possibilities different from those of adults.

The equipment used to manage these patients is important to review as well. Nasal or oral airways should not be used during initial artificial ventilations. Special backboards and other immobilization devices should be used, or the ones you have will have to be adapted to the size and shape of these patients.

About 90% of all pediatric cardiopulmonary arrests started out as a respiratory problem: obstruction of the airways due to foreign bodies, Chronic Obstructive Pulmonary Disease (COPD), such as asthma or bronchitis, and upper-airway infections, such as croup or epiglottitis.

When performing detailed physical exams, beginning with the trunk before the head is recommended.

Problems in Infants and Children

- ✔ Seizures in children are often febrile. In these cases, clothing should be removed to allow the child to release as much heat as possible.
- ✔ Poisonings are a common pediatric event. Identify and bring the substance to the hospital if possible and contact medical control for specific treatments such as activated charcoal.
- ✔ Hypoperfusion or shock in children is seldom a cardiac problem. Most often it is secondary to dehydration so be alert for histories of diarrhea, vomiting, or inadequate feeding. Vital signs associated with small children may be confusing. While the respirations may be rapid and weak, the pulse rate may actually be bradycardic when the infant is in trouble.
- ✔ SIDS, or sudden infant death syndrome, may occur in infants in their first year of life. There are many possible causes that are not clearly understood. You should try to resuscitate unless there are signs of rigor mortis.

Trauma

Trauma is the number one cause of death in infants and children with blunt injuries being most common. In assessing for traumatic injuries anticipate patterns different from those in adults. Infants and small children lead with their heads so head injuries are frequent. The skeleton is soft and pliable so there may be significant internal injuries without obvious external injuries.

Infants and children are more susceptible to environmental injuries too. Infants' total body surface area is proportionately larger than the adult so they lose heat more rapidly and burns subject them to more fluid loss and loss of ability to regulate body temperature.

Abuse

Injuries and stories that don't add up, and injuries that would seem to require more energy than the child could generate on his or her own, should be suspects of abuse and *must* be reported. Central nervous system (CNS) injuries are most lethal as is the case of "shaken baby syndrome."

Special Needs Children

Premature babies, or children with heart disease or neurologic or neuromuscular disease may have special needs for the EMT-B to address. It is a good policy to know as much as you can about these infants and children in your service area and what they might need from you.

Caring for sick and injured children is one of the hardest things the EMT-B will have to do. If things go badly, you should be prepared to talk about it and even access critical incident stress management teams.

Scenarios

1. You have been called to the scene for a sick child. The mother hands you a three-month-old male child who is lying limp in your hands. The breathing is shallow and rapid and the pulse is weak and slow. The infant's color is dusky. What do you think is happening and what can you do for him?

Solution

This infant is showing signs and symptoms of shock. Provide high-flow oxygen, conserve body heat, and consider bag-valve mask ventilations. Rapid transport to the hospital is important for fluid resuscitation.

2. What history would explain the patient's condition?

Solution

Fever with vomiting and/or diarrhea and poor feeding would be consistent with the patient's condition.

3. You are on the scene with an apparent SIDS victim. The child is pale, pulseless, and nonbreathing, but rigor mortis is not present. What should you do?

Solution

Begin resuscitation and transport as soon as possible. Also consider that the family is your patient too and it is likely that they are going to need understanding and attention.

▒▒ Review Questions

1. _____ have a fear of disfigurement.

    (A) Newborns and infants, birth to 1 year of age
    (B) Toddlers 1 year to 3 years
    (C) Preschool children 3 years to 6 years
    (D) School-age children 6 to 12 years

2. _____ want you to treat them as adults.

    (A) Toddlers 1 to 3 years
    (B) Preschool children 3 to 6 years
    (C) School-age children 6 to 12 years
    (D) Adolescents 12 to 18 years

3. The potential for airway obstruction is compounded in infants and children by

    (A) smaller airways easily blocked by secretions.
    (B) a proportionately larger tongue.
    (C) a large head causing hyperextension when supine.
    (D) All of the above.

4. For obstructed airways abdominal thrusts are eliminated in

    (A) infants less than 1 year old.
    (B) children over 1 year old.
    (C) All of the above.
    (D) None of the above.

5. Delivering oxygen to newborns should be accomplished by

    (A) strapping an adult mask to the infant upside down.
    (B) using a newborn oxygen mask.
    (C) using the blow-by oxygen method.
    (D) a nasal canula.

6. Upper airway obstruction is indicated by

    (A) stridor on inspiration.
    (B) crowing on inspiration.
    (C) wheezing on exhalation.
    (D) tachypnea without stridor.
    (E) A & B.
    (F) C & D.

7. Respiratory distress is indicated by

(A) nasal flaring.
(B) sternal or intercostals retraction.
(C) wheezing.
(D) All of the above.

8. Typical pediatric doses for activated charcoal are between

(A) 6 to 12.5 grams.
(B) 12.5 to 25 grams.
(C) 25 to 50 grams.
(D) 50 to 75 grams.

9. Vomiting, diarrhea, and fever can cause shock in newborns and infants.

(A) True.
(B) False.

10. Cardiac problems are also a frequent cause of shock in infants and children.

(A) True.
(B) False.

Answers to Review Questions

1. **C** Objective 1
Preschool-age children have fears of bodily injury and mutilation. Other fears include loss of control, the unknown and dark, and being left alone.

2. **D** Objective 1
Adolescents want to be treated as adults. They want to be involved in decisions about their care. Discuss with them how important their cooperation is and help them to calmly participate in their care.

3. **D** Objective 2
Pediatric airways are shorter and narrower; their heads are larger, causing the neck to flex when they are supine, compressing the airway. The tongue is also proportionately larger, causing obstruction when the airway is not positioned optimally.

4. **A** Objective 6
Because of the danger of damaging abdominal organs and no evidence of success, abdominal thrusts are eliminated in infants. Back blows or chest thrusts are recommended.

5. **C** Objective 7
Due to the sensitivity of the airways and the inadequacies of the available appliances, the safest and most efficient way to administer oxygen to infants is to form a tent with a towel or blanket and to blow the oxygen into the tent that the child then breathes from.

6. **E** Objective 6
Obstruction of the upper airways causes inspiratory noises. These noises are typically high-pitched crowing noises or stridor.

7. **D** Objective 4
Breathing is supposed to be effortless so any obvious respiratory signs indicate distress. These include the use of accessory muscles, nasal flaring, and sternal or intercostals retractions.

8. **B** Objective 14
The appropriate dose of activated charcoal for pediatric patients is 12.5 to 25 grams.

9. **A** Objective 8
Pediatric patients are at risk due to fluid losses with fever, vomiting, or diarrhea. Their fluid replacement needs to be managed closely or they will dehydrate and can easily go into shock from fluid loss.

10. **B** Objective 10
Cardiac arrest in children is generally secondary to a respiratory problem; therefore, the emphasis in pediatric resuscitation is on management of the airway and ventilation. Cardiac disease is rare in pediatric patients and is usually the result of birth defects.

CHAPTER 23

Ambulance Operations

SECTION 1—ALWAYS READY

■ Objectives

1. Discuss the medical and nonmedical equipment needed to respond to a call.

2. List the phases of an ambulance call.

3. Describe the general provisions of state laws relating to the operation of the ambulance and privileges in any or all of the following categories:
   - Speed
   - Warning lights
   - Sirens
   - Right-of-way
   - Parking
   - Turning

4. List the contributing factors to unsafe driving conditions.

5. Describe the considerations that should be given to

   - Requests for escorts.
   - Following an escort vehicle.
   - Intersections.

6. Discuss "Due Regard for Safety of All Others" while operating an emergency vehicle.

7. State what information is essential in order to respond to a call.

8. Discuss various situations that may affect response to a call.

9. Differentiate between the various methods of moving a patient to the unit based upon injury or illness.

10. Apply the components of the essential patient information in a written report.

11. Summarize the importance of preparing the unit for the next response.

12. Identify what is essential for completion of a call.

13. Distinguish among the following terms: cleaning, disinfection, high-level disinfection, and sterilization.

14. Describe how to clean or disinfect items following patient care.

The phases of an ambulance call include

- Dispatch
- En route
- Positioning the unit
- Arrival at the scene
- Transferring the patient to the ambulance
- En route to the receiving facility
- At the receiving facility
- En route to the station.
- Post-run

Ambulance operations include getting ready for the call. This entails checking out all of your equipment, both the gear on the ambulance and your personal equipment, daily inspections of your vehicle including fuel, fluids, lights, etc., and tests on all medical equipment including oxygen tank volume, and so on.

Knowing how your communications system and Dispatch work is also part of learning your ambulance operations systems.

Safe driving of emergency vehicles is a major concern. Intersections are the most frequent places where collisions of emergency vehicles occur, so training to prevent these events is important. Emergency vehicle operations include recommended driving courses and work practices that encourage alert driving. The use of seat belts and child seats for all passengers and crew is mandatory.

Positioning the unit is also important. Uphill from hazards and 100 feet from a wreckage are examples of planning for vehicle placement.

Post-run critiques and going over your vehicle and equipment again to make sure you're ready for the next call bring the ambulance operations full circle.

Ambulance operations also include understanding procedures for interface with aero medical transports.

SECTION 2—GAINING ACCESS

Objectives

1. Describe the purpose of extrication.
2. Discuss the role of the EMT-B in extrication.
3. Identify what equipment for personal safety is required for the EMT-B.
4. Define the fundamental components of extrication.
5. State the steps that should be taken to protect the patient during extrication.
6. Evaluate various methods of gaining access to the patient.
7. Distinguish between simple and complex access.

Gaining access to patients can be simple or complex. The role of the EMT-B is to get to the patient and care for him or her. If gaining access to the patient requires special tools and the training to use them, the EMT-B may have to stand by until rescue technicians gain access to the patient.

The EMT-B arriving on the scene will need to make an assessment as to the difficulty of gaining access. If it requires special technicians and equipment, the earlier that notification is made, the sooner it will be there to get the job done and get the EMT-B to the patient. It is important for scene safety to be determined first and for the EMT-B to have the personal protection equipment equal to the situation. In vehicular events this will include turnout gear, including coat, boots, helmet with eye protection, and gloves.

Remembering to "try before you pry" is always important, as in many cases, opening a door is simpler than it may initially appear. Working within the limits of your training and resources and knowing how to access the skilled personnel and equipment you need will be of utmost importance in all rescue situations.

SECTION 3—HAZARDS, CASUALTIES, AND DISASTERS

■ Objectives

1. Explain the EMT-B's role during a call involving hazardous materials.

2. Describe what the EMT-B should do if there is a reason to believe that there is a hazard at the scene.

3. Describe the actions that an EMT-B should take to ensure bystander safety.

4. State the role the EMT-B should perform until appropriately trained personnel arrive at the scene of a hazardous materials situation.

5. Break down the steps to approaching a hazardous situation.

6. Discuss the various environmental hazards that affect EMS.

7. Describe the criteria for a multiple-casualty situation.

8. Evaluate the role of the EMT-B in the multiple-casualty situation.

9. Summarize the basic components of basic triage.

10. Define the role of the EMT-B in a disaster operation.

11. Describe the basic concept of incident management.

12. Explain the methods for preventing contamination of self, equipment, and facilities.

13. Review the local mass casualty incident plan.

During hazardous materials incidents, the first responsibility of the EMT-B is safety. Once the incident is recognized, the EMT-B should keep himself or herself and all bystanders at a safe distance from the incident until responders trained to handle hazardous materials arrive. EMTs should be trained to the awareness level of HAZMAT training. Personnel trained at the Operations, Technician, or Specialist level will work to isolate the hazard and bring victims to the EMT-B for treatment.

The environment also presents hazards to the EMT-B. The EMT should always dress for maximum protection from the environment. The environment is also a hazard to the patient, and patients should be protected from extreme temperature. In any hot, cold, wet, or otherwise extreme environment, the EMT must first remove the patient.

Multiple casualty incidents are special situations requiring special planning. First, the EMT must summon adequate resources for the number of patients requiring care. Next, the patients must be separated into color-coded categories indicating their priority for treatment. This is triage. Red designates critical patients, the highest priority. Yellow designates serious patients, the second priority. Green designates nonserious patients—the lowest priority. The designation black indicates dead patients.

Disaster management calls for large scale organization and coordination. Incident Command provides for control direction and coordination of resources. The incident is divided into sectors that may include:

Extrications

Treatment

Transportation

Staging

Supply

Triage

Command

Individuals are placed in charge of each section and report directly to Command rather than to each other. This ensures that resources are allocated to where they are needed and that required information is gathered when critical decisions must be made.

Scenarios

1. You've arrived at the scene of a motor vehicle collision and the victims are trapped. Fire and police personnel are on the scene. What should you expect to do?

Solution

The first thing fire personnel should accomplish is to make the scene safe and gain access for EMS. Once that's done, you may be called on to give aid to patients while extrication is accomplished.

2. You are performing triage at a multiple casualty event. A patient presents who has no pulses and is not breathing. How would you classify this patient?

Solution

This patient would be Code Black, or considered dead. In multiple-casualty situations, the EMT-B should not spend time performing CPR on traumatic arrest victims. New trauma protocols call for recognizing traumatic arrest patients as being dead.

■ **Review Questions**

1. Most collisions involving ambulances occur

(A) on interstates.
(B) with oncoming traffic.
(C) at intersections.
(D) on two-lane roads.

2. Seat belts are to be worn by crew and patients.

(A) True.
(B) False.

3. In order to make sure we can find our patients, all dispatchers should get a call-back number.

(A) True.
(B) False.

4. When patients are in vehicles requiring extrication, the EMT-B

(A) may give care to the patient during extrication.
(B) is responsible for extrication.
(C) should wear appropriate protective clothing.
(D) All of the above.
(E) A & C.

5. Often the best way to gain access is the simplest.

(A) True.
(B) False.

6. In a mass casualty situation, you are checking out an alert patient with a painful swollen right ankle. This patient should be considered

(A) Red or urgent.
(B) Yellow or emergent but not urgent.
(C) Green or nonemergency.
(D) Black—dead.

7. Another patient presents with gross bleeding from a large abdominal wound. This patient should be considered

(A) Red or urgent.
(B) Yellow or emergent.
(C) Green or nonemergency.
(D) Black—dead.

8. Another patient has good vital signs but cannot move. You should consider this patient

(A) Red or urgent.
(B) Yellow or emergent.
(C) Green or nonemergency.
(D) Black—dead.

9. In regard to hazardous materials, the EMT-B should be trained to the

    (A) awareness level.
    (B) operations level.
    (C) technician level.
    (D) specialist level.

10. The EMT-B's role at a hazardous materials scene is to

    (A) stay out of the hazard and call for specially trained personnel.
    (B) get in and out of the hazard as quickly as possible.
    (C) try to neutralize the hazard.
    (D) None of the above.

Answers to Review Questions

1. C Section 1, Objective 4
The most frequent site of ambulance collisions is at intersections.

2. A Section 1, Objective 4
All crew and passengers in ambulances should be secured with belts and harnesses.

3. A Section 1, Objective 7
It is important for Dispatch center to make certain it has the ability to maintain or regain contact with the caller in case additional information is needed to find the person.

4. E Section 2, Objective 1
EMT-Bs may be called upon to care for a trapped patient during the extrication. This can be done only if the EMT-B is wearing the proper safety equipment or turnout gear.

5. A Section 2, Objective 4
The old rule of "Try before you pry" is helpful, as most often there is an easy access to the patients that does not require complex extrication.

6. C Section 3, Objective 9

The triage categories are:
Black = dead
Green = nonemergency
Yellow = emergent
Red = urgent

The patient here would be considered Green or nonemergency.

7. A Section 3, Objective 9
This patient has immediate life threats that can be managed so the rating here would be Red or urgent.

8. B Section 3, Objective 9
This patient is emergent, meaning there are injuries that could become life-threatening, but this patient can wait until after the patients with immediate life threats are treated.

9. **A** Section 3, Objective 1
Any individual that may respond to a hazardous scene needs to be trained to at least the awareness level. Operations, technicians, and specialists are trained for specific functions in securing a hazardous scene.

10. **A** Section 3, Objective 4
As we said, the EMT-B should be trained to the awareness level so that he or she can recognize a hazardous scene and stay out of it. They should call for hazardous materials specialists to control the scene and keep bystanders and other responders clear until the HAZMAT team arrives.

CHAPTER 24

Advanced Airway (Elective)

■ Objectives

1. Identify and describe the airway anatomy in the infant, child, and adult.

2. Differentiate the airway anatomy in the infant, child, and adult.

3. Explain the pathophysiology of airway compromise.

4. Describe the proper use of airway adjuncts.

5. Review the use of oxygen therapy in airway management.

6. Describe the indications, contraindications, and techniques for insertion of nasal gastric tubes.

7. Describe how to perform the Sellick maneuver (cricoid pressure).

8. Describe the indications for advanced airway management.

9. List the equipment required for orotracheal intubation.

10. Describe the proper use of the curved blade for orotracheal intubation.

11. Describe the proper use of the straight blade for orotracheal intubation.

12. State the reasons for the proper use of the stylet in orotracheal intubation.

13. Describe the methods of choosing the appropriate size endotracheal tube in an adult patient.

14. State the formula for sizing an infant or child endotracheal tube.

15. List the complications associated with advanced airway management.

16. Define the various alternative methods for sizing infant and child endotracheal intubation.

17. Describe the skill of orotracheal intubation in the adult patient.

18. Describe the skill of orotracheal intubation in the infant and child.

19. Describe the skill of confirming endotracheal tube placement in the adult, infant, and child.

20. State the consequence of and need to recognize unintentional esophageal intubation.

21. Describe the skill of securing the endotracheal tube in the adult, infant, and child.

The advanced airway elective portion of the EMT-B curriculum is not a part of most EMT-B programs. Advanced airway skills are usually performed by EMT-I or EMT-P prehospital personnel. If this was included in your training and you will be tested according to that training, you should review the respiratory anatomy as we covered it in the human body and respiratory chapters (Chapters 4 and 12). The advanced airway techniques covered should have included:

Endotracheal Intubation

This is a tube that is inserted through the mouth and past the vocal cords using a laryngoscope. A balloon is inflated to secure the tube and prevent stomach contents from fouling the airway. The patient is then ventilated using a BVM (bag-valve mask) connected to the ET tube.

Multilumen Airway Devices

These devices have a lumen or tube within a tube. They can be inserted blindly into the pharynx. Once in place, two balloons are inflated that isolate the trachea from the esophagus. There are two separate tubes that will extend from the patient's mouth. Once the balloons are inflated, one or the other will inflate the lungs when the BVM is connected.

CHAPTER 25

Final Exams

EXAM 1

1. Emergency Medical Technician-Intermediates (EMT-Is) are trained to
   (A) provide BLS to the sick and injured and transportation to appropriate medical facilities.
   (B) provide a limited amount of ALS (Advanced Life Support) to the sick and injured and transportation to appropriate medical facilities.
   (C) provide ALS to the sick and injured and transportation to appropriate medical facilities.
   (D) be first on scene to provide emergency care to the sick and injured prior to the arrival of transporting agencies.

2. EMT-Bs are trained using a National Standard Curriculum that is published by
   (A) the U.S. Department of Transportation (DOT).
   (B) the U.S. Department of Defense (DOD).
   (C) the U.S. Department Health and Human Services (HHS).
   (D) the National Highway and Traffic Safety Administration (NHTSA).

3. "A system of internal review and audits of all aspects of the EMS systems as to identify those aspects needing improvement to assure that the public receives the highest quality of prehospital care" is the
   (A) EMT oath.
   (B) definition of quality improvement.
   (C) scope of practice.
   (D) None of the above.

4. Practicing effective BSI may include wearing
   (A) gloves.
   (B) eye protection.
   (C) a face mask.
   (D) All of the above.

5. The training of EMT-Bs and their "scope of practice" are defined and regulated by
   (A) federal laws and regulations.
   (B) state laws and regulations.
   (C) a national curriculum.
   (D) a local ordinance.

6. A father standing over his dying child shouts, "No, take me!" This is an example of which stage of acceptance?
   (A) Denial
   (B) Anger
   (C) Bargaining
   (D) Depression
   (E) Acceptance

7. Your patient is acting out and exhibiting signs of the "Anger" stage of dealing with death. Your best chance at helping this patient would be through
   (A) listening to your patient.
   (B) showing empathy for your patient.
   (C) turning your patient over to the police.
   (D) Both A & B.

8. Examples of stresses the EMT-B may face include
   (A) mass casualties.
   (B) amputations.
   (C) infant, child, or spousal abuse.
   (D) All of the above.

9. Friends and family are an important part of life. You should
   (A) not discus your work with them as they may not understand.
   (B) find a way to share your work with them without frightening or making them uncomfortable.
   (C) share the most intimate details of your work with them to relieve your own stress.
   (D) share interesting stories with them about friends and famous people you have treated.

10. If faced with confined space, fire, or hazardous materials situations, the EMT-B should
    (A) approach the scene with extreme caution.
    (B) stay out of the scene until it is secured by specially trained personnel.
    (C) do what he or she can as quickly as possible.
    (D) ask for help from bystanders.

11. While working at hazardous scenes, protective clothing might include
    (A) a helmet.
    (B) gloves.
    (C) eye protection.
    (D) All of the above.

12. You are responding to a shooting. While en route, it is most important to determine
    (A) how many victims there are.
    (B) if the scene is secure.
    (C) what type of gun was used.
    (D) if the perpetrator is still on scene.

13. Just before you reach the scene you are informed that police have yet to arrive. You should
    (A) circle the block until they arrive.
    (B) continue on to the scene but stay in the ambulance with the lights and siren on.
    (C) stage a couple of blocks away with the siren and lights off.
    (D) continue on to the scene and do your best without the police.

14. While at a crime scene
    (A) do not concern yourself with evidence; the patient is your only concern.
    (B) the patient is your priority so treat the patient, but do not disturb the scene more than necessary.
    (C) collect evidence and then care for your patient.
    (D) withhold patient care until evidence is retrieved.

15. Maintaining continuing education and skills, looking after the physical and emotional well-being of your patients, and documenting honestly and completely, are examples of
    (A) the state's responsibilities.
    (B) the medical director's responsibilities.
    (C) the EMT-B's ethical responsibilities.
    (D) the employer's responsibilities.

16. You've come upon an unconscious shooting victim. You may treat by the rules of what type of consent?
    (A) Implied
    (B) Expressed
    (C) Informed
    (D) Mutual

17. In order for you to be found guilty of negligence,
    (A) there must be a duty to act.
    (B) there must have been an omission of care or inappropriate care.
    (C) your actions must have caused additional harm or injury.
    (D) All of the above.

18. Of the following, which is the EMT-B likely to be required to report?
    (A) There is an injury that appears to be the result of a crime.
    (B) You recognize the patient as a drug user.
    (C) There is possible abuse.
    (D) A & B.

19. While treating a patient you are informed that he is an organ donor. You should
    (A) treat the patient more aggressively.
    (B) treat the patient the same as any other patient.
    (C) notify medical control that your patient is a donor.
    (D) B & C.

20. Your fingers are at which aspect of your arms?
    (A) Proximal
    (B) Medial
    (C) Lateral
    (D) Distal

21. Your jawbone is the
    (A) zygoma.
    (B) mandible.
    (C) maxilla.
    (D) orbit.

22. The vertebrae in the neck are the
    (A) cervical vertebrae.
    (B) thoracic vertebrae.
    (C) lumbar vertebrae.
    (D) Coccyx.

23. The largest bones in your lower extremities are the
    (A) femurs.
    (B) patellas.
    (C) tibias.
    (D) fibulas.

24. Your mouth is part of the respiratory system and is called the
    (A) oropharynx.
    (B) nasopharynx.
    (C) retropharynx.
    (D) larynx.

25. The leaf-shaped valve that covers either the esophagus or the trachea is the
    (A) retropharynx.
    (B) oropharynx.
    (C) larynx.
    (D) epiglottis.

26. The chamber of the heart that receives oxygen-poor blood from the body is the
    (A) left ventricle.
    (B) right ventricle.
    (C) left atrium.
    (D) right atrium.

27. Blood cells that help to fight infection are
    (A) red cells.
    (B) white cells.
    (C) platelets.
    (D) tissue cells.

28. The outermost layer of the skin is the
    (A) epidermis.
    (B) dermis.
    (C) subcutaneous.
    (D) fascia.

29. The upper number of your blood
pressure is the
(A) volume pressure.
(B) diastolic pressure.
(C) systolic pressure.
(D) mean pressure.

30. You are confronted with a patient
who is covered with a dry chemical
that reacts with water. You should
(A) flush off with water.
(B) brush off as much of the chemical as possible and then flush off
with water.
(C) leave the chemical on the body
and transport as quickly as
possible.
(D) apply mineral oil to the patient
to neutralize the chemical.

31. In penetrating chest injuries, the
EMT-B should
(A) apply an occlusive dressing.
(B) apply a wet dressing.
(C) leave the wound open to air.
(D) cover the wound with
Vaseline.

32. In treating an abdominal evisceration
the EMT-B should
(A) push the organs back into the
wound.
(B) close the wounds with tape.
(C) place the patient on his or her
back with the hips and knees
flexed.
(D) cover the evisceration with a
sterile dressing moistened with
saline.
(E) A & B.
(F) C & D.

33. Which of the following are closed
soft tissue injuries?
(A) Contusions
(B) Lacerations
(C) Abrasions
(D) Avulsions

34. The long tube that connects the
pharynx to the lungs is the
(A) retropharynx.
(B) trachea.
(C) esophagus.
(D) epiglottis.

35. The normal respiratory rate for an
adult is
(A) 10–15 per/min.
(B) 12–20 per/min.
(C) 15–25 per/min.
(D) 20–30 per/min.

36. Double-walled tubular muscles that
contract to carry oxygen rich blood
through the body are the
(A) veins.
(B) trachea.
(C) arteries.
(D) esophagus.

37. The arteries that can be found on
either side of the neck are the
(A) carotid.
(B) coronary.
(C) brachial.
(D) femoral.

38. The blood cells that help to form
clots are
(A) red cells.
(B) white cells.
(C) platelets.
(D) root cells.

39. The initial survey (after immobilizing
the spine, if called for) begins with
(A) assessing mental status.
(B) assessing the airway.
(C) assessing circulation.
(D) assessing disability.

40. If the patient you are assessing came
to the door and invited you in, his
AVPU's core would be
(A) A for alert.
(B) V for verbal.
(C) P for painful.
(D) U for unresponsive.

41. You are called to the scene of a patient who was struck in the head with a bat. The patient is not moving or speaking but when you touch the injured area he moves and cries out. The AVPU score for this patient would be
   (A) A for alert.
   (B) V for verbal.
   (C) P for painful.
   (D) U for unresponsive.

42. If the patient you are assessing is talking, you may
   (A) continue to assess the airway.
   (B) assume the airway is open and assess the breathing.
   (C) assume the airway is open and assess circulation.
   (D) assume the airway is open and assess disability.

43. If you are working with a responsive patient with a respiratory rate greater than 8 but less than 24, you should
   (A) provide positive pressure ventilation.
   (B) do nothing since the patient is breathing.
   (C) provide high-flow oxygen.
   (D) provide low-flow oxygen.

44. If the patient's respiratory rate is less than 8 or more than 24, the EMT-B should
   (A) provide positive pressure ventilation.
   (B) do nothing since the patient is breathing.
   (C) provide high-flow oxygen.
   (D) provide low-flow oxygen.

45. In an unresponsive patient, the pulse that should be assessed is the
   (A) femoral.
   (B) brachial.
   (C) radial.
   (D) carotid.

46. Normally, the skin should be
   (A) warm, pale, and moist.
   (B) cool, pale, and moist.
   (C) warm, normally pigmented, and dry.
   (D) warm, normally pigmented, and moist.

47. Capillary refill
   (A) may not be useful in adult assessment.
   (B) must be done on all adult patients.
   (C) is useful in pediatric assessment.
   (D) should be done on all patients.
   (E) A & C.

48. Of the following, which should an EMT-B consider a priority patient? A patient with
   (A) chest pain.
   (B) elbow pain.
   (C) a headache.
   (D) a stomachache.

49. Significant mechanism(s) of injury include(s)
   (A) ejection from a vehicle.
   (B) falls of greater than 20 feet.
   (C) penetrating head, neck, or chest trauma.
   (D) All of the above.

50. The P in DCAPBTLS stands for
   (A) Perfusion.
   (B) Pulse.
   (C) Punctures.
   (D) Penetrations.
   (E) C & D.

51. Breath sounds should be checked at the apices, mid-clavicular line bilaterall, and at the bases midaxillary line bilaterally to determine if breaths are
   (A) present.
   (B) absent.
   (C) equal.
   (D) All of the above.

52. In order to assess the pelvis of a trauma patient, the EMT-B should
    (A) inspect for DCAPBTLS.
    (B) gently compress the pelvis to determine tenderness or motion.
    (C) Neither of the above.
    (D) Both A & B.

53. Your rapid trauma assessment has determined that your patient has been shot once in his left anterior chest with an exit wound. Your patient appears sleepy but is answering your questions. This patient should be considered
    (A) critical with an open airway, and transport should be considered before further assessment or treatment is begun.
    (B) critical with an open airway, and a more detailed assessment should be completed before transport.
    (C) noncritical with an open airway, and transport should be immediate.
    (D) noncritical, and further assessment should be done prior to transport.

54. You are called to assist a patient who has cut his finger while opening a box. Bleeding is easily controlled with direct pressure. This patient should be considered
    (A) critical; transport immediately.
    (B) critical; perform an assessment focused on the injury and the mechanism of that injury.
    (C) noncritical; perform an assessment focused on the injury and the mechanism of that injury.
    (D) noncritical; transport immediately.

55. When examining your patient's abdomen you should palpate to determine if it is
    (A) soft.
    (B) firm.
    (C) distended.
    (D) tender.
    (E) All of the above.

56. When assessing extremities, you should evaluate sensory and motor function. This includes
    (A) the ability to feel.
    (B) the ability to move.
    (C) Both A & B.
    (D) None of the above.

57. Following your focused history and physical you should
    (A) transport and monitor for changes.
    (B) obtain baseline vital signs.
    (C) perform a detailed assessment.
    (D) perform an ongoing assessment.

58. The S in SAMPLE history and physical represents
    (A) Signs.
    (B) Symptoms.
    (C) Systems.
    (D) All of the above.
    (E) A & B.

59. When reaching, the EMT-B should
    (A) avoid reaching overhead.
    (B) twist at the waist.
    (C) bend at the waist.
    (D) avoid using his or her legs.

60. Communication between the responding unit and dispatch should include
    (A) response.
    (B) arrival on scene.
    (C) transport to the hospital.
    (D) being back in service.
    (E) B & C.
    (F) All of the above.

61. The portion of the EMS run form that calls for arrival, transport, and back in service times is the
(A) patient data.
(B) check boxes.
(C) run data.
(D) narrative.

62. Of the following, which medication will not be carried on a BLS unit?
(A) Oxygen
(B) Oral glucose
(C) Nitroglycerine
(D) Activated charcoal

63. The medication an EMT-B may administer in the case of overdose or oral poisoning is
(A) activated charcoal.
(B) nitroglycerin.
(C) epinephrine.
(D) ipecac.

64. The questions an EMT-B should ask of a diabetic patient include
(A) Do you take medication and when was the last dose?
(B) When did you last eat?
(C) Are you unusually thirsty?
(D) Have you been urinating frequently?
(E) All of the above.

65. Your first priority with a patient complaining of an allergic reaction is
(A) checking the pulse rate.
(B) checking the blood pressure.
(C) checking the airway.
(D) observing the skin color.

66. Heat loss via sweating is called
(A) radiation.
(B) conduction.
(C) convection.
(D) evaporation.

67. When a person's behavior is unacceptable or dangerous to the patient, family, or community,
(A) it is a concern only for the police.
(B) it is termed a behavioral emergency.
(C) it is a private matter.
(D) None of the above.

68. Crowning indicates
(A) imminent birth.
(B) a third-trimester pregnancy.
(C) multiple births.
(D) early labor.

69. You've been called to assist a man with a laceration. You note that the bleeding from his right forearm is bright red and spurting. His bleeding appears to be
(A) venous.
(B) arterial.
(C) capillary.
(D) tracheal.

70. Injuries to the _____ vertebrae may damage the spinal cord and affect respirations.
(A) cervical
(B) thoracic
(C) lumbar
(D) sacral

71. The most common cause of seizures in children is
(A) head injury.
(B) diabetes.
(C) fever.
(D) an allergic reaction.

72. Increased respiratory effort, wheezing, and shallow respirations are
(A) normal in infants and children.
(B) signs of respiratory distress.
(C) common for sleeping adults.
(D) None of the above.

73. In a conscious adult, the initial pulse should be obtained at the
    (A) carotid artery.
    (B) brachial artery.
    (C) radial artery.
    (D) femoral artery.

74. In an unconscious adult patient, the EMT-B should seek to obtain a pulse at the
    (A) carotid artery.
    (B) brachial artery.
    (C) radial artery.
    (D) femoral artery.

75. In newborns, the pulse should be obtained at the
    (A) carotid artery.
    (B) brachial artery.
    (C) radial artery.
    (D) femoral artery.

76. When carrying a conscious patient experiencing difficulty breathing down stairs, the EMT-B should
    (A) use a chair or stair chair.
    (B) carry the patient supine on your cot.
    (C) use a spine board to keep the patient flat.
    (D) carry the patient on his or her side on your cot.

77. You have assessed the driver of a vehicle that has struck a tree to be unresponsive, with shallow and rapid breathing, a rapid weak pulse, and pale, moist, and cool skin. You should remove this patient using
    (A) a nonurgent move.
    (B) an urgent move.
    (C) an emergency move.
    (D) a standard move.

78. Getting information over the radio from the hospital on how to treat your patient is considered
    (A) offline medical control.
    (B) online medical control.
    (C) inline medical control.
    (D) operational medical control.

79. Which of the following are examples of proper documentation?
    (A) "Drunken patient requires transport to hospital."
    (B) "Patient states he's had several beers."
    (C) "Unable to obtain blood pressure."
    (D) "Unable to obtain blood pressure due to burns on arms."
    (E) All of the above.
    (F) B & C.

80. Nitroglycerin is
    (A) carried on BLS ambulances.
    (B) a medication the EMT-B may assist in administering.
    (C) a small pill.
    (D) a sublingual spray.
    (E) All of the above.
    (F) B, C, & D only.

81. The first thing the EMT-B needs to do for patients exposed to extremes of heat or cold is to
    (A) remove the patient from the environment.
    (B) remove the patient's clothes.
    (C) apply external heat or cooling.
    (D) give plenty of fluids.

82. The EMT-B's first concern at the scene of a behavioral emergency is
    (A) calming the patient.
    (B) establishing that the scene is safe before entering.
    (C) evacuating bystanders.
    (D) transporting as soon as possible.

83. A hyperglycemic patient may
    (A) appear intoxicated.
    (B) have a rapid heart rate.
    (C) have seizures.
    (D) All of the above.
    (E) A & B only.

84. During childbirth the EMT-B may insert a gloved hand into the vagina in the case of
(A) a prolapsed cord.
(B) a leg presentation.
(C) a normal delivery.
(D) a breech birth with the head undelivered.
(E) A & B.
(F) A & D.

85. The EMT-B should first try to control external bleeding with
(A) a pressure dressing.
(B) a tourniquet.
(C) direct pressure.
(D) pressure points.

86. The total number of vertebrae in the human skeleton is
(A) 23.
(B) 25.
(C) 33.
(D) 35.

87. The number of thoracic vertebrae is
(A) 7.
(B) 12.
(C) 5.
(D) 4.

88. Patients should be immobilized for possible spinal injuries when
(A) the patient complains of neck or back pain.
(B) the mechanism of injury suggests spine injuries.
(C) the EMT-B palpates a deformity along the spine.
(D) the patient is found unconscious with no witnesses.
(E) Any of the above.

89. Rapid extrication should be used when
(A) a patient in a vehicle is unresponsive with signs of shock.
(B) there is a danger to the patient.
(C) there is a danger to the rescuers.
(D) All of the above.
(E) None of the above.

90. Babies are considered newborns from
(A) birth to 3 months.
(B) birth to 6 months.
(C) birth to 9 months.
(D) birth to 1 year.

91. The number one cause of death in children is
(A) trauma.
(B) poisoning.
(C) heart problems.
(D) respiratory problems.

92. You are triaging patients at a mass casualty event and you are presented with an ambulatory patient with a painful swollen right forearm. You would tag him as
(A) Red or Urgent.
(B) Yellow or Emergent.
(C) Green or Nonemergent.
(D) Black or Dead.

93. Your next patient at this mass casualty event presents with respiratory distress. You would tag this patient
(A) Red or Urgent.
(B) Yellow or Emergent.
(C) Green or Nonemergent.
(D) Black or Dead.

94. Information on hazardous materials can be obtained from
(A) DOT Emergency Response Guidebook.
(B) National Fire Protection Administration (NFPA) 704 Manual.
(C) The Chemical Transportation Emergency Center (CHEMTREC).
(D) All of the above.

95. Which of the following are true in regard to proper radio communications?
    (A) Hold the microphone two to three inches from your mouth.
    (B) Hold the microphone against your mouth and speak softly.
    (C) Giving the patient's name over the air is acceptable and helpful to the responder.
    (D) Giving the patient's name over the air is unacceptable and a violation of the patient's rights.
    (E) B & C.
    (F) A & D.

96. When correcting an error on an EMS form, the EMT-B should
    (A) draw a line through the mistake and write in the word "error."
    (B) use white out, making sure to do so on all copies.
    (C) tear up the report and start over.
    (D) Any of the above.

97. Cyanosis is
    (A) reddened skin color.
    (B) normal skin color.
    (C) bluish skin color.
    (D) greenish skin color.

98. A stokes or basket stretcher is designed for use in (with)
    (A) normal patient transfer situations.
    (B) spine-injured patients.
    (C) confined spaces and rugged terrain.
    (D) stairways.

99. When suctioning, the EMT-B should
    (A) measure from the corner of the mouth to the ear to determine maximum length of insertion for the suction device.
    (B) limit suction to 15 seconds at a time.
    (C) keep the suction device moving while suction is applied to prevent adhering to the sides of the mouth.
    (D) All of the above.

100. Ultimately, the responsibility of maintaining the EMT-B's knowledge and skill levels lies with
    (A) the EMT-B.
    (B) the EMT-B's employer.
    (C) the state regulating agency.
    (D) the EMT-B's training coordinator.

Answers to Exam 1

1. **B** Chapter 1, Objective 2
EMT-Bs provide basic life support, EMT-Is provide a limited amount of advanced life support skills, and EMT-Ps provide advanced life support.

2. **A** Chapter 1, Objective 2
The curriculum for all prehospital care providers is developed under the direction of the U.S. Department of Transportation. That's the reason for the curriculum being described as the DOT curriculum.

3. **B** Chapter 1, Objective 1
Quality improvement is "a system of internal review and audits of all aspects needing improvement to assure that the public receives the highest quality of prehospital care."

4. **D** Chapter 1, Objective 3
Body Substance Isolation is ensured by wearing gloves with every patient contact and eye protection when there is danger of a splatter of body fluids. In extreme situations even a gown may be necessary.

5. **B** Chapter 1, Objective 1
While there is a national standard curriculum, the actual training and practice of prehospital care providers is determined by state laws and regulations.

6. **C** Chapter 2, Objective 1
The stages of acceptance in facing death are: Denial, Anger, Bargaining, Depression, and Acceptance. This person, by stating "No, take me," is bargaining with death.

7. **D** Chapter 2, Objective 1
In working with any patient in a stressful situation, listening to the patient and showing empathy toward them will help the patient to work with you honestly and better accept what is happening.

8. **D** Chapter 2, Objective 5
EMT-Bs must be prepared to face a variety of stresses. Mass casualties, amputations, and abuse situations are among the situations the EMT-B curriculum lists as stresses you must be prepared to face.

9. **B** Chapter 2, Objective 4
One of the most profound stresses EMT-Bs find themselves in is that they distance themselves from their family because of the nature of their work. EMTs may feel that their family doesn't understand them and the family may feel that the EMT-B is closed off to them and not sharing. The EMT-B must find ways of sharing things that are important to him or her and including family in this large aspect of his or her life.

10. **B** Chapter 2, Objective 7
The EMT-B should be trained at least to the HAZMAT Awareness level so as to recognize a hazard and stay out of it. The HAZMAT specialists should decontaminate and bring patients to the EMT-B for treatment.

11. **D** Chapter 2, Objective 7
Protective clothing for use around hazards will include helmets, gloves, eye protection, and possible turnout gear that is designed specifically for the hazard to be approached.

12. **B** Chapter 2, Objective 7
The most important assessment to make at scenes of violence is scene safety. In these situations if the police are not able to secure the scene, the EMT-Bs should "stage" at a safe distance until the police wave them in.

13. **C** Chapter 2, Objective 7
Until a dangerous scene is secured by the police, EMTs should stage at a safe distance.

14. **B** Chapter 3, Objective 11
Crime scene preservation is important but should not be done at the cost of patient care. The crime scene should not be unnecessarily disturbed but whatever needs to be moved to care for the patient's needs must take priority.

15. **C** Chapter 2, Objective 1
Maintaining continuing education and skills, looking after the physical and emotional well-being of the patients, and documenting honestly and completely are ethical responsibilities of the EMT-B.

16. **A** Chapter 3, Objective 4
Unconscious or incompetent patients and minors with life-threatening injuries can be treated under the rules of implied consent.

17. **D** Chapter 3, Objective 7
In order for negligence to be shown, there must be a duty to act, evidence of inappropriate care, and injury caused by the inappropriate care.

18. **D** Chapter 3, Objective 10
The EMT-B will be required to report injuries resulting from crimes, communicable diseases, and abuse to the proper authorities. There may be some particular reporting rules in your state; as an EMT-B, you are responsible to know what they are.

19. **D** Chapter 3, Objective 10
It is important to treat organ transplant candidates the same as any other patient. The patient's wishes must be communicated to medical control so that care can be followed up at the hospital.

20. **D** Chapter 3, Objective 10
Proximal means close and distal means distant so that the fingers are the distal end of the arm and the shoulder is the proximal end. Medial means inside and lateral means outside.

21. **B** Chapter 4, Objective 1
The mandible is the lower jaw or jawbone; the upper jaw is the maxilla.

22. **A** Chapter 4, Objective 1
There are 33 vertebrae total—7 cervical, 12 thoracic, 5 lumbar, 5 sacral, and 4 coccyx.

23. **A** Chapter 4, Objective 1
The femurs are the largest long bones in the body and are in the thighs. The patella is the kneecap, the tibia the anterior bone in the lower leg, and the fibula the posterior.

24. **A** Chapter 4, Objective 1, and Chapter 7, Objective 1
The pharynx is made up of the mouth or oropharynx, the nasopharynx behind the nasal region, and the retropharynx or the rear of the pharynx.

25. **D** Chapter 4, Objective 1, and Chapter 7, Objective 1
The epiglottis is a leaf-shape muscle or valve that covers the esophagus or trachea.

26. **D** Chapter 4, Objective 1, and Chapter 13, Objective 1
Blood returns to the heart through the vena cava and enters the right atrium. From there it goes to the right ventricle where it is pumped to the lungs through the pulmonary artery. The blood returns to the heart through the pulmonary veins and enters the left atrium. The blood then flows to the left ventricle where it is pumped out to the body through the aorta.

27. **B** Chapter 4, Objective 1, and Chapter 13, Objective 1
The components of the blood include the white blood cells that help to fight infections and foreign bodies in the blood, the red blood cells that carry oxygen and carbon dioxide, the platelets that assist in forming clots, and the plasma, which contains electrolytes and is the transport medium.

28. **A** Chapter 4, Objective 1, and Chapter 20, Objective 1
The epidermis is the outermost layer of the skin; the second layer is the dermis where the sweat glands and hair follicles can be found; the lowest layer is the subcutaneous or fat cell tissues.

29. **C** Chapter 5, Objective 19
The blood pressure consists of two numbers: The upper number is the systolic, which represents the pressure in the blood vessels during the contraction of the heart, and the lower number is the diastolic, which represents the pressure between contractions of the heart.

30. **B** Chapter 20, Section 1, Objective 20
Dry chemicals should first be brushed off the body as much as possible, then flushed off with water. It is important to have an unlimited supply of water particularly if the dry chemical reacts with water.

31. **A** Chapter 20, Section 1, Objective 8
Penetrating chest injuries should be covered with an occlusive dressing. If there is evidence that the wound is a sucking chest wound, the dressing should be open on one side or corner to allow air out but to limit the ability of air to enter the chest.

32. **F** Chapter 20, Section 1, Objective 10
Abdominal eviscerations should be covered. It is important that the organs not be pushed back into the opening. The inside of the dressing should be moistened so that the dressings do not adhere to the organs.

33. **A** Chapter 20, Section 1, Objective 4
A contusion is a closed soft tissue injury where damaged blood vessels leak small amounts of blood, causing swelling and discoloration. A hematoma is another closed soft tissue injury in which a large amount of blood leaking into a space causes a lump. Lacerations, abrasions, avulsions, and punctures are all open soft tissue injuries.

34. **B** Chapter 4, Objective 1, and Chapter 12, Objective 5
The trachea is the windpipe or the tube that connects the pharynx to the lungs. The esophagus is part of the digestive tract and leads from the mouth to the stomach. The retropharynx is the rear part of the pharynx, and the epiglottis is the leaf-shaped muscle or valve that protects the trachea and esophagus.

35. **B** Chapter 4, Objective 1, and Chapter 12, Objective 5
The normal respiratory rate for an adult is 12–20 breaths per minute. If the rate is much more or less than this range, the volume of air exchanged is not sufficient to maintain proper oxygen and carbon dioxide balances.

36. **C** Chapter 4, Objective 1, and Chapter 13, Objective 1
The arteries are double-walled tubular muscles that contract along with the heart to move the oxygen and nutrient-rich blood throughout the body.

37. **A** Chapter 4, Objective 1, and Chapter 13, Objective 1
The arteries on either side of the neck that provide oxygen and nutrient-rich blood to the brain are the carotid arteries.

38. **C** Chapter 4, Objective 1, and Chapter 13, Objective 1
The platelets are the blood components that help to form clots.

39. **A** Chapter 8, Section 2, Objective 2
After determining whether or not the person is a candidate for a spinal injury, the next step is to assess the mental status or responsiveness of the patient.

40. **A** Chapter 8, Objective 2
The AVPU acronym will help you to re-member what to assess during your initial evaluation of mental status. A = alert, V = responds to verbal stimulus, P = responds to painful stimulus, and U = unresponsive. This patient is spontaneously responsive so he would score an A for alert.

41. **C** Chapter 8, Section 2, Objective 2
This patient responds only when prodded so this would be a P or painful response on the AVPU scale.

42. **B** Chapter 8, Objective 6
It can be assumed that a conscious patient is breathing, which is the reason we check mental status first because if the patient can speak we know the airway is open and that he or she is breathing and has a pulse.

43. **C** Chapter 12, Objective 3
Patients in respiratory distress or pain should have high-flow oxygen, 90% to 100%, with a nonrebreather mask administered.

44. **A** Chapter 12, Objective 3
When the rate or rhythm is disrupted and the volumes are not sufficient to make adequate exchanges of carbon dioxide and oxygen, positive pressure ventilation should be provided.

45. **D** Chapter 8, Section 2, Objective 12
In an unresponsive patient it is important to be able to assess the pulse quickly. The carotid is the easiest large artery to palpate quickly.

46. **C** Chapter 8, Section 2, Objective 15
Normally skin is warm, pink, and dry. Cool, clammy, and pale skin indicates hypoxia or shock.

47. **E** Chapter 8, Section 2, Objective 18
Capillary refill is not a reliable assessment in adults but should still be used in pediatric assessments.

48. **A** Chapter 8, Section 2, Objective 19
Chest pain would be the priority patient here. Headaches and stomachaches could be significant but the threat is greater from the chest pain. The elbow pain should be evaluated but is the least of these complaints.

49. **D** Chapter 8, Section 3, Objective 1
Ejection from a vehicle, falls from greater than 20 feet, and penetrating neck and chest trauma are all significant life-threatening mechanisms.

50. **E** Chapter 8, Section 3, Objective 4
DCAPBTLS stand for **D**eformity, **C**ontu-sions, **A**brasions, **and P**enetrating injuries, **B**urns, **T**enderness, and **L**acerations.

51. **D** Chapter 8, Section 3, Objective 4
Breath sounds should be checked to see if they are present, absent, equal, and of ade-quate volume.

52. **D** Chapter 8, Section 3, Objective 4
According to the national curriculum, the pelvis should be assessed using DCAPBTLS, and the pelvis should be gently compressed to detect tenderness or motion.

53. **A** Chapter 8, Section 3, Objective 5
Penetrating trauma of this nature any-where in the trunk is critical and for these patients, definitive care is surgery. Care should be centered on rapid transport. Oxygen and other measures can be administered en route.

54. **C** Chapter 8, Section 2, Objective 19
Superficial musculoskeletal injuries are minor in nature but the patient should be evaluated considering the mechanism and any other possible injuries.

55. **E** Chapter 8, Section 5, Objective 1
The assessments to be made when doing a physical exam include palpation to see if the abdomen is soft, firm, distended, or tender. Normally, the abdomen should be soft and nontender.

56. **C** Chapter 8, Section 5, Objective 1
Extremities should be checked for pulses,
sensation, and the ability to move.

57. **B** Chapter 8, Section 4, Objective 1
Once the focused history and physical
is done, baseline vital signs should be
performed before the detailed physical
exam is performed.

58. **E** Chapter 8, Section 4, Objective 2
SAMPLE is an acronym used to help us to
remember key points of history and physical exams. S = signs and symptoms, A =
allergies, M = medications, P = pertinent
medical history, L = last oral intake, and
E = events leading up to this moment.

59. **A** Chapter 6, Objective 8
Proper body mechanics used to prevent
injury would have us avoid reaching for
things over our heads.

60. **F** Chapter 9, Objective 2
In your communications with dispatchers,
it is important to notify them that you are
en route to the scene, have arrived on the
scene, are en route to the hospital, have
arrived at the hospital, and are back in
service.

61. **C** Chapter 10, Objective 1
The run data calls for the run times. The
narrative is where you tell the story of
the EMS run. Patient data is information
about the patient including age, address,
physician, and medications.

62. **C** Chapter 11, Objective 1
Nitroglycerin is a frequently prescribed
medication that the EMT-B may assist the
patient in taking.

63. **A** Chapter 11, Objective 2, and Chapter
15, Section 2, Objective 4
Overdose patients may be given activated
charcoal to prevent absorption of the
medication or toxin.

64. **E** Chapter 14, Objective 2
When interviewing a patient with a history
of diabetes it is important to find out what
medication they have been prescribed and
when the last dose was taken. The time of
the last meal is also important. Whether
the patient has been unusually thirsty or
urinating frequently are indications of
hyperglycemia.

65. **C** Chapter 15, Section 1, Objective 3
The most frequent, life-threatening allergic
response is constriction of the airways.
There is often a rapid onset so it is important to keep an eye on the airway.

66. **D** Chapter 16, Objective 1
Heat is lost through radiation, conduction,
and convection, but evaporation is the
process through which heat is lost through
the evaporation of sweat.

67. **B** Chapter 17, Objective 1
Behavior that is unacceptable to the community is a behavioral emergency. It is also
behavior that interferes with any activity
of daily living (ADL).

68. **A** Chapter 18, Objective 4
Crowning occurs when the baby's head
appears at the vaginal opening; this
indicates imminent birth.

69. **B** Chapter 19, Objective 2
Bright red spurting blood signifies injury to
an artery. Venous blood is dark red and
flows, and capillary blood is mixed in color
and it oozes.

70. **A** Chapter 21, Objective 3
Injuries to the cervical vertebrae can disrupt the nerves that supply the muscles
of respiration, causing respirations to
cease.

71. **C** Chapter 22, Objective 11
Fever is the most common cause of
seizures in children.

72. **B** Chapter 5, Objective 3
Breathing is supposed to be effortless. Any signs of increased effort signify distress. Signs of increased effort would include the use of accessory muscles, wheezing, and shallow breathing.

73. **C** Chapter 5, Objective 5
In conscious patients the pulse should be checked at the radial artery.

74. **A** Chapter 5, Objective 5
In unconscious patients, the EMT-B should go for the large, easily accessible pulse, the carotid artery, found on either side of the neck.

75. **B** Chapter 5, Objective 5
The carotids are obscured by the newborn's short, fat neck, and the radial arteries are also obscured. Because of this, the preferred pulse is the brachial, which is palpated on the inside of the upper arm.

76. **A** Chapter 6, Objective 6
Patients having trouble breathing are more comfortable in sitting or standing positions. In extreme cases they may even stop breathing if forced to be supine.

77. **B** Chapter 6, Objective 11
Urgent moves are used when the patient's condition calls for rapid transportation to the hospital. Emergency moves are used when there is imminent danger to the patient. Nonurgent moves are used to protect the patient from further injury when there is no urgency to moving the patient.

78. **B** Chapter 9, Objective 8
Online medical control is provided by speaking directly via phone or radio to the medical director or his or her agent.

79. **F** Chapter 10, Objective 5
Proper documentation should be clear and concise; it should not include generalizations or guesses or diagnoses. It should reflect what the EMT-B saw, felt, and heard, and any history obtained during the contact with the patient.

80. **F** Chapter 11, Objective 3
Nitroglycerin is a medication prescribed to patients with chest pain and a history of angina. The EMT-B may assist the patient in taking this medication; it is supplied as a small pill or a spray to be administered under the tongue.

81. **A** Chapter 16, Objectives 3 and 4
Whenever a patient is found in a harmful environment, the priority of care will be to remove the patient from the harmful environment.

82. **B** Chapter 17, Objective 6
Scene safety must be established before entering any scene.

83. **D** Chapter 14, Objective 2
Hyperglycemic patients may appear intoxicated and have an acetone odor to their breath. The patient may also have a rapid heart rate.

84. **F** Chapter 18, Objective 14
There are only two situations in which the EMT-B may be called upon to insert a gloved hand into the vagina: First is to support the head and create an airway with a breech delivery in which the head has yet to deliver. The second situation is in the case of a prolapsed cord. In that case the EMT should hold the child's head off the cord and transport to the hospital in that position.

85. **C** Chapter 19, Objective 3
The first attempt at bleeding control should always be direct pressure. Following that, a pressure point above the bleed might be used. Tourniquets are a last resort and should never be used below the knee or elbow.

86. **C** Chapter 21, Objective 3, and Chapter 4, Objective 1
There are 33 total vertebrae. Among them are 7 cervical, 12 thoracic, 5 lumbar, 5 sacral, and 4 in the coccyx.

87. **B** Chapter 21, Objective 3, and Chapter 4, Objective 1
There are 33 total vertebrae. Among that total are 7 cervical, 12 thoracic, 5 lumbar, 5 sacral, and 4 coccyx.

88. **E** Chapter 21, Objective 7
Patients complaining of pain, having a mechanism that suggests spinal injury, having deformity along the spine, or being unconscious, should be immobilized for possible spinal injuries.

89. **D** Chapter 21, Objective 17
Rapid extrication can be used as both an emergency and/or urgent move if there is danger to the patient or rescuer or if the patient is in critical condition.

90. **D** Chapter 22, Objective 1
Infants are considered newborns until the end of their first year of life.

91. **A** Chapter 22, Objective 14
The number one cause of death in children is trauma.

92. **C** Chapter 23, Section 3, Objective 10
Ambulatory patients are considered Green or Nonemergent.

93. **A** Chapter 23, Section 3, Objective 10
This patient is critical and earns a Red or Urgent tag.

94. **D** Chapter 23, Section 3, Objective 5
Important information for use at a hazardous materials scene can be obtained from the DOT Emergency Response Guidebook, the NFPA 704 Manual, CHEMTREC, and other chemical emergency hotlines.

95. **F** Chapter 9, Objective 2
When speaking into any microphone, hold the microphone two to three inches from your mouth, speak slowly and clearly, and never give patient's name over the air.

96. **A** Chapter 10, Objective 3
When an error is made on a report form, draw a line though the error, mark it "error," and initial it. Then go ahead and make the correction. Never erase or blot out mistakes, nor should you ever tear up a report.

97. **C** Chapter 5, Objective 8
Cyanosis is blue discoloration of the skin brought about by hypoxia.

98. **C** Chapter 6, Objective 12
A stokes or basket stretcher is used on difficult terrain or in confined spaces.

99. **D** Chapter 7, Objective 7
Suctioning should be performed for no more than 10 to 15 seconds or about as long as you can hold your breath. The suction catheter should be measured from the earlobe to the corner of the mouth to determine the depth of insertion. The suction tip should be kept moving while it is in the pharynx to keep it from adhering to the inside of the mouth.

100. **A** Chapter 1, Objective 1
It is the responsibility of each EMT-B to maintain the knowledge and skills necessary to be effective in the field.

EXAM 2

1. Included in the National Highway Traffic Safety Administration's ten Standard Components of an EMS System are
   - (A) Regulation and Policy.
   - (B) Human Resources and Training.
   - (C) Facilities.
   - (D) Public Information and Education.
   - (E) All of the above.

2. Among the EMT-B's roles and responsibilities, first and foremost, is
   - (A) patient care.
   - (B) personal safety.
   - (C) following orders from medical direction.
   - (D) None of the above.

3. There are four levels of prehospital care provided by trained EMS personnel. The level of care provided by the EMT-B is
   - (A) advanced life support.
   - (B) intermediate life support.
   - (C) basic life support.
   - (D) first aid.

4. In order to ensure that the public receives the highest-quality prehospital care, there should be a system of internal and external reviews and audits of all aspects of an EMS system to identify areas in need of improvement. This process is called
   - (A) quality improvement.
   - (B) medical direction.
   - (C) accreditation.
   - (D) certification.

5. The physician responsible for overseeing the training of prehospital care providers in an EMS system, and all clinical and patient care aspects of the system, is the
   - (A) state EMS director.
   - (B) medical director.
   - (C) Chief of Service.
   - (D) system manager.

6. The laws and rules that determine how EMT-Bs should be trained and licensed are determined by
   - (A) individual states.
   - (B) the U.S. Department of Transportation.
   - (C) the U.S. Department of Health.
   - (D) each EMS system.

7. In an EMT-B, an upset stomach, dry mouth, nausea and vomiting, pounding heart, shivering or shakes, sweating, feeling clumsy, stomach cramps, diarrhea, muscle aches, and dizziness are
   - (A) warning signs of impending nervous breakdown.
   - (B) normal physiological responses to stress.
   - (C) rookie responses.
   - (D) signs of poor job preparation.

8. As you remove a deceased man from a home, his wife is pounding her fists and swearing. She is exhibiting one of many normal responses to death. It is more than likely that the phase of acceptance she is in is
   - (A) denial.
   - (B) anger.
   - (C) bargaining.
   - (D) depression.
   - (E) acceptance.

9. In dealing with the family of a dead or dying patient, as an EMT you should
   (A) identify yourself and explain your actions.
   (B) be honest and do not give a false sense of hope to the family.
   (C) assure the family that all that can be done is being done.
   (D) All of the above.

10. With family and friends, the EMT-B needs to
    (A) share work experience while protecting patient confidentiality.
    (B) make time for interests and activities that are not work related.
    (C) balance family, friends, work, and rest.
    (D) All of the above.

11. Critical Incident Stress Debriefing (CISD)
    (A) is a process of helping us deal with extraordinary circumstances.
    (B) should not be used for routine stresses of our work.
    (C) should be done within 72 hours of an event.
    (D) All of the above.

12. Which of the following is not an effective method of dealing with the stresses of EMS?
    (A) Signing up for extra shifts when things are bad at home.
    (B) Regular exercise.
    (C) A healthy diet.
    (D) Talking with family and co-workers about stress.

13. The first thing the EMT needs to evaluate on arrival is
    (A) the airway.
    (B) breathing.
    (C) circulation.
    (D) scene safety.

14. In order to avoid being infected by patients, the EMT-B should
    (A) have a history and physical by a physician.
    (B) have all recommended inoculations.
    (C) practice BSI.
    (D) All of the above.

15. When removing a victim from a vehicle involved in a collision, proper attire would include
    (A) helmet and eye protection.
    (B) gloves and protective clothing (coat and pants or boots).
    (C) gloves and goggles only.
    (D) A & B.

16. The EMT-Bs "scope of practice" is defined by
    (A) federal laws.
    (B) state laws.
    (C) the school from which the EMT graduates.
    (D) the agency that employs the EMT.

17. In order for a DNR to be honored, it must
    (A) be signed by the patient or his or her agent.
    (B) be signed by a physician.
    (C) be consistent with the system protocols.
    (D) All of the above.

18. EMT-Bs are allowed to treat unresponsive patients assuming they would consent if they were physically able. This is referred to as
    (A) expressed consent.
    (B) implied consent.
    (C) minor consent.
    (D) major consent.

19. The rules of consent dictate that
  (A) the EMT must inform the patient of the risks of not receiving treatment or transport.
  (B) the EMT must inform the patient of what care will be rendered and what the concerns are.
  (C) competent adults can refuse care and transportation.
  (D) All of the above.

20. Which of the following is not true of minor consent?
  (A) Minors cannot refuse care.
  (B) Parents can refuse care even when there is a possible life threat.
  (C) Pregnant minors cannot give consent for their own care.
  (D) None of the above.

21. If an EMT terminates a patient relationship without ensuring that care of an equal or higher level will be provided, he or she is guilty of
  (A) abandonment.
  (B) assault.
  (C) battery.
  (D) libel.

22. If the EMT-B creates an immediate fear of harm in the patient, he or she may be guilty of
  (A) battery.
  (B) assault.
  (C) negligence.
  (D) abandonment.

23. Duty to act is established
  (A) while working, once the request for aid is made.
  (B) while off duty, when contact with the patient is made.
  (C) once the EMT-B accepts licensure.
  (D) All of the above.
  (E) A & B.

24. Which of the following would be a violation of patient confidentiality?
  (A) Releasing records to the patient's attorney.
  (B) Discussing the patient with other providers involved in the patient's care.
  (C) Releasing the patient's name and history to the media.
  (D) Discussing the patient's history under subpoena.

25. Which of the following does NOT represent the EMT-Bs responsibility in regard to organ donation?
  (A) The EMT-B should ask the family of dying patients about the patient's wishes in regard to organ donation.
  (B) EMT-Bs should treat organ donors more aggressively.
  (C) EMT-Bs should treat organ donors less aggressively.
  (D) The EMT-B should treat organ donors the same as any other patient.
  (E) C & D.
  (F) A & D.

26. Which of the following would not be proper at the scene of a crime?
  (A) Entering and leaving the scene following the same path.
  (B) Staging some distance from the scene until instructed that it is safe to enter.
  (C) Touching or moving things not relevant to the care of the patient.
  (D) Cutting clothes through holes already there.

27. EMT-Bs are required to report
  (A) injuries resulting from a criminal attack.
  (B) sexual assault.
  (C) abuse.
  (D) All of the above.

28. The front of the body is the _____ surface.
    (A) anterior
    (B) posterior
    (C) lateral
    (D) medial

29. The shoulder is the _____ aspect of an arm.
    (A) distal
    (B) proximal
    (C) medial
    (D) lateral

30. The correct anatomical position is
    (A) standing facing forward with palms open and forward.
    (B) standing facing backward with palms open forward.
    (C) standing facing forward with the back of the hands facing forward.
    (D) standing facing backward with the back of the hands facing forward.

31. If you are describing something toward the head of the body it would be
    (A) anterior.
    (B) posterior.
    (C) superior.
    (D) inferior.

32. The function of the human skeleton is to
    (A) give the body shape.
    (B) protect vital organs.
    (C) make movement possible.
    (D) All of the above.

33. The portion of the spine that is made up of four fused vertebrae is the
    (A) cervical. 7
    (B) thoracic. 12
    (C) lumbar. 5
    (D) coccyx. sacral 5 / 4

34. The wings of the pelvis are the
    (A) iliac crests.
    (B) ischium.
    (C) ischial tuberosities.
    (D) pubis.

35. The bones in the forearm are
    (A) the radius.
    (B) the ulna.
    (C) the humerus.
    (D) A & B.
    (E) B & C.

36. The medial malleolus is the distal end of the
    (A) tibia.
    (B) fibula.
    (C) patella.
    (D) femur.

37. Which of the following is an example of a ball-and-socket joint?
    (A) Finger
    (B) Elbow
    (C) Hip
    (D) Wrist

38. The dividing line between the upper and lower airways is the
    (A) diaphragm.
    (B) pharynx.
    (C) larynx.
    (D) epiglottis.

39. The muscles of respiration include the
    (A) intercostals.
    (B) diaphragm.
    (C) latisimus.
    (D) dorsals.
    (E) A & B.
    (F) B & C.

40. The range of normal rate of breathing for adults is
    (A) 12–20.
    (B) 15–30.
    (C) 25–50.
    (D) None of the above.

41. Signs of inadequate respiration may include
    (A) nasal flaring.
    (B) retractions.
    (C) cyanosis.
    (D) All of the above.

42. Blood entering the left atrium comes from
    (A) the body.
    (B) the lungs.
    (C) the right ventricle.
    (D) the left ventricle.

43. In the lower abdomen, the aorta divides into two arteries, one for each leg. These are the ____ arteries
    (A) carotid
    (B) brachial
    (C) femoral
    (D) popliteal

44. Only one vein in the body carries oxygen-rich blood. That vein is the
    (A) superior vena cava.
    (B) inferior vena cava.
    (C) pulmonary vein.
    (D) saphenous vein.

45. The blood component that assists in forming clots is
    (A) the red blood cells.
    (B) the white blood cells.
    (C) plasma.
    (D) the platelets.

46. The lower number in a blood pressure reading is
    (A) systolic.
    (B) diastolic.
    (C) the pressure during contraction of the heart.
    (D) the pressure in the vessels between contractions.
    (E) A & C.
    (F) B & D.

47. The nervous system is divided into central and peripheral. Which of the following is also true?
    (A) The central nervous system consists of the brain and spinal cord.
    (B) The central nervous system consists of motor and sensory.
    (C) The peripheral nervous system consists of the brain and spinal cord.
    (D) The peripheral nervous system consists of motor and sensory nerves.
    (E) A & D.
    (F) B & C.

48. The deepest layer of skin, consisting of fat cells, is the
    (A) epidermis.
    (B) dermis.
    (C) subcutaneous.
    (D) facia.

49. Vital signs include
    (A) respirations and pulse.
    (B) blood pressure.
    (C) pupils and skin condition.
    (D) All of the above.

50. Capillary refill
    (A) is important to measure in all patients.
    (B) should be done in pediatric patients.
    (C) may be less meaningful in adults because of medical history.
    (D) B & C.

51. When assessing pupils, smaller pupils are said to be
    (A) dilated.
    (B) constricted.
    (C) midrange.
    (D) None of the above.

52. If the patient's condition is not critical, vital signs should be reassessed
    (A) every 5 minutes.
    (B) every 10 minutes.
    (C) every 15 minutes.
    (D) every 20 minutes.

53. The acronym SAMPLE refers to
   (A) the history needed to be obtained on every patient.
   (B) vital signs to be obtained.
   (C) specific fluids to be evaluated from the patient.
   (D) evaluating the scene.

54. Proper body mechanics include
   (A) using the legs and not the back to lift.
   (B) using the back and not the legs to lift.
   (C) keeping the weight as close to the body as possible.
   (D) A & C.
   (E) B & C.

55. A move to be used when there is a danger to the patient and rescuers is a(n)
   (A) urgent move.
   (B) emergency move.
   (C) nonurgent move.
   (D) specialty move.

56. Rapid extrication is an example of a(n)
   (A) urgent move.
   (B) emergency move.
   (C) nonurgent move.
   (D) A & B.

57. The direct ground lift is an example of
   (A) an urgent move.
   (B) an emergency move.
   (C) a nonurgent move.
   (D) All of the above.

58. An unresponsive patient without a spine injury should be transported in _____ position.
   (A) supine
   (B) prone
   (C) recovery
   (D) sitting

59. The trachea
   (A) is located anterior and midline in the neck.
   (B) is located posterior and midline in the neck.
   (C) conducts air in and out of the lungs.
   (D) conducts solids and liquids into the digestive tract.
   (E) A & C.
   (F) B & D.

60. The head tilt chin lift method of opening the airway should
   (A) always be used when opening the airway.
   (B) be used only when there is no suspicion of neck injury.
   (C) be used when there is suspicion of neck injury.
   (D) never be used.

61. The term used to describe difficulty breathing is
   (A) tachypnea.
   (B) bradypnea.
   (C) dyspnea.
   (D) apnea.

62. Wheezing
   (A) indicates an obstruction of the upper airways.
   (B) is common in asthma patients.
   (C) indicates an obstruction of the lower airways.
   (D) A & B.
   (E) B & C.

63. You are presented with an unresponsive 50-year-old male. He is pale and breathing rapidly. You hear gurgling noises with each breath. Once you open the airway, your next step will be to
   (A) administer oxygen with a nasal canula.
   (B) administer oxygen with a non-rebreather mask.
   (C) suction the patient's airway.
   (D) ventilate the patient using a bag-valve mask.

64. When suctioning, the EMT-B should
(A) limit suctioning to 10–15 seconds.
(B) have suction off while inserting.
(C) begin suction once the device is inserted into the mouth.
(D) keep the suction tip moving while drawing it out of the airway.
(E) All of the above.

65. The most important part, and most typical failure of bag-valve mask ventilation is
(A) attaching the reservoir to an oxygen supply.
(B) obtaining a seal between the mask and the patient.
(C) extending the reservoir fully.
(D) squeezing the bag fully.

66. During scene size-up, the EMT should
(A) assess for hazards.
(B) take BSI precautions.
(C) determine the number of patients needing care.
(D) All of the above.

67. When describing the patient's mental status using AVPU, the A stands for
(A) Alert.
(B) Ambulatory.
(C) Angry.
(D) Affect.

68. In forming a general impression the EMT is
(A) getting a "gut" sense of whether the patient is critical or noncritical.
(B) trying to determine the patient's precise problem.
(C) trying to determine what the patient thinks the problem is.
(D) trying to determine what hospital the patient will be going to.

69. Assessing the mental status of infants and children can be difficult. Steps the EMT-B can take to attempt to make this assessment include
(A) assessing the activity level of the child.
(B) asking the family if the level of activity is normal.
(C) monitoring the child's response to the exam.
(D) All of the above.

70. The EMT-B should suspect, and treat for spine injuries when
(A) the patient has pain in the neck or back.
(B) the patient has a head injury.
(C) there is deformity along the spine.
(D) there is paralysis or parasthesia.
(E) the patient is unconscious and there is no available history.
(F) All of the above.

71. Skin should be assessed for
(A) color.
(B) temperature.
(C) condition.
(D) All of the above.

72. When checking capillary refill time, it should be
(A) less than two seconds.
(B) between two and four seconds.
(C) between three and five seconds.
(D) between four and six seconds.

73. In a conscious adult, the pulse should first be checked at the
(A) carotid artery.
(B) brachial artery.
(C) radial artery.
(D) femoral artery.

74. Which of the following should be classified as priority patients?
    (A) An unresponsive patient.
    (B) A patient with pain to a forearm.
    (C) A patient with difficulty breathing.
    (D) A patient with a cut hand.
    (E) A & C.
    (F) A & B.

75. The focused trauma assessment is based on
    (A) the chief complaint.
    (B) the mechanism of injury.
    (C) the age of the patient.
    (D) the level of licensure of the responder.

76. The focused medical assessment is based on
    (A) the chief complaint.
    (B) the mechanism of injury.
    (C) the age of the patient.
    (D) the level of licensure of the responder.

77. The detailed physical exam should be
    (A) performed after the focused exam.
    (B) done in the field on noncritical patients.
    (C) done en route to the hospital on critical patients.
    (D) All of the above.

78. Once the detailed physical assessment is done, the EMT
    (A) is finished with assessments and should work on the report.
    (B) should keep an eye on the patient.
    (C) should perform a continuing assessment.
    (D) None of the above.

79. Which of the following are keys to good radio communications?
    (A) Wait for radio traffic to clear before speaking.
    (B) Wait for a moment after keying the mike.
    (C) Speak with the mike about two to three inches away from your face.
    (D) All of the above.

80. Which of the following should not be included in radio communications?
    (A) Patient's name.
    (B) Patient's condition.
    (C) The name of the ambulance company or community.
    (D) The nature of the illness or injury.

81. Hand-held radios transmitting at 1–5 watts with limited range are considered
    (A) base stations.
    (B) portable radios.
    (C) repeaters.
    (D) mobile radios.

82. The EMT will make objective and subjective assessments. Signs would be objective and symptoms would be objective assessments.
    (A) True.
    (B) False.

83. When asked if he has pain, your patient says no. Documenting that he denies pain would be
    (A) objective.
    (B) subjective.
    (C) a pertinent negative.
    (D) B & C.

84. In order for patients to refuse care
    (A) they must be competent adults.
    (B) they must understand what treatment they are refusing.
    (C) they must understand the possible negative effects of refusing treatment and transport.
    (D) All of the above.

85. The medications that will be carried on a BLS unit are
(A) glucose, oxygen, and activated charcoal.
(B) glucose, oxygen, and ipecac.
(C) diabenase, oxygen, and activated charcoal.
(D) glucose, nitrox, and activated charcoal.

86. Prescription drugs patients may carry that the EMT-B may assist in administering include
(A) epinephrine auto-injectors.
(B) nitroglycerin.
(C) inhalers.
(D) narcotic pain medication.
(E) All of the above.
(F) A, B, & C.

87. Indications that the EMT-B is providing adequate bag-valve mask ventilations include
(A) the chest rising and falling with each ventilation.
(B) the heart rate returning to a more normal rate.
(C) improvement of the patient's color.
(D) All of the above.

88. Early signs of hypoxia include
(A) nervousness.
(B) agitation.
(C) tachycardia.
(D) All of the above.

89. Patients with chest pain should be
(A) placed supine on the stretcher.
(B) allowed to sit in a position of comfort.
(C) placed prone on the stretcher.
(D) placed in a shock or Trendelenberg position.

90. Automatic external defibrillators should be placed on
(A) all chest pain patients.
(B) all unresponsive patients.
(C) any patient who has no pulse or respirations.
(D) any patient with a cardiac history.

91. A condition in which a weakened heart muscle cannot pump blood effectively and blood backs up and leaks into the lungs is called
(A) congestive heart failure (CHF).
(B) coronary artery disease (CAD).
(C) chronic obstructive pulmonary disease (COPD).
(D) arteriosclerosis.

92. Diabetes is a condition in which
(A) too much insulin is produced by the pancreas.
(B) too little, or no, insulin is produced by the pancreas.
(C) too much testosterone is produced by the pancreas.
(D) too little, or no, testosterone is produced by the pancreas.

93. The EMT-B should recognize potential allergic reactions when the patient exhibits
(A) itching and/or hives.
(B) wheezing or respiratory distress.
(C) upper airway obstruction.
(D) All of the above.

94. You are called for a 25-year-old man working in an extremely hot area in a local steel mill. He has been working all day wearing several layers of clothes. He is weak, dizzy, pale, and diaphoretic. He is likely suffering from
(A) heat cramps.
(B) heat exhaustion.
(C) heatstroke.
(D) heat blisters.

95. The priority in any environmental emergency is
(A) the airway.
(B) breathing.
(C) circulation.
(D) removing the patient from the environment.

96. The first priority in dealing with behavioral emergencies is
  (A) gaining the patient's trust.
  (B) determining which disorder the patient suffers from.
  (C) determining if drugs are involved.
  (D) scene safety.

97. The two situations in which the EMT-B may be called upon to insert a gloved hand into the vagina are
  (A) a prolapsed cord.
  (B) a breech delivery with the head undelivered.
  (C) a uterine hemorrhage.
  (D) B & C.
  (E) A & B.
  (F) A & C.

98. Tourniquets
  (A) should never be used.
  (B) should be used with all amputations.
  (C) should never be used below the knee or elbow.
  (D) should be used only as a last resort.
  (E) B & D.
  (F) C & D.

99. An open wound typified by torn jagged edges is a(n)
  (A) abrasion.
  (B) contusion.
  (C) laceration.
  (D) puncture.

100. Cushing's Triad is a collection of vital signs typical when intacranial pressure is increasing. These vital sign changes are
  (A) increasing pulse, deceasing blood pressure, and rapid breathing.
  (B) decreasing pulse, rising blood pressure, and bizarre respirations.
  (C) decreasing pulse, decreasing blood pressure, and bizarre respirations.
  (D) increasing pulse, increasing blood pressure, and rapid respirations.

Answers to Exam 2

1. E Chapter 1, Objective 1
The ten Standard Components of an EMS System Identified by the NHTSA Technical Assistance Program are:

1. Regulation and Policy
2. Resource Management
3. Human Resources and Training
4. Transportation
5. Facilities
6. Communications
7. Public Information and Education
8. Medical Direction
9. Trauma Systems
10. Evaluation

2. B Chapter 1, Objective 3
The EMT-B's roles and responsibilities include assessing and treating patients, transporting patients, and acting as an advocate for patients. The most important responsibility, however, is safety for the EMT-B, the crew, and the patient, in that order.

3. C Chapter 1, Objective 2
Paramedics or EMT-Ps provide ALS or advanced life support, EMT-Is or EMT Intermediates provide a limited amount of advanced life support, EMT-Bs provide basic life support, and First Responders provide a form of basic life support prior to the arrival of transporting agencies.

4. A Chapter 1, Objective 4
Quality improvement is the responsibility of every EMS system. This continuous audit of all aspects of EMS ensures the highest possible level of prehospital care.

5. B Chapter 1, Objective 6
The EMS system's medical director is responsible for overseeing the education of all the prehospital care providers in the EMS system and for all clinical and patient care aspects of the system.

6. A Chapter 1, Objective 7
While there is a national curriculum developed under contract to the US Department of transportation, each state enacts legislation that defines what prehospital care is, how the providers are trained, and what they are allowed to do in the field.

7. B Chapter 2, Objective 1
An upset stomach, dry mouth, nausea and vomiting, pounding heart, shivering or shakes, sweating, feeling clumsy, stomach cramps, diarrhea, muscle aches, and dizziness are all normal responses to stressful situations. EMT-Bs should be prepared for these and understand that their bodies may respond to the stress they are exposed to in their work.

8. B Chapter 2, Objective 2
Anger is the second stage of dealing with death that may be expressed by the family of a deceased person or by a person who is facing his or her own death. The wife in this question is clearly expressing anger about the loss of her husband.

9. D Chapter 2, Objective 3
EMT-Bs should identify themselves, be honest with family, never give false hope, allow the family to be with the patient as much as possible, assure the family that everything that can be done is being done, and explain to them what is happening. Honesty, disclosure of what's happening, and access to the patient will help the family face what's ahead for them.

10. **D** Chapter 2, Objective 4
One of the hazards of working in EMS is the toll it takes on friends and family. The EMT-B needs to find a way to share experiences with friends and family that do not violate confidentiality and do not offend the listener. It is also important that the EMT-B cultivate interests and activities outside of EMS.

11. **D** Chapter 2, Objective 5
CISD, also known as CISM, Critical Incident Stress Management, is effective in counteracting the negative effects of some of the extraordinary situations we find ourselves facing. It is important to recognize potentially damaging events and to get the team assembled within 24–72 hours of the event. It is also important not to trivialize the process by using it in routine situations. When many individuals appear to be distressed over an event, severe distress signals are present, behavioral changes are witnessed, errors of judgment surface, personnel is requesting help, or signs of stress persist beyond three weeks, CISD/CISM should be called upon.

12. **A** Chapter 2, Objective 5
Balancing life and all of the things that are important to us is important in limiting the effects of stress. A sure sign of trouble is retreating to work when things are difficult.

13. **D** Chapter 2, Objective 7
The EMT-B should be concerned with the ABCs of patient assessment when in contact with the patient, but before that, scene safety needs to be assured before patient contact.

14. **D** Chapter 2, Objectives 8 and 9
Having a complete history and physical and the immunizations recommended by the physician, frequent and proper hand washing, and practicing BSI are all important steps in protecting the EMT-B from the diseases he or she will be exposed to.

15. **D** Chapter 2, Objective 10
Protective clothing for assisting victims of motor vehicle collisions is full turnout gear or bunker gear. This should include helmet, gloves, eye protection, and protective clothing.

16. **B** Chapter 3, Objective 1
While there are national curricula and standards, the actual scope of practice for each EMT-B is determined by the laws and subsequent rules and regulations enacted by the state the EMT-B is certified or licensed in.

17. **D** Chapter 3, Objective 2
One of the most important facets of patient care is to honor the patient's wishes. DNRs are a way for people to ensure that their wishes are honored even if they are unable to verbalize those wishes in regard to resuscitation. Your EMS system will have policies and procedures regarding validating a DNR. They must also be signed by a physician, and the patient or the patient's guardian.

18. **B** Chapter 3, Objective 4
EMT-Bs are able to treat unresponsive patients, working under the assumption that they would consent if they were physically able to do so. This is the rule of implied consent.

19. **D** Chapter 3, Objective 3
Consent must be informed consent. For consent to be valid the EMT-B must be honest with the patient about what is happening and what the patient should expect next. The same is true for refusal of care. While patients have the right to refuse care, that refusal has to be informed. This means that the EMT-B must inform the patient of the possible repercussions of not receiving care or transportation.

20. **B** Chapter 3, Objective 5
Parents cannot refuse care for their child if there is a life threat. Pregnant minors can give consent for themselves during the pregnancy, and minors cannot refuse care for themselves.

21. **A** Chapter 3, Objective 7
Once a patient contact is made, unless the patient makes an informed refusal, the EMT-B must make certain that the patient will receive care of a level equal or higher to that provided by the EMT-B.

22. **B** Chapter 3, Objective 7
Battery is touching someone without his or her permission; assault is creating an immediate fear of harm in another.

23. **E** Chapter 3, Objective 8
The EMT-B has a duty to act in all requests for aid when on duty. When off duty, there is no duty to act in most states unless contact is made with the patient. Some states may have laws that require trained medical personnel to heed all calls for help even when off duty, so the EMT-B must review state laws and statutes.

24. **C** Chapter 3, Objective 9
Only the patient or the patient's agent can have access to patient records; otherwise, a subpoena is required for their release. It is inappropriate to release the patient's name and history to the media or discuses the patient with coworkers not directly involved in the patient's care. The EMT-B should protect patient confidentiality as a patient advocate.

25. **F** Chapter 3, Objective 10
The EMT-B should ask the family of dying patients about the patient's wishes regarding organ donation, but organ donors should not be treated any differently than any other patient.

26. **C** Chapter 3, Objective 11
The EMT-B should never touch or move anything at the scene not related to the necessary care of the patient. The EMT-B should also make sure that the scene is safe before entering, enter and exit by the same path, save all clothing removed during care, and never cut through existing holes in clothing. EMT-Bs should also be prepared to answer questions from police and in court regarding crimes involving patients they have cared for.

27. **D** Chapter 3, Objective 12
State laws may vary somewhat but EMT-Bs are required to report injuries inflicted in a criminal act, sexual assault, and abuse.

28. **A** Chapter 4, Objective 1
The front of the body is the anterior surface, the rear is the posterior, the sides are lateral, and medial is the inside or toward the midline.

29. **B** Chapter 4, Objective 1
Proximal refers to the point where an extremity attaches to the body, while distal refers to distant or farther away. The shoulder would be proximal, and the fingers distal on the arm.

30. **A** Chapter 4, Objective 1
The correct anatomical position is standing facing forward with palms open and forward.

31. **C** Chapter 4, Objective 1
Describing a part of the body in relation to other parts of the body, the nearer to the head is superior.

32. **D** Chapter 4, Objective 2
The human skeleton provides the structure from which the body takes its shape, protects internal organs, and allows for us to walk and move.

33. **D** Chapter 4, Objective 2
The spine is made up of 33 vertebrae—7 cervical, 12 thoracic, 5 lumbar, 5 sacral, and 4 coccyx. The sacrum and coccyx are fused.

34. **A** Chapter 4, Objective 2
The iliac crests are also known as the pelvic wings that are referred to as the hips. The pubis, the bone at the base of the pelvis, and the ischium are the base of the pelvis.

35. **D** Chapter 4, Objective 2
The forearm contains the radius on the thumb side and the ulna on the other. The humerus is the bone of the upper arm.

36. **A** Chapter 4, Objective 2
The medial malleolus is the distal end of the tibia. The posterior tibialis pulse is located behind it. The lateral malleolus is the distal end of the fibula, the patella is the kneecap, and the femur is the long bone in the thigh.

37. **C** Chapter 4, Objective 2
Ball-and-socket joints include the hip and shoulder.

38. **C** Chapter 4, Objective 2
The larynx or voice box divides the upper from the lower airways.

39. **E** Chapter 4, Objective 2
The intercostals and the diaphragm are the muscles of respiration, contracting with inspiration and relaxing with expiration.

40. **A** Chapter 4, Objective 2
Adults normally breathe 12–20 times per minute, children 15–30, and infants 25–50.

41. **D** Chapter 4, Objective 2
Nasal flaring, retractions, and cyanosis are signs that breathing is inadequate.

42. **B** Chapter 4, Objective 2
Blood from the body enters the right atrium. From there it goes to the left ventricle and then it is pumped to the lungs. Blood then leaves the lungs entering the left atrium before it goes to the left ventricle to be pumped out to the body through the aorta.

43. **C** Chapter 4, Objective 2
The carotids run from the chest to the head, the brachials run into the forearms from the upper arm, the popliteal runs behind the knee, and the femoral arteries bring blood to the legs.

44. **C** Chapter 4, Objective 2
The pulmonary vein carries oxygenated blood from the lungs to the right atrium.

45. **D** Chapter 4, Objective 2
Platelets assist in forming clots, white cells fight infection, red cells carry oxygen and carbon dioxide, and plasma is the transport medium.

46. **F** Chapter 4, Objective 2
The lower number in the blood pressure reading is the diastolic pressure, or the pressure in the blood vessels between contractions of the heart. The upper number is the systolic or pressure in the vessels during contractions.

47. **E** Chapter 4, Objective 2
The central nervous system consists of the brain and spinal cord, and the peripheral nervous system consists of motor and sensory nerves.

48. **C** Chapter 4, Objective 2
The outermost layer is the epidermis, the second layer containing the sweat and sebaceous gland is the dermis, and the deepest layer is the subcutaneous.

49. **D** Chapter 5, Objective 1
Vital signs include pulse, respiration, blood pressure, skin condition, and pupils.

50. **D** Chapter 5, Objective 8
Capillary refill is done in all pediatric patients but is less meaningful in adults because of medical conditions that may impair measurement.

51. **B** Chapter 5, Objective 15
Small pupils are constricted, midrange pupils are medium, and large pupils are dilated.

52. **C** Chapter 5, Objective 1
Vital signs in noncritical patients should be reassessed every 15 minutes. Critical patients should be reassessed every 5 minutes.

53. **A** Chapter 5, Objective 1
SAMPLE refers to the history to be evaluated on every patient. It includes

   S = Signs and symptoms

   A = Allergies

   M = Medications the patient is taking

   P = Pertinent past medical history

   L = Last oral intake

   E = Events leading up to this call

54. **D** Chapter 6, Objective 1
Proper body mechanics calls for keeping the weight as close to the body as possible and lifting using the legs and not the back.

55. **B** Chapter 6, Objective 11
Emergency moves should be used when there is imminent danger to the patient and/or rescuers.

56. **D** Chapter 6, Objective 11
Rapid extrication is used as both an urgent and emergency move.

57. **C** Chapter 6, Objective 11
Direct ground lift is a nonurgent move.

58. **C** Chapter 6, Objective 10
The recovery position places an unresponsive patient on his or her side; in the event of vomiting, it protects the airway from aspiration.

59. **E** Chapter 7, Objective 1
The trachea, also known as the windpipe, is located anterior and midline in the neck and conducts air in and out of the lungs.

60. **B** Chapter 7, Objective 4
The head tilt chin lift maneuver should be used to open the airway except when there is the possibility of a neck injury.

61. **C** Chapter 7, Objective 3
Dyspnea is the term for difficulty breathing. Tachypnea means rapid breathing, bradypnea means slow breathing, and apnea means not breathing.

62. **E** Chapter 7, Objective 3
Wheezing is an airway noise heard when mucus accumulates in the lower airways and with bronchospasm. It is commonly heard in COPD patients. These are patients with asthma, emphysema, and chronic bronchitis.

63. **C** Chapter 7, Objective 7
The gurgling noises signify obstruction of the airway. Once the airway is open, the priority is to clear it to prevent aspiration of the obstruction.

64. **E** Chapter 7, Objective 8
The suction catheter to be used should first be measured from the earlobe to the corner of the mouth to determine how deep to insert it. Suction should be off until the catheter is inserted and once in, the suction tip should be withdrawn while keeping it moving around in the mouth to keep it from adhering to the inside of the mouth. The suctioning should be completed within 10–15 seconds, or about as long as the EMT can hold his or her breath.

65. **B** Chapter 7, Objective 10
The most important part of bag-valve mask ventilation, and the most common failure, is obtaining a tight seal between the mask and the patient. Without a good seal, air will leak out of the mask and not enter the lungs.

66. **D** Chapter 8, Section 1, Objectives 1–6
Scene size-up calls for the EMT to assess the scene for hazards and clues as to the mechanism of injury, determine the number of patients and the need for additional resources, and approach the scene taking BSI precautions.

67. **A** Chapter 8, Section 2, Objective 2
AVPU is an acronym used to represent a patient's mental status:

A = Alert

V = Responds to verbal stimulus

P = Responds to painful stimulus

U = Unresponsive.

68. **A** Chapter 8, Section 2, Objective 1
The EMT-B needs to form a general impression quickly to determine whether or not the patient has immediate life threats or not. The manner in which the patient is assessed and treated depends on this early assessment.

69. **D** Chapter 8, Section 2, Objective 3
Assessing the mental status of infants and children is difficult. Assessing their activity level is important. A child should be excited or afraid in an emergency, particularly when handled by strangers. A child who responds sluggishly or not at all is behaving in a significant way. Asking the family about the child's activity levels, if they have changed, for example, is also helpful.

70. **F** Chapter 8, Section 2, Objective 5
The EMT-B needs to provide spinal immobilization whenever there is cause to suspect injury to the spine. Unconscious patients with no history, patients complaining of pain or inability to move or feel extremities, patients with a deformity over the spine, and patients with head injuries are all suspect for spinal injury and should be immobilized.

71. **D** Chapter 8, Section 2, Objectives 15–17
As a part of assessing circulation, the skin should be checked for color, temperature, and condition. Normally, skin color varies based on a patient's race, and should be warm and dry. Patients who are perfusing poorly will be pale, cool, and clammy or diaphoretic. Patients with infections may be hot, dry, and flushed.

72. **A** Chapter 8, Section 2, Objective 18
Capillary refill should be checked in pediatric patients but is less reliable in adults. When evaluating capillary refill the nail bed or skin on the forehead should be compressed and the color should return in less than two seconds.

73. **C** Chapter 8, Section 2, Objective 12
The radial pulse is the first pulse to check in conscious adults. In unconscious adults the carotid is checked, and in infants the brachial is checked.

74. **E** Chapter 8, Section 2, Objective 19
Priority patients include any patient with an immediate life threat. This would include any disruption in the ABCs. Airway or breathing problems, impaired circulation, or changes in the level of consciousness are all priority situations.

75. **B** Chapter 8, Section 3, Objective 1
The focused exam on trauma patients is based on the mechanism of injury. Using the mechanism, the EMT should determine the potential injuries and look for signs consistent with those injuries during the exam.

76. **A** Chapter 8, Section 4, Objective 1
The focused exam in medical patients is based on the chief complaint. The chief complaint, whether it is chest pain or difficulty breathing, is considered in assessing for life threats relative to that complaint.

77. **D** Chapter 8, Section 5, Objective 4
Detailed physical exams should follow the focused exam. If the patient is critical, the detailed exam can be delayed or withheld but should be done en route to the hospital if possible. Otherwise, with non-critical patients the detailed exam should be done in the field, prior to transport.

78. **C** Chapter 8, Section 5, Objective 1
Once the initial, focused, and detailed assessments are done, the EMT-B should be performing a continuing assessment of the patient for as long as the patient is in his or her care. As a part of this, the vital signs should be repeated every five minutes in critical patients and every 15 minutes in noncritical patients.

79. **D** Chapter 9, Objective 5
Radio communications are enhanced by good radio etiquette. Waiting for radio traffic to clear, pausing a moment after keying the mike, speaking slowly with the mike two to three inches away from your mouth, are all keys to good radio communications.

80. **A** Chapter 9, Objective 6
The patient's name should never be given out "over the air" as it might be overheard by people who monitor radio communications. To do so would be a breach of patient confidentiality.

81. **B** Chapter 9, Objective 1
Hand-held radios transmitting at low watts in a limited range are called portable radios. Mobile radios are vehicle mounted and transmit with more power in the 20–50 watt range.

82. **A** Chapter 10, Objective 3
Signs are objective or measurable like pulses and breathing. Symptoms are subjective and relative to the person's tolerance or senses like pain or difficulty.

83. **D** Chapter 10, Objective 1
Documenting things the patient denies is called a pertinent negative and it is also subjective as it is dependent on the patient's description and not observable.

84. **D** Chapter 10, Objective 4
In order for patients to refuse care, they must be competent adults. The EMT must also have explained what the treatment is that they are refusing and what the complications of refusing care and transport might be.

85. **A** Chapter 11, Objective 1
The drugs carried on a BLS ambulance are oxygen, glucose, and activated charcoal.

86. **F** Chapter 11, Objective 4
EMT-Bs may assist patients in taking their own epinephrine, nitroglycerin, and inhalers.

87. **D** Chapter 12, Objective 7
Signs of adequate bag-valve mask ventilations include the rise and fall of the chest, breath sounds on auscultation, color improving, and pulse rates returning to more normal ranges.

88. **D** Chapter 12, Objective 7
Early signs of hypoxia include nervousness, agitation, and tachycardia or a rapid heart rate. Worsening hypoxia results in decreasing levels of consciousness.

89. **B** Chapter 13, Objective 2
Chest pain patients should be placed in a position of comfort, sitting up to facilitate breathing.

90. **C** Chapter 13, Objective 10
Automatic external defibrillators should be used only in pulseless nonbreathing patients. They should never be placed on conscious patients or patients with pulses.

91. **A** Chapter 13, Objective 1
Congestive heart failure is the condition in which the heart muscle, weakened due to muscle damage, is unable to pump all of the blood returning to the heart. Due to this, blood begins to back up into the lungs causing pulmonary edema or fluid/blood in the lungs. The patient will have rales or crackles on auscultation and may have pink-tinged sputum.

92. **B** Chapter 14, Objective 1
Diabetes is a condition in which the islets of Langerhans in the pancreas produce too little insulin, produce no insulin, or produce insulin erratically, impairing the body's ability to get glucose into the cells for metabolism.

93. **D** Chapter 15, Objective 1
Patients with allergic reactions can have local or central responses. Central responses include respiratory problems or shock, and peripheral problems can be localized redness, swelling, and itching. Itching and hives can also be a central response if the entire body is involved or if it occurs remote to the exposure.

94. **B** Chapter 16, Objective 4
Heat exhaustion is the second level of heat exposure sickness and can be recognized by complaints of nausea, dizziness, and weakness, and pale, cool, and clammy skin. The first sign of heat exposure is often heat cramps and the final stage is heatstroke in which the patient loses consciousness and the ability to dissipate heat. The skin will be hot, dry, and flushed.

95. **D** Chapter 16, Objectives 1 and 2
The first and most important thing to do for any patient suffering from exposure to an environment is to remove the patient from that environment.

96. **D** Chapter 17, Objective 6
The most important thing to determine in a behavioral emergency is safety of the scene. These patients can be violent and the EMT-B should not enter the scene without police support.

97. **E** Chapter 18, Objective 14
The EMT-B may have to insert a gloved hand into the vagina to open an airway when the head does not deliver in a breech birth. The EMT-B may also have to insert a gloved hand into the vagina to hold the head off the cord in deliveries where the cord protrudes from the vaginal opening. This is called a prolapsed cord.

98. **F** Chapter 19, Objective 3
Tourniquets should be used only as a last resort and never below the elbow or knee.

99. **C** Chapter 20, Section 1, Objective 6
Lacerations are open wounds typified by torn jagged edges.

100. **B** Chapter 21, Objective 11
Cushing's Triad occurs as a response to increasing intracranial pressure. The pulse rate drops, the blood pressure rises, and bizarre respiratory patterns such as Cheyne-Stokes respirations or neurogenic hyperventilation occur.

Glossary

Abandonment. Termination of patient-provider relationship without assuring continuing care at a level equal to or greater than that provided prior to termination.

Abdomen. The portion of the body between the diaphragm and the pelvis.

Abortion. Spontaneous or intentional termination of pregnancy prior to the twentieth week of pregnancy.

Abrasion. An open soft tissue injury caused by scraping away the superficial layers of skin.

Acceleration. The rate of increasing speed.

Acute. Rapid onset, severe, and short in duration.

Alkali. A strong base.

Allergic reaction. A hypersensitivity to a substance that results in potentially life-threatening reactions.

Allied Health. Referring to health care providers other than physicians, including nurses, technicians, therapists, EMT-Bs, EMT-Is, and EMT-Ps.

Alpha radiation. The lowest level of nuclear radiation that can be stopped by a sheet of paper.

Advanced Life Support (ALS). Patient care given in the hospital or by paramedics in the field, which includes the use of defibrillators, intravenous and drug therapy, and advanced airway interventions.

Alveoli. Air sacs in the lungs at the end of the bronchioles that take carbon dioxide from the pulmonary capillaries in exchange for oxygen.

Alzheimer's disease. A progressive degenerative disease that attacks the brain, impairing memory, thinking, and behavior.

Amniotic fluid. Fluid in the amniotic sac that surrounds and protects the developing fetus.

Amniotic sac. Membranes that contain the amniotic fluid, surrounding and protecting the developing fetus.

Amputation. Partial or complete severing of a part of the body.

Anaphylaxis. Severe allergic reaction that can be rapidly fatal.

Anatomy. The study of living body structures.

Aneurysm. Bulging area of a weakened blood vessel.

Antibiotics. Medications given to combat bacterial infections.

Antidote. Substance given to counteract the effects of another substance.

Anxiety. A feeling of apprehension, uneasiness, or dread.

APGAR scoring. Numerical system used to describe a newborn's condition by evaluating appearance, pulse, grimace, activity, and color.

Apnea. Absence of breathing.

Arachnoid membrane. Middle layer of meninges that surround the brain.

Arteriosclerosis. A thickening and hardening of the veins and arteries that limits their flexibility.

Asphyxia. Increasing carbon dioxide and decreasing oxygen levels caused by cessation of, or insufficient, breathing that ultimately results in death.

Aspiration. Foreign bodies, solid or liquid, drawn into and obstructing the airway and lungs.

Assault. A violent physical attack; places a person in fear of bodily harm.

Atherosclerosis. The most common form of arteriosclerosis in which fatty deposits collect on the insides of medium to large arteries, narrowing them and limiting blood flow.

Auscultation. Listening to sounds made by internal organs.

Autonomic nervous system. The part of the nervous system that controls involuntary body functions.

Avulsion. An open soft tissue injury where tissue is gouged or torn away completely or leaving a flap of skin.

Axial loading. Extreme compression of the cervical vertebrae.

B

Bacteria. Small, independent living organisms that can cause infections or assist in body functions.

Ballistics. Study of the motion of projectiles and their effects on the objects they strike.

Battery. The unlawful touching of a person without that person's consent.

Battle's sign. Discoloration behind the ears that can indicate basilar skull fractures.

Beta radiation. Medium nuclear radiation that can be blocked by clothing or the outer layers of the skin.

Bile. Greenish yellow fluid secreted by the liver and stored in the gallbladder that aids in the digestion of fats.

Bradycardia. Heart rates below 60.

Bronchi. Branches of the trachea leading into the lungs.

Bronchioles. Smaller extensions of the bronchi leading to the alveoli.

Burnout. Losing interest in one's job following constant unresolved stress.

C

Capillary. Microscopic blood vessels that connect small arteries to veins.

Capillary refill. An assessment of the circulatory system that measures the time it takes for the capillaries to refill with blood after compression.

Cardiogenic shock. Shock caused by failure of the heart to act as a pump.

Cardiovascular disease. Disease that affects the heart and/or the blood vessels.

Cavity. Hollow spaces in the body (i.e., chest and abdomen) that contain the body's organs.

Cell. The basic unit of life, which makes up and is specific to every body tissue.

Cerebrospinal fluid. Clear fluid surrounding the brain and spinal cord, providing cushioning and nutrition.

Cerebrum. Largest part of the brain, divided into two hemispheres and responsible for consciousness and higher mental functions such as thought, memory, and emotions.

Cheyne-Stokes respirations. A respiratory pattern common in brain-injured patients in which the rate and volume of respirations increase then abruptly subside and begin again, repeating the cycle.

Chronic. Of continuing or long duration.

Chronic Obstructive Pulmonary Disease (COPD). Diseases that impair breathing that include asthma, emphysema, and chronic bronchitis.

Circumferential. Encircling or going all the way around something.

Civil law. Law dealing with noncriminal issues.

Coma. A state of unconsciousness.

Command post. A fixed location set up to coordinate efforts of multiple companies and or agencies operating at a large event.

Compensated shock. The body's compensation for blood loss that involves constriction of blood vessels and increasing the heart rate to maintain adequate circulation.

Computer-aided Dispatch (CAD). Enhanced dispatch systems that have the capability of storing information on addresses and occupants and helping to manage response capabilities.

Concussion. A brain injury that is typified by a momentary loss of consciousness.

Conduction. Moving electrons, heat, or energy through a medium. For example, water is a good conductor, while air is a poor conductor.

Consent. Permission to treat.

Contrecoup. Something occurring on the opposite side; a blow to the forehead causing injury to the rear of the brain.

Contusion. A closed soft tissue injury in which the skin is unbroken but underlying tissues are damaged.

Convection. Transferring heat through air or water currents.

Cranium. The boxlike part of the skull that houses and protects the brain.

Crepitation. A grating or crackling sensation associated with subcutaneous emphysema or bone endings rubbing together.

Cricothyroid membrane. A thin membrane located between the cricoid and thyroid cartilages.

Criminal law. Laws dealing with crimes against society.

Critical Incident Stress Management. A plan to provide support from peers and professionals in the event of exposure to critical incident stress.

Critical incident. An event that carries the potential for strong, potentially damaging emotional impact.

Croup. Viral infection common in children that causes swelling of the upper airways and is characterized by a barklike cough.

Crowning. Presentation of the baby's head in the vaginal opening that signifies imminent birth.

Cerebrovascular accident (CVA). Death of brain tissue caused by either blockage of a blood vessel or rupture of a blood vessel.

Cyanosis. Bluish color to the skin caused by hypoxia.

D

Deceleration. The rate at which something that is moving comes to a stop.

Decompensated shock. Failure of the compensation mechanism in which the blood vessels dilate causing the blood pressure to drop precipitously and making circulation inadequate.

Decorticate posturing. Posturing in which an unresponsive patient's arms are flexed with clenched fists and the legs extended. This posturing is typical of patients with brain injury above the upper brain stem.

Defibrillation. The process of using an electrical charge to cease disorganized electrical activity in the heart allowing organized electrical activity to restart.

Dehydration. Loss of body fluids through elimination or evaporation (sweating).

Delirium tremens (DTs). Body tremors and hallucinations suffered by alcoholics when blood alcohol drops too low.

Delirium. Acute alteration in mental functioning.

Delusion. False belief held despite evidence to the contrary.

Dementia. Frequently progressive and irreversible deterioration of mental status.

Depression. An overpowering feeling of hopelessness.

Dermis. The second layer of skin that produces the epidermis and contains the blood vessels and nerve endings.

Diabetes mellitus. Condition in which the pancreas either fails to secrete insulin or secretes insulin erratically, causing the patient to be unable to utilize sugar as fuel to cellular metabolism.

Dialysis. A mechanical process used in place of failed kidneys to filter impurities out of the blood.

Diastole. The relaxation phase of the heart's contraction cycle.

Diastolic. The bottom number in blood pressure readings representing the pressure in the vessels between contractions.

Direct medical control. Medical direction given directly to field personnel via radio or phone.

Disentanglement. The process of removing a vehicle from a trapped occupant.

Dislocation. Disruption of the proper position of the bones in a joint.

Dispatch. The center that receives requests for service and the exchange of information with the responding units.

Dura mater. The outermost layer of meninges that covers and protects the brain.

Durable power of attorney. Legal designation of responsibility to one person for another.

Dyspnea. Difficulty breathing.

E

Ecchymosis. Bruising.

Ectopic pregnancy. A fetus developing outside the uterus.

Elderly. Patients over 65 years of age.

Emboli. A clot or other particle that lodges in a blood vessel.

Emergency medical dispatcher. Dispatcher who is trained following the DOT curriculum for dispatchers.

Emergency medical services. The prehospital emergency care delivery system.

EMT-Basic. An individual trained according to the DOT curriculum for basic life support.

EMT-Intermediate. An individual trained according to the DOT curriculum for intermediate life support, which includes a limited amount of advanced skills.

EMT-Paramedic. An individual trained according to the DOT curriculum for advanced life support.

Epidermis. The outermost layer of skin.

Epidural hematoma. A pool of blood that accumulates between the dura and the cranium.

Epigastrum. The abdominal area directly below the sternum.

Epiglottis. Leaf-shaped muscle that covers either the trachea or esophagus depending on whether one is swallowing or breathing.

Ethics. The rules, standards, or morals that govern the activities of professionals within a society.

Evaporation. The process through which a substance changes from a liquid to a gas.

Expressed consent. The act of an individual actually giving written or verbal consent to a health care professional.

Extrication. Removal of an entrapped person from his or her confinement.

F

Flail chest. Describing two or more ribs broken in two or more places creating a free-floating section of the chest wall.

Fontanelles. Soft areas on an infant's head where the bones of the skull have not yet fused together.

Fracture. Any break in the continuity of the bone.

G

Gag reflex. A reflex that protects the airway from foreign bodies by creating a spasm and cough to clear the airway.

Gamma radiation. The third and strongest level of radiation that requires lead shielding to block.

Genitalia. Reproductive organs.

Geriatrics. The study of the special needs of the elderly.

Glasgow coma scale. A scoring system used to evaluate the neurological status of patients that looks at eye opening, verbal responses, and motor response.

Glottis. Opening between the vocal cords.

Golden hour. The time in which definitive care must be provided following injury for the best chance of survival.

Good Samaritan laws. Laws that provide for protection from liability for good-intentioned individuals providing emergency care.

Gran mal seizures. Seizure activity characterized by tonic clonic muscular contractions.

Greenstick fracture. Common fracture in children that causes bones to bend and fray.

Guarding. Positioning to minimize pain.

H

Hallucination. Seeing or hearing things that are not real.

Hazard zone. The area around an emergency that requires special protective equipment and training and isolation from bystanders.

Heat cramps. Painful muscle spasms associated with exposure to heat and subsequent dehydration.

Heat exhaustion. Weakness, dizziness, and nausea associated with vasodilation secondary to exposure to heat.

Heatstroke. Loss of consciousness due to exposure to heat.

Hematemesis. Vomiting blood.

Hematoma. Blood pooling beneath the skin from broken blood vessels.

Hematuria. Blood in the urine.

Hemoglobin. The part of red blood cells that enables the transport of oxygen and carbon dioxide.

Hemoptysis. Coughing up blood.

Hemothorax. The collapse of a lung due to the accumulation of blood in the chest cavity.

Hypertension. Elevated blood pressure.

Hyperthermia. Abnormally high body temperature.

Hypoglycemia. Low blood sugar levels.

Hyperglycemia. Elevated blood sugar levels.

Hypothermia. Unusually low body temperature.

Hypoxia. The state of low oxygen blood content.

I

Implied consent. The rule that allows for unresponsive patients to be treated with the assumption that they would consent to care if they were able to.

Incident Command System (ICS). The system that provides for command and supervision of all of the functions at an emergency scene.

Incident commander. The individual with ultimate authority and responsibility at an emergency scene.

Incision. A very clean precise laceration made by a sharp instrument.

Indirect medical control. Medical control provided with standard operating procedures.

Informed consent. The provision that in order to give consent or remove treatment a patient must be informed as to their condition and possible complications from nontreatment.

Ingestion. Swallowing a substance entering the body through the digestive tract.

Inhalation. Breathing in a substance entering the body through the respiratory tract.

Injection. Describing a substance entering the body by breaking the skin, such as a sting, bite, or needle.

Inspection. Visual exam of the body.

Insulin. The hormone secreted by the pancreas to facilitate transport of sugar into cells.

Intercostal muscles. The muscles between the ribs that facilitate breathing.

Intracerebral bleeding. Bleeding directly into tissues of the brain.

Intracranial pressure (ICP). Pressure within the skull exerted on the brain.

Intubation. Passing a tube through the vocal cords into the trachea to facilitate ventilation and isolation of the airway from the potential for aspiration.

Involuntary consent. Consent obtained against the wishes of the patient.

Iris. Portion of the eye that contains the pigment that gives the eye its color.

K

Ketoacidosis. Condition created in a diabetic whose insulin production is insufficient to transport sugar out of the blood and into the cells. This accumulated sugar causes the blood to become more acidic. Without sugar making it into the cells to produce energy, the patient will eventually lose consciousness and without treatment, die; also called diabetic coma.

Kinetic energy. The energy of motion.

Kussmaul's respirations. Deep, gulping breaths, common in diabetic emergencies; also called air hunger.

Kyphosis. Exaggerated curvature of the spine; generally causes the patient to appear stooped.

L

Labor. The period of childbirth.

Laceration. An open soft tissue injury characterized by a tear in the skin with jagged borders.

Laryngospasm. Normally a mechanism to protect the airway against aspiration; this spasm of the vocal cords can also block the airway and cause asphyxiation.

Libel. Make false accusations or statements that injure a person's reputation.

Licensure. Verification that a governmental unit has authorized a person to practice a given, regulated profession.

Ligament. Connective tissue connecting bone to bone and holding joints together.

Litigation. The act of filing a lawsuit against another person.

Living will. A document that instructs providers on what type of care the patient wishes and which care the patient refuses. In the event that this patient is unable to give consent, this document is to be honored in place of that consent.

M

Magill forceps. A curved forceps used to position tubes into the airway or to clear foreign bodies from the airway.

Mammalian diving reflex. An ancient reflex that decreases circulation to every area of the body except the brain. This reflex can be stimulated by submersing the face into water.

Maxillary. Referring to the maxilla or jawbone.

Mechanism of injury. The events and physical activity that create injury.

Meconium. Dark green material in the amniotic fluid. It is the product of fetal distress causing the fetus to move its bowel into the fluid. It also refers to the first bowel movement of the newborn.

Mediastinum. Space between the lungs and the sternum and spine.

Medical director. Physician responsible for the training of and protocols for prehospital care providers.

Medulla oblongata. Lower portion of the brain stem responsible for maintaining respirations.

Melena. Black, tarry, especially foul-smelling stool caused by blood decomposing in the lower intestines.

Meninges. Membranes covering and protecting the brain. There are three of them: dura, arachnoid, and pia.

Meningitis. An infection of the meninges, the layers of tissue covering and protecting the brain.

Mesentery. Folds of tissue within the body that support and supply organs with blood.

Midbrain. The portion of the brain that connects the pons and the cerebral hemispheres.

Minute volume. The amount of air inhaled and exhaled in one minute.

N

Nares. The openings in the nose that lead into the airway.

Nasal flaring. Excessive widening of the nares with respirations.

National standard curriculum. The curriculum for prehospital care providers prepared under the direction of the U.S. Department of Transportation.

Negligence. Deviation from standard of care that causes injury.

Neonate. Term used to describe infants from birth to one month old.

O

Organ. Group of tissues with a common function.

Overdose. A drug taken in excess of its intended dose causing a potential threat to life.

P

Packaging. Preparing a patient using stretchers, boards, blankets, pillows, and whatever else is necessary, for safe transport to the hospital.

Palpation. Assessment using the sense of touch.

Palpitation. A sensation that the heart is pounding, or a strong, rapid heartbeat that the patient feels.

Paradoxical movement. Referring to a section of the chest wall that moves in a direction opposite from the direction it should move during respiration. This is caused by two or more ribs being broken in two or more places creating a free-floating section of the chest wall.

Parasympathetic nervous system. Part of the nervous system controlling vegetative function.

Parietal pleura. A thin sheath of tissue covering the inside of the chest wall.

Patent. Secure and open; a patent airway is a secure and open airway.

Patient assessment. Examinination of a patient to determine his or her condition.

Percussion. Striking an area or object to elicit a sound or vibration.

Perfusion. Fluid flowing into and out of tissue providing nourishment and removing waste.

Pericardial tamponade. Any fluid accumulating in the sac surrounding the heart that inhibits the contraction of the heart muscle.

Pericardium. Double-layered sac surrounding the heart.

Peripheral vascular resistance. Pressure exerted back against the flow of blood from the heart by the peripheral vascular bed.

Peristalsis. Wavelike muscular contractions of the digestive tract that help to move the food along as it is digested.

Petit mal seizure. Form of seizure activity that may or may not involve a loss of consciousness; may be a twitch of a single extremity or a person may "black out" for a moment.

Physiology. The study of the function of the body and its parts.

Pia mater. Innermost of the three meningeal layers covering and protecting the brain.

Placenta. The organ that is attached to the wall of the uterus and supplies the growing fetus with its blood supply.

Plasma. The fluid portion of the blood that transports the blood cells and platelets.

Pleura. Membranes that line the inside of the chest wall and covering the lungs.

Poison control center. A resource center staffed with trained personnel to give up-to-date information on poisons and the proper response to poisonings.

Poisoning. Taking harmful substances into the body.

Postpartum. The period after the birth of the child.

Prenatal. The time period before the birth of the child. Another term for this period is antepartum.

Primary assessment. Rapid initial assessment designed to identify any immediate life threats.

Professional. A person who exhibits the qualities and conduct characteristic of a practitioner in a given field.

Protocols. Policies and procedures addressing all aspects of an EMS system.

Proximate cause. Legal term that refers to being able to determine that an injury is the result of another person's negligent action or inaction.

Psychosis. Change in personality that prevents a person from behaving normally.

Pulmonary embolism. Blood or other type of clot that lodges in pulmonary blood vessels impairing pulmonary function.

Pulse oximeter. Device that measures oxygen concentration in the blood.

Puncture. Open soft tissue injury typified as a hole punched into or through tissues.

Q

Quality assurance (QA). Process that evaluates service performance for compliance to protocols and measures outcomes.

R

Radio. An electronic communication device that transmits sound waves and telemetry over distances.

Rales. Lung sounds heard on auscultation, also described as "crackles" when fluid accumulates in lungs.

Rebound tenderness. Tenderness noted when gentle pressure is released on palpation of abdomen, signifying peritoneal irritation.

Reciprocity. Certification or licensure granted in recognition of similar licensure or certification granted by another agency.

Repeater. A radio booster designed to amplify a radio signal received by a weaker transmitter.

Rescue. To remove someone from a hazardous or dangerous situation.

Research. Establishing fact through diligent investigation and experimentation.

Resource. Personnel and equipment available to responders.

Respiration. Exchange of gasses between a living organism and its environment.

Retraction. Drawing-in motion as in "sternal or intercostal retractions" seen in infants with difficulty breathing.

Retroperitoneal. Posterior abdominal space containing the kidneys and abdominal descending aorta and inferior vena cava.

Rhonchi. Rattling sounds heard when mucus or fluid is in the upper airways.

S

Safety officer. Specially trained responder who supervises the safety of a scene and the personnel working it.

Scapula. Large, flat, wing-shaped bones forming the posterior part of the shoulders.

Schizophrenia. Mental disorder characterized by disturbances in thought, mood, and behavior.

Sebaceous glands. Sebum (oil)-secreting gland found in the dermis.

Sebum. Fatty oil secreted by the sebaceous glands that keep the skin pliable and waterproof.

Secondary assessment. Detailed history and physical exam that seeks to determine the patient's condition.

Sector. Referring to an area of an incident that has been sectioned off and assigned to a sector officer for management by incident command.

Seizure. Spasm or loss of motor function due to disorderly discharge of neurons in the brain.

Senile dementia. Decline of mental functions common in elderly patients.

Sepsis. Infection in the blood.

Septic shock. Infection in the blood causing vasodilation and hypotension.

Shock. Inadequate tissue perfusion. Different types that describe the underlying cause include hemorrhagic hypovolemia, metabolic or nonhemorrhagic hypovolemia, neurogenic, psychogenic, anaphylactic, and septic.

Size up. A quick assessment of the scene to determine immediate needs.

Slander. Injure a person's reputation by making false statements.

Snoring. Audible noises created by upper airway obstruction.

Staging. Describing a place for equipment and personnel to congregate until they are needed or until the scene is made safe for their entry.

Standing orders. Predetermined orders written by the system medical director for specific patient situations, allowing field personnel to administer care without contacting medical control for orders.

START. An acronym that stands for Simple Triage and Rapid Treatment. The system is designed to triage a large number of patients in a short period of time to enable assembling and utilizing necessary resources.

Status epilepticus. A state in which a patient has multiple and continuous grand mal seizures without regaining consciousness between them.

Sternocleidomastoid muscles. Muscles that attach to the mastoid bones on both sides of the neck and connect to the clavicle and sternum. These muscles serve as accessory muscles to breathing in patients in respiratory distress.

Stimulus. Any provocation that creates a response as in verbal or painful stimulus applied during assessment of a patient.

Stridor. High-pitched crowing sound caused by constriction of the upper airways.

Stroke. Injury to the brain caused by an interruption of blood flow to the brain. Dysfunction is directly relative to the area of the brain involved.

Subcutaneous emphysema. Air trapped in subcutaneous tissues causing a swollen appearance and a crackling sensation when palpated.

Subdural hematoma. Blood accumulating beneath the dura meninges covering the brain.

Subluxation. Incomplete dislocation of a joint that causes deformity while the bone ends are still in contact with one another.

Sudden infant death syndrome (SIDS). Death due to undetermined causes during the first year of life.

Surfactant. Material secreted by cells in the lungs contributing to elastic properties necessary to normal pulmonary function.

Sympathetic nervous system. Part of the autonomic nervous system that allows the body to respond to stress. Sympathetic stimulis cause the heart and respiratory rates to respond to the stress.

Synapse. Space between nerve cells across which chemicals conduct electrical impulses.

Syncope. A momentary loss of consciousness caused by an interruption in blood flow to the brain.

Systole. Contraction of the heart muscle.

Systolic. The top number in blood pressure readings representing the pressure in the vessels during contractions.

T

Tachycardia. Heart rate above 100.

Tachypnea. Rapid breathing.

Tendon. Connective tissue that attaches muscle to bone.

Tension pneumothorax. Condition in which air accumulates in the chest, collapsing one lung and compressing the uninvolved lung and the heart and large blood vessels between the lungs, resulting in increased dyspnea and decreased cardiac output.

Tentorium. Extension of the dura mater that separates the cerebrum from the cerebellum.

Transient ischemic attack (TIA). Temporary interruption of blood flow causing temporary dysfunction relative to the area of the brain involved.

Tissue. A group of cells with a common function, such as skin, muscle, or bone.

Tonic phase. Phase of a seizure characterized by contraction of muscles.

Toxins. Poisonous substances.

Tracheal tugging. Retraction of tissues in the neck of a patient attempting to breathe with obstructions of the airway.

Trajectory. The path that a projectile follows.

Transfer of command. The planned process of transferring command from one individual to another in an incident command situation.

Trauma. Injury called by a violent intentional or unintentional act.

Trauma center. A hospital that has been designated to treat trauma patients due to its commitment to specialized equipment, personnel, and training.

Traumatic asphyxia. Severe compression injury to the chest causing disruption of the organs in the chest cavity and impairing circulation and breathing.

Triage. Picking, choosing, and sorting patients according to the severity of their condition.

U

Umbilical cord. Cord that contains nerves and blood vessels, connecting the fetus to the placenta and providing blood supply and nutrients to the fetus.

Umbilicus. Also called naval or belly button; a remnant of the umbilical connection to the placenta during fetal development.

Universal precautions. Another term for BSI or Body Substance Isolation referring to precautions responders take to prevent exposure to any body substances.

V

Vallecula. A depression between the epiglottis and the base of the tongue.

Valalva's maneuver. Maneuver used to slow a patient's pulse rate by increasing intra-abdominal and intrathoracic pressure. This can be brought about by forcing exhalation against a closed glottis as in trying to blow up a rigid balloon.

Velocity. The rate of speed at which an object is traveling.

Vertigo. Dizziness and a sense that everything around you is moving.

Virus. Microscopic organism, smaller than bacteria, that require another living host and are the frequent causes of disease.

Visceral pleura. Pleural lining covering the lungs.

Vitreous humor. Clear watery fluid within the posterior portion of the eye.

W

Wheezing. Audible whistling sound heard in patients suffering from obstruction of the lower airways as in asthma and emphysema.

Index